Zed Books Titles on Development and Humanitarian Assistance

The era of international aid is by no means over. What is happening, however, is that significant changes are occurring in the purposes of aid and the ways in which it is being delivered, including much more emphasis on targeted forms of humanitarian assistance and intervention in situations of acute conflict. Zed Books has published a considerable number of titles in this area.

Crewe, Emma and Elizabeth Harrison *Whose Development? An Ethnography of Aid*

Duffield, Mark *Global Governance and the New Wars: The Merging of Development and Security*

Engberg-Pedersen, Poul and John Degnbol-Martinussen *Aid: An Analysis of International Development Cooperation* (in preparation)

Macrae, Joanna *Aiding Recovery? The Crisis of Aid in Chronic Political Emergencies*

Pirotte, Grunewald and Bernard Husson (eds) *Responding to Emergencies and Fostering Development: The Dilemmas of Humanitarian Aid*

Sogge, David *A Helping Hand? Foreign Aid in the New Century*

For full details of this list and Zed's other subject and general catalogues, please write to: The Marketing Department, Zed Books, 7 Cynthia Street, London N1 9JF, UK or email Sales@zedbooks.demon.co.uk

Visit our website at: http://www.zedbooks.demon.co.uk

Evaluating International Humanitarian Action: Reflections from Practitioners

Edited by Adrian Wood, Raymond Apthorpe
and John Borton

Zed Books
LONDON • NEW YORK

in association with

ALNAP
LONDON

Evaluating International Humanitarian Action: Reflections from Practitioners was first published by Zed Books Ltd, 7 Cynthia Street, London, N1 9JF, UK and Room 400, 175 Fifth Avenue, New York, NY 10010, USA in 2001

in association with the Active Learning Network for Accountability and Performance in Humanitarian Action (ALNAP), c/o ODI, 111 Westminster Bridge Road, London SE1 7JD.

Distributed in the USA exclusively by Palgrave, a division of St Martin's Press, LLC, 175 Fifth Avenue, New York, NY 10010, USA.

Cover designed by Andrew Corbett
Set in Monotype Ehrhardt and Franklin Gothic by Ewan Smith
Printed and bound in the United Kingdom by Biddles Ltd, Guildford and King's Lynn

A catalogue record for this book is available from the British Library

Library of Congress Cataloging-in-Publication Data: available

ISBN 1 85649 975 8 cased
ISBN 1 85649 976 6 limp

Contents

Maps, Figures and Boxes

Maps

Figures

Boxes

Abbreviations

ADF	Australian Defence Force
AFOR	Albania Force (NATO)
AHC	Australian High Commission
ALNAP	Active Learning Network for Accountability and Performance in Humanitarian Action
AusAID	Australian Agency for International Development
CCD	Commission Coopération Développement
CDC	US Centers for Disease Control and Prevention, Atlanta
CEBEMO	Catholic Organization for the Co-financing of Development
CIDA	Canadian International Development Agency
CRC	Convention on the Rights of the Child
CTA	Chief Technical Adviser
DAC	Development Assistance Committee
Danida	Danish International Development Agency
DFAT	Department of Foreign Affairs and Trade (GOA)
DFID	Department for International Development (UK)
DHA	Department for Humanitarian Affairs (UN)
DP	delivery point
EADI	European Association of Development and Training Institutes
ECHO	European Commission Humanitarian Office
EMA	Emergency Management Australia
ETC	ETC Foundation UK
FAO	Food and Agriculture Organization (UN)
FDF	Fondation de France
FTS	Fast Tracking System
fYROM	former Yugoslav Republic of Macedonia
GOA	Government of Australia
GOPNG	Government of Papua New Guinea
IASC	Inter-Agency Standing Committee
IASER	Integracion de Aplicaciones de Seguridad de Tiempo Real

ICRC	International Committee of the Red Cross
ICVA	International Council for Voluntary Agencies
IDPs	internally displaced persons
IFRC	International Federation of Red Cross and Red Crescent Societies
INGO	international non-governmental organization
IOB	Policy and Operations Evaluation Department of the Netherlands Ministry of Foreign Affairs
ISSAS	Institute of Social Studies Advisory Service
JEEAR	Joint Evaluation of Emergency Assistance to Rwanda
JEFF	Joint Evaluation Follow-up, Monitoring and Facilitation Network
LWF	Lutheran World Federation
MAE	Ministry of Foreign Affairs (France)
MFA	Ministry of Foreign Affairs
MILONG	MAE's Mission for Liaison with NGOs
MSF	Médecins Sans Frontières
NATO	North Atlantic Treaty Organization
NDES	National Disaster and Emergency Services of GOPNG
NGO	non-governmental organization
NLG	Netherlands guilders
OAU	Organization of African Unity
ODA	Official Development Assistance
ODI	Overseas Development Institute (UK)
OECD	Organization for Economic Co-operation and Development
ONS	Operating National Red Cross/Red Crescent Society
PIA	Performance Information and Assessment Section in AusAID's Office of Program Review and Evaluation
PNG	Papua New Guinea
PNS	Participating National Red Cross Societies
PRO	Protracted Relief Operations (WFP)
QIPs	quick impact projects
RAG	Review Advisory Group
REST	Relief Society of Tigray
RPF	Rwanda Patriotic Front
SCA	Swedish Committee for Afghanistan
SCHR	Steering Committee for Humanitarian Response
SEPHA	Special Emergency Programme for the Horn of Africa (UN)
Sida	Swedish International Development Agency
TL	Team Leader
TOR	Terms of Reference

TRCS	Tajikistan Red Crescent Society
UN	United Nations
UNAMIR	UN Assistance Mission in Rwanda
UNHCR	United Nations High Commissioner for Refugees
UNICEF	United Nations Children's Fund
UNITAF	UN International Task Force (Somalia)
UNPROFOR	United Nations Protection Force (former Yugoslavia)
UNREO	United Nations Rwanda Emergency Office
UNTAC	United Nations Transitional Authority in Cambodia
URD	Urgence-Réhabilitation-Développement
USAID	United States Agency for International Development
VOICE	Voluntary Organizations in Cooperation in Emergencies
WFP	World Food Programme (UN)
WHO	World Health Organization (UN)

ALNAP: Active Learning Network for Accountability and Performance in Humanitarian Action

ALNAP is an international interagency forum working to improve learning and accountability across the humanitarian system. Established in 1997, ALNAP's membership comprises over forty-six Full Members encompassing bilateral and multilateral donor organizations; UN agencies and Departments; NGOs and NGO umbrella organizations; the International Red Cross and Red Crescent Movement; and selected consultants, academics and research institutes. To create a context that encourages self-criticism and learning, ALNAP is structured so that no single type of organization is able to dominate the discussion or set the agenda. ALNAP is funded by over twenty of its Full Members on a voluntary basis. It is governed by a Steering Committee of eight Full Member Representatives and is serviced by a three-person Secretariat located in the Humanitarian Policy Group at the Overseas Development Institute in London. This publication was one of the outputs of ALNAP's 2000–02 Workplan, which was constructed around three themes: Making the Evaluation Process More Effective; Strengthening Accountability Frameworks within the Humanitarian System; Improving Field-Level Learning Mechanisms. An extensive database of evaluative reports of humanitarian assistance is maintained by the Secretariat with key sections stored in fully searchable format on the ALNAP website <www.alnap.org>.

Acknowledgements

The editors would like to express their appreciation to AusAID and all the contributing authors for their efforts and patience in seeing this venture through to fruition. We are grateful to those members of the ALNAP Steering Committee and the two ALNAP members who peer-reviewed sections of the volume and made many helpful comments. As ever, Ted Kliest was particularly supportive and constructive. We are equally grateful to Steve Pratt of Huddersfield University for his assistance in preparing the maps in this book. Finally, we are indebted to two members of the ALNAP Secretariat: Felicity Heyworth for single-handedly organizing the workshop of contributors in March 2000 and giving this process its initial impetus; and Kate Robertson for her invaluable rigour and assistance in finalizing the text.

While this book was going to press we learned of the untimely death of David Lea, author of Chapter 8. We take this opportunity to express our condolences to his family, our appreciation for his contribution to the book and participation in the Workshop and our respect for his indomitable spirit.

Huddersfield, London, Sydney

About the Editors and Contributors

Editors

Adrian Wood has a BA in geography from Durham University and a Ph.D. from Liverpool University. He is a reader in geography at the University of Huddersfield. His work focused initially on migration and agricultural and aid policy, and later on environmental policy, including national conservation strategies. In 1974 work with the Ethiopian Relief and Rehabilitation Commission provided his first experience of humanitarian action studies. Since 1983, he has been involved in numerous development and humanitarian evaluations. In 1991 he led the evaluation of NORAD's late 1980s Ethiopia programme, and in 1995 he was responsible for the Ethiopia section of the evaluation of Sida-supported emergency operations in the Horn of Africa. He has wide consultancy experience with national and international organizations and has edited six volumes published by Earthscan, IUCN, Iowa State University and Leeds University. He is the author of over forty consultancy reports and fifty journal articles and chapters in academic volumes. He lectures at universities in Europe and Africa.

Raymond Apthorpe has a D.Phil. in social theory from Oxford University and currently (since 1995) is visiting professor at the National Centre for Development Studies, Australian National University (ANU). He was a professor at the Institute of Social Studies in The Hague from 1977 to 1986, the founding professor in Development Studies at the University of East Anglia from 1975 to 1977, and before that a professor at Makere and Ibadan universities. Other positions held include visiting professor at Addis Ababa University, Ecole des Hautes Etudes en Sciences Sociales, Witwatersrand University, the University of Bath, the University of Zimbabwe, the University of Colombo, the Asian Institute of Technology, the University of Wales and the University of Khartoum. He has worked as a policy adviser and consultant for UN, governmental and non-governmental organizations and has published extensively. His evaluation experience spans some forty years. In 1994 he led the evaluation of the 1990–94 Sida-supported Horn of Africa emergency operations, and in 1996 he led the evaluation of WFP's food aid policy in the Liberian sub-region. Since 1997 he has co-run an annual course in humanitarian assistance and evaluation at ANU. He was a delegate to the OECD's Development Assistance Committee's task force meetings and was at the time of writing this book part-time evaluation training and research adviser to ALNAP.

John Borton has a BA in geography from Oxford University and an M.Sc. in agricultural economics from Reading University. He is coordinator of ALNAP Secretariat and a research fellow at the Humanitarian Policy Group, Overseas Development Institute. From 1980 to 1983 he worked for the Botswana government, becoming planning officer for the National Drought Relief Programme in 1981. In 1985 he joined the International Disaster Institute (IDI), beginning a 15-year period of research and evaluation on disasters and humanitarian action. In 1991 he joined ODI as a research fellow and, in 1993, he founded the ODI Relief and Rehabilitation Network (now the Humanitarian Practice Network). In 1995–96 he led Study 3, 'Humanitarian Aid and Effects', of the Joint Evaluation of Emergency Assistance to Rwanda, and in 1997 he initiated ALNAP. He is a trustee and board member of the UK Disasters Emergency Committee (DEC) and a member of the International Advisory Panel of the British Red Cross Society.

Contributors

Wiert Flikkema has an MA in the human geography of developing countries from the University of Utrecht and is a freelance consultant who works primarily on evaluations and reviews commissioned by the Netherlands Ministry of Foreign Affairs. He has worked in the South Pacific region, Sri Lanka, Eastern and Central Africa and the Balkans. A major focus of his activities is the field of humanitarian assistance, covering both emergency aid and rehabilitation.

Véronique de Geoffroy is an emergency expert with a legal specialization. She has worked in Colombia, former Zaire, Angola and Bosnia-Herzegovina with NGOs, especially Médecins du Monde (MDM). She now works as a legal adviser in Groupe URD and follows the relations between state actors (including the military) and humanitarian agencies.

François Grunewald has a diploma in agricultural engineering from the Institut National Agronomique Paris-Grignon and is chair of Groupe URD, a post he has held since 1997. He is an agricultural engineer with

20 years of field experience in over twenty countries in Africa, Asia and Central Europe. He is specialized in emergency agricultural rehabilitation and crisis management and has held a number of posts including that of technical adviser to the Special Representative of the UN Secretary-General for Humanitarian Assistance to the Cambodian People (1985–88) and ICRC coordinator for Emergency Agricultural Rehabilitation Programmes (1992–97).

John Kirkby has a BA in geography from Cambridge University and an MA in applied geography from Newcastle University. He is senior lecturer in geography at Northumbria University. He has undertaken consultancy work for 15 years with ETC (UK). He has field experience in over twenty countries through research and consultancy work in humanitarian assistance and development issues. He has special interests in environmental and beneficiary perceptions in humanitarian assistance.

Ted Kliest has an MA in human geography from the University of Utrecht. He is senior evaluator in the Policy and Operations Evaluation Department of the Netherlands Ministry of Foreign Affairs. Previously he worked as a staff member of the Department of Human Geography of Developing Countries at the University of Utrecht and the African Studies Centre at Leiden. He has 15 years of field experience, mainly in sub-Saharan Africa, and has been involved as an evaluation manager/evaluator of humanitarian aid in Somalia and Rwanda and as a reviewer of an evaluation of Danish humanitarian aid.

The late **David Lea** had a BA in geography from Adelaide University and a Ph.D. from the Australian National University. He was emeritus professor, and formerly head of the Department of Geography and Planning, at the University of New England, Australia. He worked at a number of universities as well as being head of the Department of Geography at the University of Papua New Guinea. He undertook research and consultancy work in Papua New Guinea and other developing countries for over thirty years, and worked as a consultant for many Australian and international organizations on development issues.

Claes Lindahl has a BA in social sciences from the University of Lund and a Ph.D. from the University of Lund. He is co-founder and partner, since 1997, of Management Perspectives International, which is involved in economic development, governance, evaluation and institutional assignments in industrialized and developing countries. Previously he worked as an economist and a monitoring and evaluation specialist for the World Bank and the United Nations Development Programme and as an independent consultant. He has experience of working in more than twenty-five countries, primarily in South-east Asia, sub-Saharan Africa and the Middle East.

Phil O'Keefe has a BA in geography from Newcastle University and a Ph.D. from University College London. He is reader in geography at Northumbria University and director of ETC (UK), a not for profit institute that undertakes research into development and humanitarian issues. Over the last decade he has been involved in 22 evaluations of humanitarian assistance. He has worked in more than forty countries. He has been senior research fellow in the Royal Swedish Academy of Science, and associate professor at Clark University, Worcester, Massachusetts, and was a member of the editorial boards of *Review of African Political Economy* and *Antipode*.

Claire Pirotte is a medical doctor with long experience with NGOs in Latin and Cental America, Africa and the Middle East. She was MSF field coordinator during the Kurdistan crisis in 1991. She served as executive coordinator to Groupe URD from 1993 to 1996. She currently manages Groupe URD's health files.

John Telford has an MA in economic and social studies from Trinity College Dublin. He has been a freelance consultant in emergency and disaster management since 1993, as director of his company, EMMA Ltd. He specializes in evaluations and training for humanitarian protection and assistance programmes, including disaster preparedness and mitigation. He has 20 years of experience in international development and humanitarian aid, including six years as a senior emergency officer with UNHCR, serving in Jordan, Turkey, Iraq, Central and South America, the Caucuses and widely in the former Yugoslavia. Since then, he has worked with a wide range of NGOs, donor governments and UN organizations worldwide, including Africa and Asia.

Peter Wiles has a BA in English from Oxford University and has been a freelance consultant since 1992, specializing in evaluations and reviews of humanitarian and development programmes, as well as management reviews. He has worked with a wide range of agencies including Danida, the European Commission, IFRC, Overseas Development Institute, Oxfam GB and the UN Office for the Coordination of Humanitarian Affairs. He has been involved in NGO development and humanitarian work since 1972, including work in South-east Asia, India and East, Central and Southern Africa, primarily with Oxfam GB.

Foreword

Throughout the past decade, international humanitarian activities have continued to manifest themselves in unprecedented ways, in terms of both nature and spread. Humanitarian actions have become more frequent and more complex. The rapid expansion of humanitarian resources has coincided with major crises such as the Gulf War, Somalia, the Rwandan genocide, Bosnia, East Timor, Hurricane Mitch and the Balkans. These crises have engendered a growing sensitivity towards affected people whose needs demand international assistance and protection – women, children, internally displaced, refugees, returnees, those deprived of freedom, wounded, sick, missing and separated from their families. Responding to their needs is a complex international humanitarian network of donor and local governments, United Nations agencies, the Red Cross Movement (the ICRC, the Federation and National Red Cross and Red Crescent Societies in donor and recipient countries), international and local NGOs, military groups and private sector interests.

The evolution of the international humanitarian system has also taken place against a backdrop of public sector reform. In the early 1990s governments were absorbed by budget deficits, the erosion of public confidence, aid fatigue, declining official development assistance and public perceptions that programmes failed to produce significant results. In an attempt to transform systems where learning was perceived to be unnecessary and change considered a threat, public sector reform has signalled greater attention to performance issues. This performance focus takes account of client needs and preferences; stakeholder involvement in the design and delivery process; results achievement; decentralization of management authority and responsibility; and shifting attitudes towards knowledge management and organizational learning. For many public sector organizations, the 'performance and accountability bar' has been raised from a preoccupation with 'doing' to one of 'achieving results that address client needs'.

Today, many humanitarian agencies are involved in some form of effort, individually and collectively, to improve their accountability and learning systems. This process has been driven by a recognition that significant improvements are needed to ensure the timely and effective delivery of humanitarian assistance, especially under harsh conditions where conflict and insecurity predominate. Hence interest in the evaluation of humanitarian activities has never been higher, with international humanitarian organizations being asked fundamental questions – are victims being reached? Does assistance and protection make a difference? What are the impacts? Is learning occurring? Is performance improving?

However, the art of evaluating humanitarian programmes is in its infancy, with its own concerns around process and output: how is the evaluation actually done? Are the programmes properly set up to address the task? Are the right questions asked? Is the quality adequate? Is there duplication? Are evaluation findings being used? For those of us involved in evaluations, the learning curve is steep and although we draw on techniques developed for other fields, these do not necessarily lend themselves to the specificities of the new humanitarian context. Development of the humanitarian programme evaluation process is necessary if we are to optimize our efforts to improve accountability, learning and performance within the humanitarian community.

The idea of a volume of case studies on the experience of undertaking humanitarian evaluations emerged from a workshop organized by two of the editors (Raymond Apthorpe and John Borton) at the Australian National University in March 1998, and funded by AusAID (Apthorpe 1998). The proposal met with ALNAP Full Members' approval in April 1999, and, as the current Chair of ALNAP, it is exciting and rewarding to see it become a reality in the shape of ALNAP's first major publication.

Not only does this book 'open up' a process that has for too long remained hidden, it also provides clear pointers as to how evaluators, evaluation managers and humanitarian managers/practitioners can improve the 'doing' of evaluations of humanitarian operations and thereby the effectiveness of the evaluation process.

This book would not have been possible without the financial assistance provided through the Australian Government's Overseas Aid Program. On behalf of ALNAP, I would like to express my sincere thanks to the Office of Program Review and Evaluation of AusAID (Australian Agency for International Development), one of ALNAP's 46 full members, for supporting this publication.

We are also indebted to the contributors of the nine case studies. The act of writing up and reflecting critically on an evaluation process is never easy. This is particularly true when the writing has to be done alongside 'normal' work in an author's spare time. Evaluations of humanitarian operations are often intense experiences, involving considerable judgements about the perceived success or limitations of an action. Evaluators work under difficult conditions under considerable time pressures and in the face of high expectation. To dissect and share that experience has required the contributors to reflect carefully and critically on their own roles. For all, it has a been demanding process involving a measure of courage and self-discovery.

Finally, this book would not have been realized without the creative and steadfast commitment of Adrian Wood, his two co-editors Raymond Apthorpe and John Borton, and colleagues in the ALNAP Secretariat at the Overseas Development Institute. Inasmuch as this book is widely circulated, closely read and serves as a guide for improving humanitarian programme evaluation performance, their efforts will have been richly rewarded.

Wayne MacDonald, Chairman of ALNAP
(Head of Planning, Monitoring and Evaluation,
International Committee of the Red Cross
Geneva)

Introduction

Adrian Wood, Raymond Apthorpe and John Borton

Every day humanitarian relief operations, mounted in response to needs created by natural disasters and conflict, are taking place in at least twenty and as many as fifty different locations around the world.[1] Perhaps three or four times a year, these crises become so grave as to make headline news around the world and enormous resources are mobilized by donor and disaster response agencies of national governments, the United Nations (UN), the Red Cross and non-governmental organizations (NGOs) in response. While the bulk of this assistance is resourced by 'official funding' derived from taxes, a significant proportion is made up of private donations by the general public. How effective is such assistance? How do these organizations know that their aid 'got through' and that their actions were beneficial? How do they learn from their experiences so that they can improve their response to the next hurricane or the next mass movement of refugees?

Over the last decade evaluation has become a key tool, arguably *the* key tool used by donor organizations and humanitarian agencies to assess how the assistance was used and what lessons might be learned. A situation has now been reached where evaluations are almost *de rigueur* for 'respectable' organizations at the end of large humanitarian operations. For example, the international response to humanitarian needs created by the 1999 conflict in Kosovo has led to at least ten conventional evaluation reports and many more evaluative or audit-style exercises (Apthorpe 2000). How are such studies carried out? Who are these evaluators and how are they recruited? What methods do they use? How do they arrive at their conclusions and recommendations? How do they cope when the agencies being evaluated press for their report to be less critical? How effective are they at identifying what went wrong, what went right and what lessons should be learned from the experience? By bringing together, for the first time, reflections on evaluations by those involved in undertaking them, this book seeks to explain and analyse these issues and contribute to efforts to improve the existing guidance on how best to carry out such evaluations.

Who is this Book for?

As the first book to chart and analyse the application of evaluation approaches, methods and methodologies in the humanitarian field, this book will be of interest to a wide range of readers within the evaluation community, the humanitarian relief community, teachers and students, the media, and members of the general public.

The evaluation community is extensive and rapidly growing, and must now involve tens of thousands of people around the world. Evaluation is now applied to almost every form of human activity, whether road construction, health systems delivery or teaching methods used in schools. Professional evaluation associations are active in many countries on all the continents and more are being established each year. The national associations are now being complemented by regional evaluation associations and networks forming around particular types of evaluation. Within this extensive community are a wide range of roles and perspectives, including:

- methodologists (specialists in methodological issues of evaluation) who analyse and contribute to the continuing development of evaluation methods;
- evaluators, often working for commercial organizations or on a freelance basis, who undertake evaluation studies for client organizations; and
- evaluation managers who, on behalf of their organizations, oversee and manage the evaluation process from inception and commissioning through to delivery and follow up the completed studies.

This book will be of interest to those methodologists, and also those evaluators and evaluation managers, who are interested in the extension and application of evaluation into this comparatively new field and the ways in which the methods are being adapted to this very particular context and role. By providing accounts of the actual practice of humanitarian evaluation it is hoped to draw them into the discussions and debates about the evaluation of humanitarian assistance, which to date have only involved a small, but growing, number of individuals.

Only a very small proportion of the total number of those in the 'evaluator' and 'evaluation manager' categories within the evaluation community are involved in the evaluation of humanitarian assistance. Indeed, most of those who are involved will be working for the very organizations and agencies that comprise the humanitarian community. Nevertheless, there is significant movement of evaluators and evaluation managers into and out of humanitarian evaluation, and the recent rapid increase in the number of humanitarian evaluations has drawn in many evaluators who had no previous experience of such evaluations. Thus the book is of interest not only to those currently involved in such work but also to those who are about to move into the field and those who may be contemplating such a move.

The 'humanitarian community' includes thousands of individuals working around the world for a wide variety of organizations – national governments, UN agencies, the Red Cross movement and NGOs. Most of these organizations have sections responsible for evaluation and lesson-learning. The staff of these sections represent the points of overlap between the 'evaluation community' and the 'humanitarian community'. For the staff of these sections this book will be highly relevant and professionally of central importance. The book will also be of interest to many of their colleagues, whether working in head offices or 'in the field' involved in operations. Many will have read evaluation reports and wondered about the process by which they were prepared, or will even have experienced 'being evaluated' by virtue of their programmes being covered by an evaluation.

Staff in humanitarian agencies whose programmes have been evaluated often emerge from the experience unhappy about the process and its outcomes. Part of the purpose of this book is to open up the process (warts and all!) in order to demystify it and contribute to a more informed debate within the humanitarian community about the benefits and potential value of the evaluation process, and also the limitations of evaluation as it is currently practised.

So far very few training courses on how to evaluate humanitarian assistance have been established. Existing courses on evaluation methods in the field of development assistance have not been quick to recognize the increase in the number of humanitarian programme evaluations taking place or to develop additional components for their courses. With the encouragment and help of the sponsors of this volume, the Active Learning Network for Accountability and Performance in Humanitarian Action (ALNAP)[2], this situation is about to change. Simultaneously with the publication of this book, ALNAP will be: initiating courses aimed at evaluation managers and humanitarian desk officers; providing support to the development of components for postgraduate courses aimed at current and future evaluators; and developing curricula and materials to enable existing training providers, whether in the humanitarian or evaluation communities, to introduce modules on humanitarian programme evaluation. For the teachers, students and participants in any of these courses this book will be an invaluable resource.

The role of the media in humanitarian crises and operations is varied.

At times it can be hugely influential in terms of awareness-raising, moving a particular situation or crisis up the international agenda and provoking governments and the public to donate to the international response. It can also focus the spotlight upon aspects of the humanitarian system that appear not to be functioning as they should. While all journalism is investigative to some degree, investigative journalism when focused upon the functioning of a particular operation comes close to evaluation. Indeed, it is a form of 'instant evaluation'. The personnel of humanitarian agencies often welcome and actively encourage media coverage of their work, but there are times when they bitterly resent what they regard as partial and ill-informed journalism – similar, perhaps, to the way in which one-sided evaluations might be regarded. This book will be of interest to those in the media who cover humanitarian or disaster 'stories' and wonder about how the humanitarian system assesses its performance long after the cameras have gone. Perhaps introducing some of the ideas and techniques used in evaluation and described in this book might lead to improvements in the quality of media coverage of future humanitarian operations.

Finally, this book may also be of interest to members of the general public who have donated to fundraising appeals by agencies at times of particular disasters. While the book does not directly answer their most frequently asked question – 'did the aid get quickly to those who needed it?' – it focuses upon on one of the principal ways in which organizations assess and reflect upon their performance and thereby answer such questions for themselves.

The International Humanitarian System and Trends in Humanitarian Assistance

In order to understand the context in which humanitarian programme evaluation takes place, it is necessary to consider the structure and functioning of, and recent trends within, the international humanitarian system.[3]

Figure 1.1 shows the principal resource flows within the international humanitarian system and thereby the principal types of organization that comprise the system and their broad relationship. The system is fuelled by tax-derived and privately donated resources, principally from within the richer nations. The tax-derived resources are managed by bilateral donor organizations that occupy a very influential position within the overall system. Resources from these two sources are channelled to the beneficiaries within the affected population via intermediate organizations such as United Nations agencies, NGOs and the Red Cross and Red Crescent movement (ICRC, IFRC and national societies). Assistance and resources also flow laterally within affected countries from wealthier and less affected

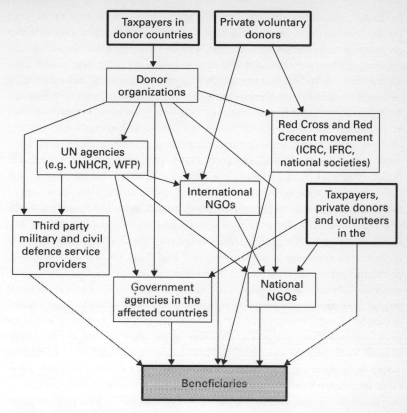

FIGURE 1.1 Principal resource flows and routes between donors and beneficiaries within the international humanitarian system (*source*: Borton 1993, adapted)

sections of the society, but such resource flows are very rarely measured and are of uncertain scale.

The types of organization commonly involved in the provision of humanitarian assistance include:

- national relief structures (where they are still operating) or relief structures linked to particular groups (such as warring factions in a conflict);
- national and 'local' NGOs;
- UN agencies;
- international NGOs; and
- different components of the ICRC, IFRC and national societies.

The above group may expand as a result of operations taking place in particular contexts. For example, where displaced populations cross international borders, refugee agencies will become involved together with the authorities in the asylum countries. In some operations, bilateral and multilateral donor organizations may expand their presence beyond their existing aid missions through the establishment of local field teams providing funding and coordinating directly funded projects and agencies.

When combined with the numbers of organizations typically represented within any of these different organizational categories, the overall numbers of organizations present in an operation can be surprisingly high. While many operations may involve a maximum of perhaps twenty humanitarian organizations, in the largest operations, such as those mounted in the Great Lakes region of Africa during 1994–95 and in the Balkans during the 'Kosovo crisis' of 1999, the total number of organizations involved exceeded two hundred and may even have reached three hundred. A 'medium-scale' operation will typically involve seven or eight UN agencies, the ICRC, IFRC (perhaps working in different areas with the ICRC operating in the areas of active conflict) and the National Red Cross/Red Crescent movement; and perhaps fifty or more international and local NGOs. The various organizations and agencies present may be funded by twenty or more official governmental donor organizations supplemented by funds raised privately.

The prime source of such variation in the numbers of organizations present is invariably the NGO sector. In some countries – Bangladesh would be a good example – the NGO sector may already be very active prior to a disaster and the numbers of 'new' NGOs establishing operations in the wake of the disaster comparatively limited.[4] However, in many operations significant numbers of 'new' NGOs are attracted to establish operations in response to a humanitarian crisis. The number of 'new' NGOs involved in an operation is heavily influenced by the scale of the humanitarian need and also by the level of media coverage of the situation. Frequently, but by no means in every case, these two factors work in tandem to provide incentives (in terms of the availability of funding) and pressures (from their traditional supporters, who expect them to establish operations in the affected country) influencing the number of 'new' NGOs.

Another point that needs to be borne in mind when considering NGOs and the capacities that they represent is the enormous variation in their capacities. While most of the larger international NGOs have the capacity to work simultaneously in several sectors (such as health, shelter, food and nutrition, and water and sanitation) in large parts of the affected area, many NGOs are highly specialized, concentrating on the needs of a particular population group (children, elderly, disabled) or confine their work to a particular locale.

Humanitarian agencies invariably operate alongside other actors within other domains. For instance, human rights agencies and organizations seeking to resolve conflicts (through the provision of mediation channels or by building links between opposing communities) are increasingly active in areas of ongoing conflicts. In some conflicts international peacekeeping or peace-enforcement forces may be deployed, either by the UN or by regional bodies such as the Organization of African Unity (OAU) or the North Atlantic Treaty Organization (NATO). Such military interventions may involve troop contingents from a variety of countries. In these situations humanitarian activities will run alongside the peacekeeping/peace-enforcement operation. Depending on the context and the effectiveness of what are referred to as 'civil–military cooperation arrangements', the level of cooperation and collaboration between the humanitarian and the military operations may vary greatly.

Though almost invisible on the ground, diplomatic activity operates around and alongside the humanitarian system. Such activity typically involves neighbouring states and more powerful distant states with an interest in the area or an interest in seeing a particular outcome to a conflict. Such 'interests' may range from the comparatively benign interest in achieving an early cessation of a conflict to a more malign interest in seeking the victory of a favoured side or faction, and may involve the use of both covert and overt means.

A recent analysis of trends in overall expenditures on humanitarian aid by rich country governments[5] reveals 'a distinctive pattern: periodic increases in humanitarian aid tend to be followed by a plateau and then another rise. Funding does not fall back to its pre-plateau level' (IASC 2000).

Figure 1.2, expressed in inflation-adjusted rather than cash terms, is useful for comparison of inter-period changes. It reveals broadly stable levels of bilateral humanitarian assistance from 1971 through to 1984, when the famines in Ethiopia and Sudan and the wider food crisis in Africa led to a doubling in the levels. In 1991, with the Kurdish refugee crisis and the aftermath of the Gulf War, the overall expenditures doubled again and rose to a peak in 1994 – the year of the genocide in Rwanda and the massive refugee movements in the Great Lakes region of Africa. Assistance levels declined from this peak over the next three years, but even in 1997 they were still more than twice the average for the late 1980s. In 1998 the figures increased again as a result of the international response to the devastation in Central America caused by Hurricane Mitch, and it is expected that when the data for 1999 become available the total will be substantially higher as a result of the conflict and consequent population displacements in and around Kosovo. When the data are considered in cash terms, the peak in 1994 was US$5.7 billion, a figure that exceeded 10 per cent of total

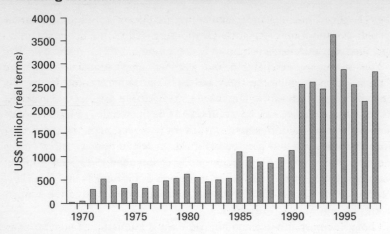

FIGURE 1.2 Long-term trends in bilateral humanitarian assistance
(*source*: IASC 2000)

official development assistance provided by the Development Assistance
Committee (DAC) member governments.

The boom in funding in the first half of the 1990s was closely related
to the ending of the Cold War period. Throughout the Cold War the USA
and the USSR freely used their veto powers on the UN Security Council
to prevent direct UN peacekeeping interventions in ongoing conflict
(Parsons 1995). The pattern was typically that peacekeeping forces were
deployed only once peace agreements had been signed and there was
literally 'a peace to keep'. For the most part humanitarian assistance from
government sources during this long period was provided only to those
who could escape from the conflict zones and cross, as refugees, into
neighbouring countries. The provision of humanitarian assistance in areas
of ongoing conflict was almost the sole preserve of NGOs. As well as
some of the well-known international NGOs, the NGOs involved in these
operations at the time also included solidarity groups such as the Swedish
Committee for Afghanistan (SCA) and the relief arms of rebel groups
such as the Relief Society of Tigray (REST). These were formed with the
express purpose of providing assistance to populations in the areas controlled by rebel groups. Initially the NGOs involved in the provision of
assistance in zones of ongoing conflict were entirely dependent on voluntary funding from private sources. Fearful of being seen as contravening
the sovereignty of the internationally recognized authorities, Western
governments were extremely cautious in their support to NGOs providing
relief assistance in such areas. However, towards the end of the Cold War

Western governments were channelling significant levels of resources through NGOs into areas such as northern Ethiopia and *mujahideen*-controlled areas of Afghanistan.

The end of the Cold War period saw the virtual cessation of the use of their veto powers by the USA and the Russian Federation from 1989 onwards, and a readiness by key states to undertake military intervention in conflicts in the pursuit of substantially humanitarian objectives. The watershed in this regard was the April 1991 intervention to create safe havens for displaced and persecuted Kurds in northern Iraq, and this was quickly followed by the January 1992 creation of the United Nations Protection Force in the former Yugoslavia (UNPROFOR) and the December 1992 deployment of US troops in Somalia as part of the United Task Force (UNITAF) operation.

These changes had a profound impact on the international humanitarian system. UN agencies and NGOs could now operate alongside, and to some extent under the protection of, UN-sanctioned peacekeeping and peace enforcement forces (Weiss 1999). Even in conflicts where the UN-sanctioned troops were not present, NGOs and UN agencies increasingly operated more directly, though often at far greater risk to the safety of their personnel. In such ongoing conflicts, UN agencies were often unable to use the structures of the host governments, as natural partners of the UN in more stable contexts, to undertake the delivery of assistance. Structures of the host governments were frequently rendered ineffective as a result of the conflict in that they did not cover areas of the country controlled by rebel groups or, within those areas under rebel control, could not be relied upon to distribute assistance fairly to those in need. Consequently the humanitarian system was forced to make greater use of NGOs as 'implementing partners' and increasingly NGOs entered contractual 'relief delivery' relationships with the UN and bilateral donor agencies.

This direct 'on-the-ground' role in ongoing conflicts placed all agencies on a very steep learning curve. Models of relief assistance that had been developed in relation to natural disasters, or in relation to refugee camps located away from conflicts, now required major adaptations (Roberts 1996). For instance, NGOs that had previously been open about their solidarity with particular groups were now forced to adopt consciously the principles of 'neutrality' and 'impartiality' that had long been integral to the approach of the Red Cross and Red Crescent movements. The needs of internally displaced populations (IDPs), virtually invisible previously due to their ambiguous legal status and the lack of dedicated organizational capacity within the system for responding to their needs, were now placed firmly on the agenda. Then, from the middle of the 1990s onwards, came growing criticism that humanitarian assistance was actually prolonging conflicts by providing resources that were diverted and manipulated by warring factions and that relief was actually 'doing harm' (de Waal 1997; Anderson 1999). The pressures increased substantially for humanitarian agencies to learn from their experiences, so as to inform the process of adaptation and to protect themselves from damaging criticism.[6]

In parallel to these pressures was the increased questioning of the effectiveness of the expenditures on humanitarian assistance within donor organizations by their respective parliamentary and congressional scrutiny bodies. As long as humanitarian expenditures within the DAC had remained at comparatively low levels, the effectiveness of humanitarian assistance expenditures had escaped close scrutiny by DAC Members of DAC countries. However, when expenditures reached levels of 20 per cent or more of the aid programme in some bilateral donor organizations and the overall levels of official development assistance approached (and in 1994 exceeded) the 10 per cent level, the resources devoted to humanitarian assistance became too significant to ignore.

It was this combination of factors that contributed to the upsurge – some prefer the term 'boom' – in the evaluation of humanitarian assistance, which is the focus of, and provides the raw material for, this book.

The Growth of Humanitarian Evaluation

Although its precise meaning has been the subject of considerable debate, the term 'evaluation' is generally taken to mean 'the process of determining the merit, worth or value or something, or the product of that process' (Scriven 1991: 139). While the roots of what we now call evaluation can be traced back to the 1920s (Guba and Lincoln 1989), evaluation, as a field of professional practice, effectively commenced in the United States of America during the 1960s (Patton 1997). The 'Great Society' legislation of the 1960s poured massive Federal expenditures into poverty alleviation programmes, desegregation, housing, welfare and the education sectors. Such large expenditures led to the development and application of evaluation, and indeed in many programmes was actually required by the legislation, in order to assess the effectiveness of the programmes and decide how best to use the funding available. By the mid-1970s two professional organizations were established in the USA that in 1984 were to merge and form the large and highly influential American Evaluation Association.[7] National evaluation associations were being formed in other countries too, and in 1995 the first International Evaluation Conference was held (Patton 1997).

It was not long before the techniques developed in the USA were being applied in the field of international development assistance. The decolonization process of the 1950s and 1960s led to the establishment of new departments and ministries to administer the aid programmes. Evaluation was increasingly utilized to assess effectiveness and assist in decisions about how best to allocate the funds available.

During the 1960s some of these departments established evaluation units. By the end of the 1970s most aid-administering organizations had evaluation units of some form. Under the auspices of the Organization for Economic Cooperation and Development (OECD), representatives of these units formed a Group on Aid Effectiveness (precursor to what is now the DAC Working Party on Aid Evaluation)[8] and began meeting regularly (Kjekshus 1991; Cracknell 2000).

However, the application of evaluation to the field of humanitarian aid (or emergency assistance or disaster relief as it was known) was comparatively slow. A combination of attitudinal, technical, practical and methodological factors contributed to this delay, including the following:

- Organizations involved in disaster relief were, initially at least, resentful of the evaluation process, the attitude in effect being 'we did our best under extremely difficult circumstances and do not accept that someone who was not involved in the operation should come and criticize us'.
- Natural disasters and conflict are both highly dynamic situations involving rapid change, and the baseline information that is usually available for evaluations of development assistance is usually unavailable for humanitarian evaluations.
- The pressure to respond rapidly and the difficulties of the operational context often result in poor and incomplete documentation by the agencies involved.
- The nature of the interventions by humanitarian agencies are often highly multidisciplinary, covering health, logistics, food and nutrition, water and sanitation, and this creates organizational barriers to initiating and undertaking evaluations.

The story of how these factors were gradually addressed and overcome covers at least the last thirty years. It is primarily a story of gradual shifts in the face of increasing pressure for the system to be more accountable – a pressure fuelled by the increasing level of resources used by the international humanitarian system and also wider changes in the approach to accountability within Western societies.

The Sahelian droughts and famines of 1972–74 resulted in three US studies, although none was strictly speaking an evaluation commissioned by an aid organization. One was a report to Congress (USAID 1977). The other two were research assessments (Sheets and Morris 1974; Glantz 1976; Chambers et al. 1986). In 1984 an excellent account of the international response to the conflict and genocide in Cambodia and the consequent refugee crisis was published by William Shawcross (Shawcross 1984), yet this was a book by an investigative journalist, not a commissioned evaluation report. Not until the mid-1980s, when the United States Agency for International Development, the UK Overseas Development Administration (now the Department for International Development) and the International Federation of Red Cross and Red Crecent Societies commissioned evaluations of their respective response to the famines in Ethiopia and Sudan and the wider African Food Crisis (USAID 1986; Borton et al. 1988; Chambers et al. 1986), did evaluation procedures, as applied to development assistance, began to be applied to 'emergency assistance'.

Although evaluations of such assistance increased in the years following the African Food Crisis, the numbers carried out were limited until around 1993, when the 1991 upturn in humanitarian expenditures started to feed through into increased numbers of evaluations. The Dutch evaluation undertaken in Somalia that forms the second chapter of this volume can rightly claim to be the first attempt to evaluate humanitarian assistance provided in response to a conflict or a complex emergency. Curiously, the very event that produced the upturn in humanitarian expenditures – the Kurdish refugee crisis – was never subjected to a conventional evaluation process, although a number of internal studies were undertaken in aid agencies, including the United Nations High Commissioner for Refugees (UNHCR), and in those military forces involved in the operation.

The Joint Evaluation of Emergency Assistance to Rwanda, part of which is described in Chapter 6, proved influential in several ways. One was the initiation of a process to develop initial guidance material for undertaking humanitarian evaluation in complex emergencies, assisted by a productive workshop held in Canberra in March 1998 and supported by AusAID (Apthorpe 1998). The process resulted in two differently oriented guidance documents – one aimed at relief workers (Hallam 1998) and the other at evaluation managers in bilateral and multilateral donor organizations (OECD–DAC 1999). Because of the timing of their publication, these guidance documents were available only to the last two case studies in this volume. Yet such is the pace of change in the sector that more types of humanitarian evaluation have emerged since 1997–98, and gaps in the guidance have already been identified.

Introduction to the Case Studies

The nine case studies presented in the following chapters were undertaken between 1993 and the end of 1999. They therefore represent a sample from within the 1990s 'boom' in humanitarian evaluation. By virtue of the seven years spanned, the sample may provide glimpses of whether the 'art' of humanitarian programme evaluation has evolved during the decade, and, if so, the ways in which it has evolved.

In assembling this collection we used the generally accepted definition of evaluation, i.e. a study to assess the merit, worth or value of a programme, its policy and its projects. The grounds on which such value judgements are made, and the methods used, vary. While there tends to be much commonality, for instance around the concept 'humanitarian', emphases vary considerably. Some put the heaviest value on matters of principle. Other focus on material inputs, outputs, outcomes or even impacts.

We attempted to select a range of types of evaluation (own performance, performance of partners, system-wide), involving a range of agencies (bilateral donor, UN agency, NGOs and the IFRC) and different field conditions and locations. Most studies were undertaken independently. Some, however, were undertaken jointly. One case involved a major collaboration of the donor community. A further consideration was to draw evaluations from across the world and to focus not only on complex emergencies and not only upon Africa, where the editors had most contacts and experience.

The volume starts with the 1993 Somalia study undertaken by the Netherlands Ministry of Foreign Affairs evaluation department working jointly with a number of consultancy groups. As well as assessing the Dutch assistance in Somalia, this study sought to explore whether or not it was possible to evaluate humanitarian assistance in complex emergency situations, where armed conflict makes it difficult to address humanitarian needs as well as assess humanitarian responses. The study showed that the evaluation of humanitarian programmes in complex emergencies is possible, something that other donors and field agencies increasingly recognized during the 1990s.

The Swedish International Development Agency (Sida) was one of the bilateral donor agencies that was particularly keen to review its expanding funding of humanitarian activities, which had increasingly cut into its development budget during the late 1980s and early 1990s. During 1993 and 1994 it commissioned a series of three studies of its assistance in complex emergency and natural disaster situations. Two of these are reported in this volume. Sida's Horn of Africa study, undertaken by a university-based consultancy organization, found that the diversity of partners and projects, as well as the timing of the evaluation – several years after most of the field activities had stopped – raised questions about what conclusions could be drawn from this work. The team's view was that lessons could be learned, but most usefully at programme and policy

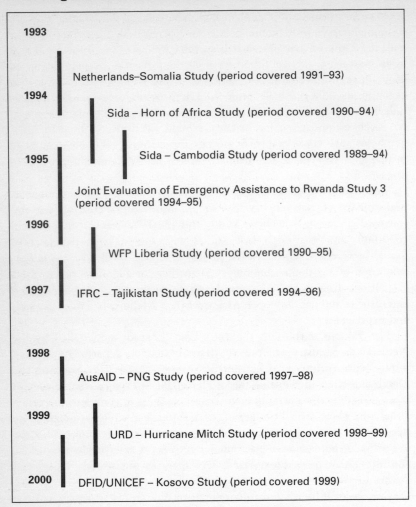

FIGURE 1.3 Timeline of the case studies. Vertical lines show approximate
duration of studies from start of work to completion of final report

levels, rather than at project level. These were generally well received and
provided Sida with guidance about how to think about and plan its humanitarian assistance.

Sida's Cambodia evaluation differed in some important respects from
the Horn of Africa evaluation. Its team was recruited directly by the agency.
While both teams were largely made up of country specialists, the Horn
of Africa study had focused on an integrated approach and the Cambodia
study followed a sectoral and specialist approach.

That the version submitted to Sida contained two concluding chapters reflecting the majority and minority views in the team was the result of tensions that are often present within evaluation teams but rarely surface in such an open fashion. In this case the conflicts seem to have come not so much from differing field experiences as from different methodological approaches within the team and debates over the importance of a historical perspective when a long-time period of assistance, six years in this case, is being considered.

Starting in January 1995, and with the results published in March 1996, there was what was, and probably will remain, the largest humanitarian evaluation – the Joint Evaluation of Emergency Assistance to Rwanda (JEEAR). This considered the humanitarian assistance and protection provided in response to the conflict and genocide in Rwanda and the consequent population displacements. Uniquely this study was commissioned by the donor community almost in its entirety, and was made up of four separate studies and a synthesis study. The whole process was steered by a large committee involving UN agencies, the Red Cross movement and NGO umbrella organizations, but was managed by a group of five bilateral donor organizations. This study was seminal in many ways, not least because it pointed out that humanitarian programmes could not be properly evaluated without reference to the political situation. In particular, it showed that humanitarian assistance had been used by Western donors in effect as an alternative to military intervention. This 'system-wide' study also highlighted the problems of coordination in complex emergency situations and was especially critical of the UN system for its failings in this respect.

In contrast to this multi-agency, system-wide study is the evaluation by the World Food Programme (WFP) of its food aid in the Liberia region, which was undertaken in 1996. Using a team that had at its core a majority of independent team members but also drew personnel from within the WFP and a sister agency, this study sought to explore the reality of food aid provision under the very difficult field conditions in this part of West Africa. The problem of gaining access to beneficiaries, the field conditions, and the historical nature of the activities being studied (a six-year period), led the team to conclude that it could work credibly only at the policy level. However, it was also able to identify where a number of key conceptual misunderstandings were occurring and to propose new ways in which these could be addressed in the operations concerned.

The Tajikistan study covers a review of the IFRC programme in that country. The study shows how evaluations are part and parcel of planning and programming on many types of occasion and not only as end of activity assessments for learning lessons. In this case the evaluation was called an external review, perhaps to make the evaluatory nature more acceptable but also because the agenda was clearly to provide clearance for further funding by the Federation to one of its member organizations – the Tajikistan Red Cross Society. At the same time the study was undertaken to identify lessons that could be used in the programming of future work by the Tajikistan Red Cross Society.

The Papua New Guinea study provides an interesting case of conflicts between a commissioning agency and an evaluation team. It highlights the need to ensure that an appropriate effort is put into ensuring that the study is accepted and likely to be used by the commissioning agency. Despite a commendable methodology, which focused on beneficiaries at the end of the distribution chain, this study will probably be remembered more for the disagreements with the team than for the lessons learned. The idea of separating some of the stages in the evaluation process is raised here in order to focus specifically on field performance and policy issues.

The need for a dialogue between those being evaluated and the evaluators in order to ensure that lessons are learned from an evaluation is explored by the last but one study, an evaluation of the response of French NGOs to Hurricane Mitch. This study came about primarily as a result of the interests of those agencies operating in the field. It involved a more inclusive and explicitly lesson-learning approach. It shows especially how networking and feedback can contribute to a very open and constructive learning process. However, it still shows some of the tensions of the decade over the approach, with a conflict between the funding agency interested in accountability and the team (from Groupe Urgence-Réhabilitation-Développement) and NGOs whose primary concern was with lesson-learning.

The Kosovo study is the most recent in the volume. This is a joint evaluation between a donor, the UK Department for International Development (DFID) and the United Nations Children's Fund (UNICEF), of activities undertaken by UNICEF and funded by the DFID. The study shows how jointly selected teams with internal and external staff can work effectively. However, problems can occur easily in such joint evaluations, so there is a special need to keep all the parties in each organization informed about the basis on which it is carried out as a joint inquiry.

The Contributors

The authors of these studies are drawn from several parts of the world, although by no means do they form a fully representative sample. Despite invitations to a wider range of potential contributors to the volume, none of the eventual contributors is from Africa, Asia, South America or North America. Overall the contributors are predominantly white Northern males of 'mature' years (40–70). Only two are women. The Anglo-Saxon cultural zone is the origin for almost half of the authors, but a range of nationalities across the Western donor countries is included – France, Sweden, Netherlands, Ireland, and Australia, as well as the UK.

All the contributors are committed to humanitarian evaluation and have contributed in different ways to the development of humanitarian evaluation and to the thinking about how such evaluations should be done. They include:

- full-time consultants specializing in humanitarian evaluation, who come from a variety of professional backgrounds, which include working with NGOs in the field on humanitarian assistance, or with donor agencies, etc;
- the coordinator of ALNAP, whose responsibilities include encouraging improvements in humanitarian evaluation; and
- university-based professors and researchers who have worked as consultants in variety of roles including humanitarian and development evaluations.

Learning from the Case Studies

The case studies that follow explore the doing of evaluations from the perspective of one or more team members, often, but not always, the Team Leader. The authors were asked to reflect on their experience and to discuss, in a primarily chronological order, the experiences they felt were most important and influential. Common guidance was given but contributors have interpreted this in their own way so that the chapters have their own particular emphases and distinctive styles. This, we hope, will help bring alive to the reader the debates and experiences the authors are presenting.

From these studies the editors have drawn a series of issues and ideas that are common to a number of the chapters and require further thought. These are explored in the conclusions, which identify specific areas that need attention for the practicalities of both doing and managing evaluations, as well ideas about the conceptual ways of approaching evaluation in the future.

Notes

1. The figure of 50 is given in IASC 2000.

2. ALNAP's structure and activities are described at the front of this book. ALNAP's website is at <www.alnap.org>.

3 The use of the word 'system' to describe the complex of governmental, non-governmental and multilateral organizations involved in funding, channelling, coordin-

ating, transporting and delivering humanitarian assistance is not universally accepted. In his classic text Randolph Kent (1987) prefers the phrase 'network of actors'. Nevertheless, 'system' is used here in part because the complex of organizations broadly share the same goal of saving lives and reducing the suffering and economic and social impacts of disasters and conflicts. However imperfectly, the complex grouping of organizations frequently behave in aggregate as a system and are generally perceived by outsiders as constituting a system. Finally, the more the word is used the more those within the various organizations who view their role only in terms of their own organization will be encouraged to view their role and their organization's as part of a larger system.

4. 'New' is used here to describe those NGOs that did not exist or have programmes in the affected country prior to the disaster or crisis. New national NGOs may be established in response to the event, and established international NGOs may establish programmes (usually relief but sometimes more developmental in their focus) in response to the disaster or crisis.

5. These figures refer only to 'official development assistance' provided by governments that are members of the Development Assistance Committee (DAC) of the Organization for Economic Cooperation and Development (OECD). For example China, Korea, the United Arab Emirates, India and Saudi Arabia are not members of the DAC and so their contributions are not included by the data. Neither do the data cover voluntary flows from private sources. Such flows are extremely hard to measure and the available datasets are very patchy. A reasonable guess would be that such flows are equivalent to perhaps 15 per cent of annual official development assistance flows, with the proportion rising to as much as 40 per cent in those operations that receive intense media, especially television, coverage.

6. Part of the response to such pressures has been the initiation of a number of accountability initiatives within the humanitarian system. This began with the 1994 Code of Conduct for the International Red Cross and Red Crescent movements and NGOs in disaster relief <www.ifrc.org/pubs>; ALNAP and the Sphere Project, which has produced the Humanitarian Charter and Minimum Standards in Disaster Response <www.sphereproject.org>.

7. For more information on the American Evaluation Association the website addess is <www.eval.org/>. Other useful sites are: the UK Evaluation Society <www.evaluation.org.uk>; the European Evaluation Society <www.europeanevaluation.org> and MandE NEWS <www.mande.co.uk/news>. An African Evaluation Society was formed in 1999 and there are also regional evaluation societies in Asia and Latin America. The sites of many of the other national and regional societies can be accessed from those given above. The International & Cross-Cultural Evaluation Topical Interest Group (I&CCE) provides evaluators who are interested in cross-cultural issues with opportunities for professional development. Its website is at <http://home.wmis.net/~russon/icce/>.

8. The Group has since evolved, initially in 1982 into the DAC Expert Group on Aid Evaluation and subsequently into the DAC Working Party on Aid Evaluation. The Working Party meets regularly to share experience to improve evaluation practice and strengthen its use as an instrument for development cooperation policy. It currently consists of 29 representatives from OECD member countries and multilateral development agencies, the World Bank, regional development banks and the UN Development Programme. <www.oecd.org/dac/evaluation>.

2

Somalia: Towards Evaluating the Netherlands' Humanitarian Assistance

Phil O'Keefe, Ted Kliest, John Kirkby and Wiert Flikkema

The rise in humanitarian expenditure during the 1990s was associated with the growth in complex emergencies which, in turn, was a consequence of the collapse of the Soviet Union and the end of a bipolar world. Cambodia, Afghanistan, the Caucasus, Iraq, former Yugoslavia, the Horn of Africa, West Africa, southern Africa, in particular the Lusophone countries, and Nicaragua were world trouble spots. Bosnia dominated and, there especially, the issues of humanitarian intervention were tied into diplomatic and military considerations.

The Policy and Operations Evaluation Department (IOB) is the independent evaluation unit of the Netherlands Ministry of Foreign Affairs. Its evaluation reports, based on desk and field studies carried out by IOB's own staff and external experts, are written by IOB and published under its responsibility. Depending on the subject evaluated, IOB reports directly to the minister of foreign affairs or to the minister for development cooperation. The minister concerned submits these reports to Parliament to be discussed by the Permanent Committee on Foreign Affairs; follow-up actions are then considered.

After questions were raised in Parliament in November 1992 about the effectiveness of humanitarian aid given its growing volume, the minister for development cooperation decided to commission IOB to review the matter. In preparing the evaluation, several questions were raised. Where should the evaluation take place? Mozambique, Sudan, Somalia and Cambodia were possible theatres discussed; all were places where humanitarian aid monies were spent. Another issue was whether humanitarian assistance could be evaluated. If so, would the focus of the evaluation be largely on the implementation of activities rather than the results? And finally, there was the ethical issue that evaluators might hinder aid delivery, that evaluators would 'get in the way' of those providing the humanitarian assistance. Quite simply, at the early stages of discussing the possibility of evaluating

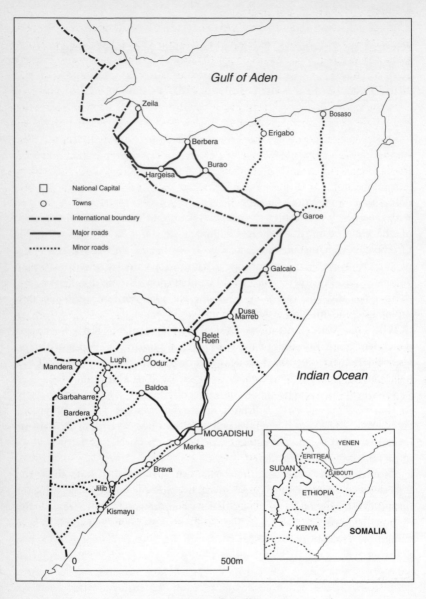

MAP 2.1 Somalia

humanitarian aid there were severe doubts among IOB's staff about the feasibility of such an undertaking.

After consultation with the Emergency and Humanitarian Aid Section of the Ministry of Foreign Affairs, it was decided to evaluate the humanitarian assistance provided to Somalia (Map 2.1) during the period January 1991 to June 1993. Somalia was chosen because of the volume of the Netherlands' assistance to that country (NLG 74.5 million over 30 months). Also, the mix of different humanitarian interventions, focusing on providing immediate relief and rehabilitation programmes, as well as the number of different agencies involved, made it a suitable contemporary example. Desk studies, some interviews with key stakeholders and preparation for field studies took place from June to October 1993; fieldwork was carried out in November and December 1993; analysis, reporting and preparing for publication ran from late December 1993 to April 1994.

Objectives of the Study

The central purpose of our evaluation was to question whether humanitarian aid in Somalia was relevant, effective and efficient in relation to the general principles for the Netherlands' humanitarian assistance. We examined the organization and strategies of the humanitarian interventions and considered the problems that were encountered in aid delivery. Questions about both the theory and practice of humanitarian assistance were dealt with in the context of the complex Somali emergency, although the political situation was not subject to analysis. Specifically, the Terms of Reference (TOR) required:

• a description of Dutch policy and decision-making in the provision of humanitarian aid to Somalia in general; and
• a review of the ways in which the humanitarian aid activities in Somalia have been/are executed with an emphasis on the decision-making process including an assessment of the emergency situation and the affected population, the choice of channels/implementing agencies, the type of activities and the process of planning and execution as well as results (effectiveness and efficiency).

Designing the Evaluation

After selecting Somalia as the subject of the evaluation, there was the challenge of designing the study. This evaluation can be considered a 'pioneer effort' since, at that time, in 1993, other major evaluations of humanitarian assistance, such as the Sida-sponsored evaluation of humanitarian action in the Horn of Africa (Apthorpe et al. 1995), were still on the drawing-board. Moreover, Larry Minear's critical review of the international relief system, which provided new insights for designing evaluations of humanitarian assistance, was published well after our evaluation was finished (Minear 1994). In other words, methodological guidance other than the 'common' Organization for Economic Cooperation and Development–Development Assistance Committee (OECD–DAC) evaluation criteria for evaluating structural development aid (OECD–DAC 1986, 1988, 1992) was hard to find.

The question we had to face was whether the DAC criteria, of 'relevance', 'efficiency', 'effectiveness' and 'sustainability', could be used to evaluate humanitarian assistance. We felt that relevance was perhaps better addressed as appropriateness; efficiency was difficult to define because intervention in disaster was immediately necessary, irrespective of cost implications; and effectiveness was difficult to judge not least because of the lack of baseline data and the disappearance of the beneficiary population through death or movement. Sustainability was essentially a judgement about rehabilitation rather than the detailed criteria developed by OECD–DAC. Our discussion of the evaluation design also involved the need to address the relationship between disaster and development because of arguments about creating an aid dependency culture. The difficulty was in defining the 'cut-off point' for emergency assistance.

Another issue we faced was how far the political context of a complex emergency should be the subject of the evaluation. In the event, we decided to omit any direct reference to this, although relevant issues would arise in the context of aid delivery. There was also discussion on the importance of leadership in addressing humanitarian activities, as field performance was expected to be variable. Our decision was to deal with leadership issues in context, thus avoiding an implied ranking of institutions. Finally, we decided that this evaluation, like most others, would not address the theoretical underpinnings of the intervention, the assumption that humanitarian aid was the necessary intervention.

We decided to undertake first a desk study at the Ministry covering all programmes and projects approved for Somalia with the aim of obtaining initial insights from the results of these interventions, and from this to select cases for further investigation. The desk study, however, found little documentary evidence of results and so the critical issue became how such information could be obtained in a meaningful way and at reasonable cost.

This issue was addressed by developing an evaluation strategy that would focus on Netherlands-financed interventions that were ongoing or only recently finalized. We chose six case studies: four project-type interventions and two programmes. The project case studies were the Lutheran

World Federation's (LWF) airlift operating from Nairobi; Concern's use of King's Recovery Food in its therapeutic feeding centres throughout Somalia; Médecins Sans Frontières-Holland's (MSF-H) medical emergency programme in Baidoa; and projects within the seeds and tools programme of the United Nations Children's Fund (UNICEF). The two programmes were the countrywide Emergency Plan of Action by the International Committee of the Red Cross (ICRC) and the Cross-Border Cross-Mandate Operation by the United Nations High Commissioner for Refugees (UNHCR) (see Box 2.1 for details).

We selected the case studies in consultation with the Emergency and Humanitarian Aid Section in the Ministry of Foreign Affairs. The criteria for selection were the type of activity, the kind of implementing agency and the size of the allocation. Although the sample cannot be considered representative from a statistical point of view, the cases represented a cross-section of the humanitarian assistance financed by the Netherlands and accounted for more than 50 per cent of the total Netherlands humanitarian aid to Somalia in the period 1991–93. Allocations to the World Food Programme (WFP) were excluded because IOB was, at the time, also engaged in a multi-donor evaluation of the WFP.

A three-stage process for the evaluation was envisaged from the outset, with desk studies followed by field investigations leading to case study reports that subsequently would be synthesized in a final report. What was not planned from the outset was the heavy involvement of one of the consultancy teams (see below) in the final stage, this being due to the lack of capacity within the IOB management team to get the study finalized. It was only at a later stage that it was decided to have a very interactive writing up of the final report.

Compiling the Teams and Preparing for Work

The design of the evaluation was carried out by two of us, IOB staff member Ted Kliest and a consultant, Wiert Flikkema. For the implementation of the study, Georg Frerks of IOB subsequently joined us. We decided to sub-contract the case studies separately to individual consultants using direct contracting. Selection criteria were technical expertise and experience with evaluation studies, preferably of humanitarian interventions.

The programme evaluations of ICRC and UNHCR were led by ETC (UK). This firm was chosen because of its work on refugees in IOB's earlier evaluation of the Sector Programme for Rural Development. Part of the task for ETC (UK) included compiling a working document on famine and complex emergencies, building on the geographic tradition of natural hazard research. This was to provide a common framework initially

Box 2.1 List of interventions selected for study

Activity	Agency	Details	Netherlands' contribution
Emergency feeding	Concern (NGO, Ireland)	Purchase, transport and use of 100 Mt 'Kings Recovery Food'	NLG 0.8 million
Emergency medical assistance	MSF-Holland (NGO)	Emergency healthcare. Secondary activities include water, sanitation, shelter and feeding	NLG 2.6 million
Miscellaneous emergency support	International Committee of the Red Cross (ICRC)	Protection and tracing, food distribution, medical assistance, water and sanitation, support to detainees, veterinary campaign, etc.	NLG 13.0 million
Miscellaneous emergency support to refugees	UNHCR	Programme of cross-border and cross-mandate relief assistance as part of the 100-Day Action Plan for Somalia. Relief and rehabilitation activities include food provision, Quick Impact Projects, transport and household essentials	NLG 13.8 million
Operational and logistical support	Lutheran World Federation, through CEBEMO (and NGOs)	Airlift of high-quality food aid and medicine	NLG 9.8 million
Rehabilitation activities	UNICEF (and NGOs)	Provision of seeds and tools to promote household food security and help in re-establishment of returnees	NLG 1.0 million

for the ETC (UK) work, although it was used subsequently for the analysis
of all case studies and the writing up of the final report. The four project
evaluations were allocated to four Netherlands consultancy groups. GEM
Consultants conducted the study on the airlift operations of LWF; the
Institute for International Health, University of Nijmegen carried out the
study on the use of King's Recovery Food in Concern's therapeutic feeding
centres; Medi Vision investigated the medical emergency programme
carried out by MSF-Holland in Baidoa; and Quest Consult evaluated
UNICEF's seeds and tools projects.

Preparatory work for the evaluations of the respective cases included
discussions between each consultant and IOB's management team. Although
a start-up seminar was envisaged, no such meeting took place. Other
conflicting commitments by the various consultants made it difficult to
bring them together. Ultimately, the teams were briefed individually. IOB's
management team informed the different organizations being evaluated of
the study's objectives and approach, forwarded to them the general terms
of reference and provided particulars about the consultants selected to
conduct the different case studies. The consultants were responsible for
coordinating their work schedule with the respective organizations being
studied.

Documents, reports and publications, from a variety of sources, relating
to emergency relief and conditions in Somalia were consulted before the
fieldwork began. All files on the Ministry's allocations of funds from January
1991 to June 1993 were studied, using a format especially drawn up for this
purpose and first tested to ensure inter-researcher reliability. An analysis
was made of the context of aid delivery as it affected the various operations
in Somalia. This analysis was based on secondary sources and on fieldwork,
both in Somalia and in Nairobi. The IOB management team also conducted
detailed interviews in Geneva before going to Nairobi and Somalia.

Analytical Approach

Three separate, but closely linked, analytical categories were employed:
broad questions; concepts; and the 'logic' of intervention.

Seven broad questions were asked about humanitarian assistance:

- What is the context?
- Is it effective?
- Is it efficient (that is, are the funds efficiently spent)?
- What are its side-effects?
- Is it sustainable (in the case of rehabilitation)?
- What lessons are to be learned from each intervention and from an
  examination of its strong and weak points?

- Is it in line with the Netherlands' policies?

With respect to the concepts, we considered that notions of changing vulnerability are powerful aids to understanding the changing impacts of disaster. We included Sen's (1981) concept of entitlement and the exploration by Watts and Bohle (1993) of the interrelations between poverty, hunger and famine. The latter authors set out to define the 'space of vulnerability'. This space is defined in 'locally' and 'historically specific configurations of poverty, hunger and famine'.

It is in this context that another central concept in this evaluation must be understood. We refer throughout to the disaster in Somalia as 'complex'. This implies that any single agent of disaster, such as a drought, exposed other agents, such as low levels of entitlement. Drought, combined with Somalia's immediate political and economic past, which led to civil conflict, a breakdown of civil society, the massive displacement of people and so on, all conspired to create a web of catastrophe. We believe that a disaster may be described as 'complex' when its origins are multiple and its effects compound one another.

Finally, for our study of the logic of intervention, we developed a framework relating to the decision-making, planning and implementation of humanitarian aid. Elements of this framework were:

- the understanding of the emergency, its underlying causes and its development;
- the distinction between relief and rehabilitation within humanitarian assistance, which implies that the definition of the start and end of humanitarian activities is linked to a particular stage of the emergency; and
- that the distinction of procedural stages within relief and rehabilitation are similar to those discerned in the 'project cycle' for structural development activities.

Scope and Limitations of the Evaluation

The Terms of Reference for the study were the template for the five consultant companies. No specific methodology, such as discourse analysis, was required, although the analytical framework (outlined above) and a checklist of key issues and questions (see Box 2.2) was drawn up and shared between the teams. The point of entry for the studies was an analysis of the vulnerability and entitlements of the beneficiary population in a complex emergency that was compounded by drought.

From the beginning, we were acutely aware that the evaluation could not cover the total Somalia experience. With the exception of the inquiry into one of the seeds and tools projects of the UNICEF programme, aid interventions in Somaliland (northern Somalia) were omitted and the field evaluation concentrated, for practical reasons of security, largely south of Mogadishu, particularly along the Juba river.

The study was confined to assistance financed from the 'humanitarian aid' budget vote, i.e. it focused only on relief and rehabilitation activities. Moreover, we could consider only the policies in force during the implementation of the activities. This meant that new policy documents, such as *A World in Dispute* (Netherlands Ministry of Foreign Affairs 1993a) and *Humanitarian Aid between Conflict and Development* (Netherlands Ministry of Foreign Affairs 1993b), published during the course of the evaluation, were taken into account only obliquely. The lack of analysis of the political and military issues made it impossible to come to the conclusion that would dominate later evaluations, notably the Rwanda case (JEEAR 1996),

---

Box 2.2 Checklist for case studies

1. The executing agent: organization, procedures and approach

2. The intervention framework

- needs assessment and identification of intervention
- design of intervention (including goals, instruments, activities, plan of operation and budget)
- appraisal and commitment
- implementation (input, activities, output/delivery, effects, impact)
- reporting/monitoring/evaluation
- follow-up and feedback

3. Discussion

- summary of strong and weak points
- summary of problems and constraints
- compliance of results with the intervention's goals/terms of reference/proposal
- impact
- effectiveness
- efficiency
- sustainability
- policy relevance

4. Discussion

- conclusions, lessons learned, recommendations

that humanitarian aid was used as a substitute for political and diplomatic initiatives.

We also faced limits imposed by the nature of the phenomena to be examined. Much humanitarian assistance is immediately consumed and its temporary institutions dismantled; many of the people involved, both as workers and as beneficiaries, move on to other places and cannot be reached; in the fury of action, paperwork is frequently forgotten or inadequately executed so records are poor or non-existent.

Other limits, springing from the nature of the case, were the impossibility of specifically identifying the contribution made by the Netherlands to co-financed operations as well as the difficulty of estimating the effect of one form of intervention when conditions are changed by a multiplicity of interlinked endeavours. Finally, some limits were imposed on our work by the continuing difficulty of movement within Somalia because of the security situation. Therefore, events had necessarily to be reconstructed from incomplete evidence.

Approaches to the Evaluation of the Cases

Different approaches were taken in the evaluation of the six activities studied. In the case of the 'LWF Airlift' we sought to determine the results of the airlift and its effects on the direct beneficiaries, i.e. the organizations requesting goods to be transported into Somalia. This involved analysis of written materials (project proposals, statistics, reports) as well as interviews with key staff involved in the airlift and members of organizations that used the airlift. Fieldwork in Somalia was confined to participation in one of the airlifts and no ultimate beneficiaries were interviewed.

In the study of the 'King's Recovery Food in Concern's Feeding Programme' we had to rely on only the documentary evidence (found in the Ministry's files and in the Dublin offices of Concern), and interviews with Concern personnel who previously worked in the feeding centres and their headquarters.

A similar desk-based study addressed 'MSF-Holland's medical emergency programme carried out in Baidoa'. As the project had been terminated, its target group could no longer be identified and staff involved in its execution had been transferred. The evaluation method used was restricted to an analysis of documentary evidence (e.g. proposals, statistics and reports) and interviews with key informants involved in decision-making and actual project execution.

'UNICEF's rehabilitation projects' were evaluated through fieldwork in the Lower Juba Valley and in Somaliland. As the interventions had been in a fragmented and unstable society, attention had to be paid to the degree to which the specific context had determined decision-making in project planning and implementation. The evaluation focused on the link between rehabilitation and a more developmental approach. It also looked at the implementation process and through this assessed the results of the interventions.

Some of the elements in 'ICRC's Emergency Plan of Action' were still ongoing, such as tracing people, and in medical, water and sanitation, agricultural and veterinary programmes, and these were visited. However, the study was seriously limited by ICRC's refusal to give access, due to confidentiality, to any materials other than technical documents and the reports drawn up for donors. As a result we were unable to substantiate some of their observations and comments. A framework that reconstructed the logic and evolution of ICRC's activities, with slight variations depending on context and the available time, was used in nearly every interview. This was used with a wide range of NGOs as well as ICRC staff so that an overall view was obtained. Discussions with the beneficiaries of ICRC's work had less to do with the programme than with their own personal situations and survival mechanisms. While Somalis are articulate, as a result of their oral tradition, perceptions are subjective and prone to distortion. Even the months in which activities started could not be agreed upon and at times it was possible for us to get dates for major parts of the operation only by referring to the available documentation. This emphasizes the need for access to the full documentation so that events and issues can be treated adequately.

We held interviews with the United Nations High Commissioner for Refugees (UNHCR) headquarters staff and also with staff in the field concerning the 'Cross-Border Cross Mandate Operation'. A range of documents was obtained that detailed the Kenyan programme and the UNHCR approach. We spent three weeks in Kenya and across the border in Somalia evaluating the programme. A total of almost a hundred Quick Impact Projects (QIPs) were visited in Somalia, some finished, some under construction and some abandoned. By November 1993, some 360 QIPs had been initiated. Those studied were selected, with guidance from UNHCR, to exemplify as wide a range of activities as possible, but there was a bias towards ones with some tangible output. In most cases, two of us worked together in field visits and interviews so as to allow an informed sharing of opinions. In view of the methodological limitations, justice could not be done to all the relevant factors affecting UNHCR's operation.

With five different consultancy teams, keeping some common approach to the evaluation was difficult. In Nairobi, the IOB management team, which was also undertaking its own interviews, interacted several times with the evaluation teams from ETC (UK), GEM Consult and Quest Consult, while they were making their field investigations. This linkage was critical for establishing a shared understanding of the TOR as well as being able to reflect on the issues emerging from the field investigations and to triangulate some views. Constant returning to the TOR ensured that the evaluation was not overcome by anecdotes of our various experiences. While the TOR were not negotiable at this stage, and were not revised or adapted by the consultants, the continuing discussions, in the light of the field experience, led to a deeper understanding of them and helped ensure that they were fully covered. If this had been undertaken at the start we might have generated a different set of TOR.

Fieldwork: Understanding the Situation on the Ground

In the field the evaluators experienced difficulties in obtaining documentation. Moreover, many records were unclassified and not stored in an orderly fashion. As the evaluation teams needed to produce a timeline of events in Somalia to triangulate information, substantial time and manpower (including the hiring of extra staff) were needed for collating the unclassified documents.

Without a timeline, it is almost impossible to triangulate information. The triangulation of information is critically important for humanitarian aid evaluations, because scattered and incomplete documentary information means that much emphasis is placed on the integrity of the evaluation team. The evaluation team must rely on informants, largely those responsible for implementation, to tell their stories of the action. These stories must be tested against the beneficiaries' viewpoint until the evaluation team is confident it can tell a story from beginning to end. The story, however, has to have a purpose, a moral. Evaluation of humanitarian aid is the writing of disaster fables.

Other problems that we faced included the fact that institutions running the two programmes we were evaluating were undergoing profound change stimulated by the Somalia situation. In the case of ICRC, it had faced severe criticism about its hiring of gunmen to guarantee delivery of aid, thus compromising its neutrality, and because of its withdrawal from Somalia as fighting escalated. In the case of UNHCR, the cross-border operation flew in the face of much existing legal practice, including *refoulement*, but was a necessary response as the Kenyan government did not wish to support large numbers of refugees. The cross-mandate gave UNHCR lead coordination responsibility for international humanitarian efforts delivered from Nairobi, but with little leverage on the military or other resources delivered directly into Somalia.

Mandate creep was another problem that recurred throughout the evaluation, not just for ICRC and UNHCR but for other UN organizations, international and local NGOs. For UNHCR the situation was unusual in that it was operating across an international border and intervening directly in Somalia through the QIPs programme. This was an extension of its normal mandate to support refugees in a country of refuge, in this case Kenya. Moreover, although this was not the first time that QIPs had been attempted by UNHCR, the scale of the programme was large and the agency was moving into fields of activity that were not envisaged in the mandate and entailed the development of a new range of skills. The management of what were arguably development programmes was seen by UNHCR and ourselves as new ground for the agency.

For the NGOs, including those contracted by UNHCR, humanitarian assistance had become the single largest area of growth in development aid and every agency was competing in the market. Many NGOs had little, if any, experience of working in emergencies and had to reinvent themselves as humanitarian agencies. For some NGOs this was mandate creep. For others it was mandate transformation. Competition produced some startling results. For example, from 1991 to 1993, over two thousand local NGOs sprang up in Somalia. Several international NGOs, with no field implementation experience, were drafted in as major players and some experienced a fifty-fold increase in staff. Evaluation of UN agencies and NGOs in these changing, metamorphosed, novel and unaccustomed roles is an unusual challenge, but we had to assess the implications of these innovations in cross-border and cross-mandate activities.

The substitution role by NGOs was, to some extent, understandable. Somali state structures, including the judiciary and local government, had not just collapsed but had disappeared. In their place was everything and nothing. In Lugh, there was a militant Islamic mini-state with its own police and border guards. In Baidoa, the UN military operation was using a Polish political commissar to reconstitute civil society under a Botswana infantry umbrella. In Bardera, there was nothing except continuing fighting. Responsibility was a patchwork quilt of ceased opportunity. That also had to be coped with in the field.

In trying to understand the situation, we faced, above all, the problem of who was genuinely a refugee, who was registered for rations and repatriation. In an area that covered three countries (Somalia, Kenya and Ethiopia), which has a moving population of nomadic pastoralists, combined with continued ethnic clashes, there was no easy answer. Even in the refugee camps themselves, it was difficult to address problems. For example, the reluctance of women to press charges of rape against men, when rape was clearly a problem in the camps, created tension between Western, human

	Relief agencies		Somali community	
	Self	**Somali community**	**Self**	**Relief agencies**
Dominant image	Benefactor 'Here to help'	Aggressive	Coping	Imposing
Organizational characteristic	Structured	Anarchic	Negotiating	Coercive
Decision-making framework	Professional	Exploitative	Fate and Somali	Bureaucratic
Economic assumptions	Efficiency and effectiveness	Welfare recipients	Satisficing	Source of money
Negotiation assumptions	Neutral	Partisan	Decentralized	Authoritarian
Negotiation characteristics	Rational and objective	Unreasonable	Continuous	Regulation without dialogue

FIGURE 2.1 Contrasting perceptions of agencies and recipients
(*source*: Operations Review Unit 1994: 98)

rights approaches to emergency assistance and the approaches of beneficiaries in the different political and cultural environments into which it
was being delivered.

In trying to understand these tensions between the formal and informal
local structures in Somali society and the aid community, we reverted to
making an inventory of perceptions. These perceptions are brought together
in the overview presented in Figure 2.1, which is based on comments made
to us, in the field, by members of each of the communities. Although these
contrasting perceptions cannot do justice to the cultural complexity underlying the delivery of humanitarian assistance, they subsequently played an
important role in helping us explain the various phenomena observed during
the evaluation. The IOB team was very conscious of the significance of the
field teams' perceptions of actors in the emergency and carefully read each
report with this in mind, debating the findings with the consultants and
demanding evidence to substantiate the findings and conclusions.

Getting to Conclusions

The story of Somalia, limited because the political and military issues
were not addressed, was captured by the punchline: 'Too much, too late

for too long'. In other words, our focus was on efficiency and effectiveness of humanitarian aid with attention paid to the lack of an exit strategy. Initially this punchline, developed during the fieldwork, was strongly debated between the IOB management team and the teams involved in the case studies.

This debate largely revolved around interpreting the following 'one-line conclusions' drawn from the evaluations of the six projects and programmes. The LWF airlift continued after ground transport became an option not least because there is a dominant, and profitable, culture of emergency flights out of Nairobi. Concern's emergency feeding programme, boosted by a promise of additional supplies following the visit of the Dutch minister for development cooperation to the feeding centres that offered additional medical supplies, nearly ordered materials that could have had a detrimental impact on the therapeutic feeding programme. External medical advice saved the day, but the evaluation team was always conscious that the project had only just avoided the tabloid headlines of 'Minister kills babies'. The MSF-H emergency medical programme, like many humanitarian medical projects, was not really emergency assistance but the establishment of hospital outpatient departments. UNICEF's seeds and tools programme lacked a gender focus and there was little organizational history of implementing agriculture. Most importantly, the issue of forced change of land ownership in the Juba valley, the key agricultural area, was not addressed. ICRC's programme raised issues of the use of armed guards to protect ICRC lives and resources and clearly raised issues of how neutrality was interpreted: to arm all equally is hardly neutral. ICRC's involvement with a veterinary programme was a substantial expansion of its mandate. Mandate expansion was also the core critique of UNHCR, whose Quick Impact Projects (QIPs) were implemented as 'Les Phares' – lighthouses to attract refugees back from Kenya. However, they were not linked to the rehabilitation process: for instance, social sector QIPs, especially in education, did not carry sufficient revenue to support staff.

All this sounds negative, but the evaluation team struggled to tell an accurate story of humanitarian intervention where also models of good practice were shared. The ability to piece together an accurate (that is, a good) story is a necessary skill in evaluation of emergencies. It is not, however, sufficient in itself and the story must be supported by critical appraisal of objective evidence. In the Somalia case, we interpreted the story in the specific and unique context in which the aid was delivered. Because the TOR did not cover the political/military issues, the context was, however, incomplete.

The dedication of humanitarian aid workers, frequently working in environments of considerable risk, was impressive. When programme judgements came to be made, where, for example, it was concluded that UNHCR's QIPs were 'a quarter good and a quarter poor or worse' (Operation Review Unit 1994: 280), it was a judgement that would not reflect badly on development programmes. Intervention clearly saved lives.

Writing Up

Although the six case study reports could be considered as free-standing accounts of separate interventions, it was also necessary to synthesize the findings in order to be able to make some overall judgements and produce a final report. This entailed comparison between agencies with different characteristics, undertaking very different activities, which had been evaluated using very different methodologies – desk studies or field studies. Further practical problems were the facts that not all evaluators adhered to the originally agreed checklist and that writing skills tended to differ substantially. As a result the reports were individually of differing quality, which made drawing overall judgements much more difficult. The IOB management team had planned to hold a meeting involving all consultants to enter into a dialogue and compare the findings of the separate studies. Unfortunately, this plenary meeting did not materialize due to the commitments of the various teams. Instead individual discussions were held with each consultant team.

From the completion of the individual case study reports to the production of the synthesis report involved a peer review process of an intensity not matched in any work we had experienced before. First, the IOB management team read each case study report and often demanded substantiation of findings and conclusions of the individual evaluation teams. Second, the revised manuscripts were sent to those evaluated who, as this was the first major evaluation they had experienced in many cases, made copious comments on the drafts. The manuscripts were submitted for comments to all sections of the Ministry of Foreign Affairs involved in the humanitarian relief activities and to the Netherlands Embassy in Nairobi. Whenever relevant they were also sent to the Netherlands Permanent Missions in New York and Geneva. Internal working documents, drafted by IOB's management team, were also presented for comments to different sections in the Ministry.

The writing and compilation of the final synthesis report was a cooperative effort of IOB's management team and ETC (UK), with IOB having the final responsibility for its contents. This in its final draft form was also presented to all above-mentioned actors for their comments.

The entire process took considerable time since the organizations whose activities were evaluated provided extensive comments that had to be taken into account. In many instances these organizations provided additional information that previously had not been made available to the evaluation teams. This new information frequently led to further analytical work.

The draft final report was subsequently subjected to a stringent external peer review process involving experts from the University of Northumbria at Newcastle, the London School of Hygiene and Tropical Medicine, the Disaster Preparedness Centre in Cranfield and the Oxford Centre for Disaster Studies. This review process allowed the story line to tighten. Finally, before IOB adopted the report, there was the usual internal review involving IOB's director and its evaluation staff.

The IOB management team wanted to complete the work quickly to meet a deadline to present the report to Parliament. The first draft of the final report was completed within three months after the consultants finalized their case studies. Final publication took an additional two months due to the various review rounds and time required for printing. This tight timetable was achieved only through close collaboration. During this period we spent considerable periods of time together in ETC's office in Newcastle upon Tyne to finalize the work. Central to the whole process was the engagement of an editor who had final say not over content but over sense. In hindsight, the editor's engagement from the start of the project would have greatly increased the efficiency of the write-up.

In parallel with the write up, a short video was produced, based on 200 slides taken during the fieldwork. The production of the video was not without problems. The text of the video had to be written in parallel with the text of the evaluation. To the dismay of the video-makers, the text kept changing because of the review process outlined above. Nevertheless it was a worthwhile exercise as the video had a powerful impact, enabling some 335 pages of evaluation to be captured in a 25-minute presentation.

While writing up the individual case studies faced its own difficulties, the key problem in the final synthesis report was whether generic conclusions could justifiably be based on a single country study. This issue was debated at length among us. We concluded that generic conclusions could be made on, for example, administrative aspects, such as the handling of the project cycle by the Ministry of Foreign Affairs, and in particular the Emergency and Humanitarian Aid Section. The capacity of the Emergency and Humanitarian Aid Section and the Nairobi Embassy to respond to the complex humanitarian emergency in Somalia (a staffing issue) could also be dealt with generically. Some other issues, such as effectiveness and efficiency, could be covered only in relation to the specific situation of the study area. Our major findings are summarized in Box 2.3.

Self-evaluation

On the positive side we would suggest that the decision to undertake the study, against the advice of IOB colleagues, was justified by the findings. Similarly, the decision to involve the Emergency and Humanitarian Aid Section in the evaluation contributed to the quality and effectiveness of the report. Sufficient time was available for the desk study, even though little information was available, and all the consultants had sufficient time to prepare for the evaluation. It was appropriate to allow the evaluated

---

Box 2.3 A summary of major evaluation findings

The context of aid delivery The complexity of the disaster, the high levels of insecurity, the lack of counterparts and the collapse of physical, institutional and state infrastructure all made the delivery of humanitarian aid very difficult. Delivery was also complicated by the differences of perception and operational norms between the Somalis and the aid community. The study concluded that factors such as understanding the culture of the country in which the emergency takes place, comprehension of the physical and socio-economic context of the emergency and knowledge of its origins and development should be understood by those planning and implementing the humanitarian action.

Policy relevance, effectiveness and efficiency While the activities concerned were in accordance with the Netherlands' overall objectives for humanitarian aid, by and large they did not meet all specific operational criteria defined for such assistance. The channels chosen to carry out the interventions were generally considered to be appropriate and all activities studied were effective in meeting the aim of alleviating human suffering and restoring human dignity. Single components of the interventions studied, however, proved less effective. The judgement on efficiency was based mainly on qualitative evidence. Since relevant data were absent in most cases, the calculation of unit cost per beneficiary was impossible. Given the overall Somali context, the operations were efficiently executed, and it was concluded that a substantial and overall improvement of operational efficiency and cost-effectiveness would have been difficult to achieve without putting lives at risk. Nevertheless, better management and more effective negotiation could have secured improved humanitarian access.

Side-effects Several side-effects resulted from the humanitarian institutions and the operational departments (Humanitarian Desk, Nairobi Embassy and Permanent Netherlands Representatives in New York and Geneva) an opportunity to respond to both the draft case study reports and draft final report.

Where we did less well was in the writing up of the reports, especially the final report. We did not expect this to be so arduous and difficult. The whole evaluation would have benefited from an earlier literature search for concepts relating to humanitarian assistance and complex emergencies. This was done by ETC only after the field studies. Thus we discovered the lack

---

assistance. Negative side-effects included a slow return to commercial agriculture and inflated prices for labour, rental, vehicle hire and other local services. Dependency on aid agencies led to problems of disengagement. Positive side-effects were the creation of employment and the growth of local capacities.

Strong and weak points Strong points of the operations included the availability of funding for relief operations, the hard work, courage and dedication of both Somali and expatriate staff, the formation of a number of genuine local NGOs and the willingness and ability of individual agencies to learn from experience. A major weak point was the failure of the agencies to coordinate their activities. In a situation where there are so many agencies with differing mandates, decision-making structures and procedures and organizational cultures, there are no easy solutions to the problem of coordination. However, it appeared that not everyone was prepared to be coordinated and the agencies responsible for coordination or liaison lacked the capacity for the task and were therefore not accepted by some of the organizations involved.

Administrative aspects The most telling criticism of the way in which humanitarian aid was administered was that, while appraised broadly on a number of relevant aspects, proposals were judged on the Ministry's experience with the executing agency. It was found that most proposals either did not include a rationale or objectives, or these were imprecisely defined. Many did not define the target group and its location or did not provide detailed budgets, approaches and work plans. In most instances the issue of gender was not addressed. Quite simply, these findings were a clarion call for normal paradigms of administrative practice to be applied to humanitarian aid. Without these, it was impossible to judge relevance, efficiency, effectiveness and impact.

of theoretical framework in which to contextualize the findings. The failure to hold a workshop to allow discussion of the methodological issues with all consultants before the field investigations were undertaken led to variations in the quality of the field studies. Finally, it was not anticipated that the Emergency and Humanitarian Aid Section would react so defensively to the draft report. It was thus necessary to organize an external peer review group of experts. Such a group should have been constituted at an earlier stage of the evaluation process.

Impact and Follow-up

In August 1994, the final report and the policy reaction of the minister for development cooperation on the findings and conclusions were presented to the Netherlands Parliament. Subsequently, discussions took place in the Permanent Committee on Foreign Affairs.

The immediate impact was on the Emergency and Humanitarian Aid Section in the Ministry of Foreign Affairs, which instituted a more structured approach to granting humanitarian assistance, requiring significantly more reporting from implementing agencies, as well as a database on implementing agency capacity. This Section also started to commission evaluative studies of its own accord.

In retrospect, the biggest achievement was to show that it was possible to do evaluations of complex emergencies using the 'normal' OECD–DAC evaluation criteria. The report also stimulated a number of other debates, particularly about the need for exit strategies and the disaster continuum (see Frerks et al. 1995 and Kirkby et al. 1997).

But there were also problems with the impact of the evaluation. It was impossible to return to Somalia to present the final evaluation to the beneficiaries so that they could know they had been heard. Some implementing agencies were still doubtful about the ethics of evaluating humanitarian aid, as it seemed to question the humanitarian imperative. The lack of a political and military focus meant that the key issue of humanitarian aid as a substitute for diplomatic solutions was not addressed. The issue of leadership in emergency assistance was not directly addressed, although it is a key to success since the same institution with different teams produces quite different results. Most fundamentally, the theoretical necessity of humanitarian aid was never raised. But you can't do that, can you?

3

Exploring the Swedish Emergency Relief Experience in the Horn of Africa

Adrian Wood

This chapter reflects on the experience of a team that in 1994 undertook an evaluation of emergency relief projects in the Horn of Africa (Map 3.1) funded by the Swedish International Development Agency (Sida) (Apthorpe et al. 1995). This was one of three studies that Sida's Evaluation Department commissioned from different organizations as part of a global review of its involvement in emergency relief. The contract for this second study in the series was obtained by the Institute of Social Studies Advisory Service (ISSAS), which during the 1980s and early 1990s undertook a number of consultancy activities with staff from ISS and external consultants. I have written this chapter on the basis of close and detailed discussions with the Team Leader (TL), but contact with the other team members was not possible.[1]

My aim in this chapter is to give a narrative of the evaluation from a personal perspective, identifying what appeared to me to be the key stages in the process and the critical experiences that affected the evaluation. The chapter focuses on the particular stages in which I was heavily involved, especially the setting-up phase. Nevertheless, conclusions are drawn considering the implications of the overall practical experience upon the evaluation report that was produced.

Landing the Contract

The process of landing a contract for an evaluation often involves some of the prospective team members. In this case, one of the full-time academic managers of ISSAS, not a team member, prepared the bid. It appeared to the team that ISSAS was quite confident about how the evaluation proposal should be constructed in response to the invitation to bid. As prospective team members we were involved very little, having only to provide our CVs and offer names of key persons in the field area

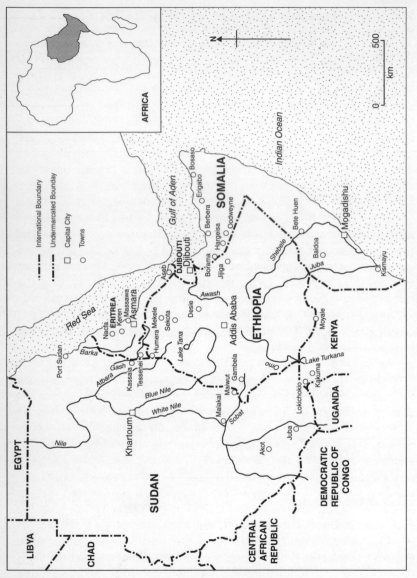

MAP 3.1   Horn of Africa

whom we felt might be helpful in the study. In fact throughout the evaluation none of the team members, not even the TL, saw the proposal that ISSAS submitted. Instead it was always the Terms of Reference (TOR) that were used as the basis for any discussions between ISSAS, or Sida, and ourselves over how the study was to be undertaken.

The limited involvement of the team at this stage may be explained by the financial costs involved in employing prospective team members. It may also have been affected by ISSAS's belief that a more coherent proposal could be made if the task was kept 'in house'. Further, ISSAS appeared to be confident in making the proposal, believing that Sida was looking for an academic institution, outside Scandinavia, to undertake the task in contrast to the Swedish consultancy group that had undertaken the first study in this series of three.[2]

Compiling the Team

The process of compiling the team was based on personal contacts and recommendations within ISS in support of a person's CV. Recruitment never seemed to be openly competitive. While ability to work together was perhaps valued, it was not a deciding factor for recruitment. We were specifically chosen because of our current experience in the countries to be studied and to a lesser extent our expertise in evaluation and emergency relief matters. Nationality considerations were not seen as crucial either by Sida or by ISSAS, although ISSAS clearly wanted its own people on the team as much as possible. In the end this was only one person out of four.

Probably the key criterion for selection was availability. In academic, if not consultancy, terms this involved very limited notice. However, in the end the availability of the team members led to the study being delayed slightly to the middle of the Northern Hemisphere summer. In many respects this was not the best time of the year for the evaluation – many donor representatives were on leave, and the weather was poor for travel in Ethiopia and southern Sudan. The delay in the start of the study also nearly impacted upon the preparations, as it was only just possible for two of us to complete the necessary briefings with Sida before most of the staff in Stockholm went on their summer leave.

In letting our names go forward for membership of the evaluation team we each had different personal motivations. Unusually for such evaluations, these included our personal applied research interests, as well as a specific strategic commercial interest on the part of the full-time consultant.[3] As a result, a peculiar combination of applied research interests dominated this team, and this accounts for a number of particular aspects about the way this evaluation occurred and the materials it produced. (See Field Process below.)

In appointing the TL, ISSAS decided that it needed a more senior person than anyone within the initial three-person team it had compiled. In particular, they wanted someone who had a successful track record with them and was known to be effective in this role. The TL was asked to accept the post having had no say whatsoever in the team's composition and not knowing any of the other three, except through the publications of one.

As a team for consultancy evaluation we were rather unusual in being dominated by three university-based researchers who had specialist interests in the region of study, more than in the subject area of emergency relief. Only one of the team members was a professional consultant, although all had some consultancy experience, and only two had extensive experience of emergency relief. This composition in part reflected ISSAS's location within an academic institution but also the reported wish by Sida to have the study undertaken by a different type of team in order to generate some new ideas.

A key aspect of the team was the disciplines brought together, these being sociology, economics and geography. These specific disciplines were not a major concern to us but they did help ensure that a variety of perspectives were presented in the study, from which it benefited. In addition the choice of team members with a wide range of experience assisted the evaluation process because of the comparative experience this could provide. No Chief Technical Adviser (CTA) was proposed for this team. This was not even considered by us as a possibility, although it must be recognized that the senior ISSAS staff did offer some limited advice in such a role during the writing up stage.

We were all outsiders to the organizations involved in the implementation of Sida's relief activities, and had no previous links with Sida. One of us had related field experience, having worked in a non-governmental organization (NGO) with links to one of the field areas studied (Eritrea and Tigray), while another had worked with one of the other organizations studied when undertaking research. While independence is necessary, some prior experience to assist in getting to terms with the complex reality can be helpful. Further assistance of this sort was arranged for me in Ethiopia, the country with the largest number of operations, where a former Sida relief official provided support for a few days.

We received supplementary research assistance to improve our understanding of the field in Eritrea, where one local consultant was employed, and in Ethiopia, where two local consultants worked with us. However, identifying and managing such resource persons proved time-consuming.

As a result they were involved primarily in a few specific studies and were not as widely used as might have been desirable. Consequently, in the end, this element of the field budget was underspent.

Familiarization and Preparing for the Planning Meeting

Once the contract was obtained a number of steps were taken in preparation for the first meeting of the team.

Field contacts Two of the team made initial contacts with Sida staff when passing through the study area on other business. This started the process of familiarization. While this seemed to be useful at the time, it was perhaps too early in the process to be of much value and the impact on the final work appeared to be negligible.

Stockholm visits Far more important and significant for our output were two visits of several days made to Sida's headquarters in Stockholm.

The first visit, for three days in early May 1994, involved me, as I happened to be available, and the ISSAS official who had been negotiating the contract. On that visit briefings were provided on a number of topics, including:

- the context of this study, i.e. within a series of three evaluations of emergency relief;
- clarification of the TOR with the head of Sida's Evaluation Department and also with Sida's consultant for this evaluation series;
- a review of the time period the study should consider, with coverage sought for the full five years but effectiveness focusing on the last three years;
- data availability on projects and possible criteria for the choice of projects to be studied;
- concerns about the possibility of following up individual projects given their completion and the turnover of staff among different partners, and
- relative importance to be accorded in our work to projects versus the Sida relief system.

With respect to the latter point a major question raised by this visit was whether or not Sida's strategy for emergency relief, especially complex emergencies, was sufficiently clear, proactive and comprehensive. There was concern that Sida's relief system, while priding itself on flexibility and rapid response, might lack guidance for consistent and quality decision-making. Sida officials suggested that money appeared to be 'thrown' at the problem and that little was known about the overall pattern of this funding and its impact given the limited monitoring and the reporting schedule. Hence the question was raised of whether a more judicious and directed use of such funds might be better.

These various discussions led to two key conclusions that affected the evaluation. The first was the realization that Sida staff were concerned about the emergency relief process more than about the individual projects that had been funded. As a result questions were raised about whether greater emphasis upon a programme or process evaluation rather than a project evaluation was necessary. The second point concerned the information about the emergency relief programme and whether this was adequate and was managed properly to allow appropriate decisions to be made. Both these points tended to suggest that further time was needed to review the situation in Stockholm.

An additional task on the first visit to Stockholm was addressing our need for data with which to plan the fieldwork. As a result we made arrangements for a junior researcher to be employed to assist the team by translating critical documents and compiling project summaries for all the activities funded during the period to be covered by the study. The latter was a major task (four to five weeks), but critical as it meant that at its first meeting the team had an understanding of the activities that had been supported, the range of partners and the relative importance of the financial support by country, partner and activity. The diversity of activities was quite considerable: locust control, industrial plant establishment and institutional development as well as the usual food distribution, health and rehabilitation activities. The actors receiving funds were also many and diverse, with 63 different ones in seven major categories, while further complexity occurred once implementation on the ground was considered (Apthorpe et al. 1995: Chapter 3).

A second visit to Stockholm was made by the TL. Unfortunately this took place before he could meet the team, as he had wished. It involved the usual round of formalities, including some rather uninformative handshakes with people not involved in the study area. It was requested that funds should be made available for all the team members to visit Stockholm on this occasion, but this was refused. We all felt that this was a mistake, as it meant that two of us could have no personal knowledge of the situation in Stockholm, or any first-hand understanding of the issues being raised by staff there. In addition, contact with Sida staff, especially the heads of Evaluation and Relief Statistics, led to a sense of personal responsibility among those of us who met these people.

This second visit confirmed the importance of policy and programme review within the TOR. During this visit there were two critical meetings in which the discussions with officials exposed a number of underlying issues and questions that Sida needed to have answered. These included the following:

- How should we think of emergency assistance?
- What is the nature of emergencies?
- How should we balance funds for relief against those for development?

These questions became important for our discussions in the team about how to operationalize the TORs. No questions were raised about the link of relief and development, nor was the issue of NGOs raised. They were taken for granted as key elements in the work.

Meeting Up

Our initial team meeting was held at ISS in mid-June 1994. After a briefing by one of the ISSAS staff, we were left to decide for ourselves how the study would be undertaken. This appeared to be a major change after the tight control and management by ISSAS of the bidding and early contacts with Sida. While the limited input from ISSAS staff at this stage left some of us wondering if we had been abandoned, this actually proved essential as we were able to develop our own modes of interaction and understanding of the task without having to look over our shoulders at our employers.

Terms of Reference and framework   The TOR and the field operations were the main issue discussed in detail at our first team meeting. This discussion started with a review of the data obtained from the analysis of Sida's records. This preliminary data analysis, which I had managed, revealed that there were over five hundred projects, or expenditure decisions, within our remit. With the time and the resources available for the evaluation it was clear that it would not be possible to complete an adequate sample of project evaluations across the six countries concerned. The project evaluation approach was also undermined by the fact that the projects had been implemented up to six years earlier, which would make it difficult to find appropriate persons who had been involved in these activities or the beneficiaries of them. In addition, it was recognized that in most cases we would not have a baseline from which to measure impact. Hence despite the evaluation having been designed by Sida as a performance analysis, it was decided that this was not going to be possible. This, combined with the feedback from the visits to Stockholm, led us to the conclusion that what was needed was an issues-driven review of policy, programme and partners. This was communicated to Sida and was accepted, apparently because, at this stage of the three-study review process, there was a growing wish to begin to move towards drawing higher-level generalizations that were already in our TOR (see Box 3.1).

In order to reach conclusions, we recognized that it would be necessary to transcend particularities and to identify the broad lessons that could be learned rather than the specific experiences of individual projects, although some particularities were required to meet some of the TOR. Of the various ways of transcending the particular, we opted to devise and model a theoretical view of relief as a process to which to relate our observations and conclusions.

 This involved developing a timeline model of famine, concerning early signs, how it strikes, and the phasing in and out of interventions. This narrative model included consideration of both 'structural' and 'situational' dimensions of disasters and the relief required, with the structural issues including policy issues.

In the process of agreeing this theoretical model we decided that the focus would be upon famine and famine relief, rather than humanitarian aid, and that it would build up a narrative of that experience, with the emergency aspects of war, refugees and political change added to that. We did not make a model of complex emergency situations as we felt that it

---

 Box 3.1 Summary of the main aspects of the Terms of Reference

The scope of the study was all decisions for Eritrea, Ethiopia, Somalia and Sudan funded by the Emergency Relief vote between 1990 and 1994. Special emphasis was placed on reconstruction in Eritrea and Ethiopia, the peace process and intervention during conflict in Somalia, and the use of UN channels and intervention during conflict in the Sudan.

Key criteria were: the impact of assistance, the preparatory process including project identification, conflict situations in which to operate, channels used for relief distribution, donor coordination, cooperation with recipient countries, logistics, the refugee situation and its implications, the purposes for which Sida funds are used, the comparative advantage of Sida aid funds, flexibility of funding, impacts on rehabilitation and reconstruction, and impacts on gender issues and children.

Conclusions were sought at two levels, one for the Horn of Africa and one for Sida as a whole, focusing on lessons learned, comparability and suggestions for future operational arrangements.

would be difficult to achieve this in a way that would be relevant to the different cases in the region.

Division of labour   The initial team meeting also agreed the division of labour in the field. This was undertaken with little reflection, as a division had seemingly been settled for the team by the ISSAS proposal to Sida and it agreed with our individual interests and experience. Three of the team were to work individually in different countries, these being chosen on the basis of their previous experience and current contacts. The TL was to focus on the relations with the multilateral organizations and to circulate among the various countries in order to ensure an overview and to identify any gaps. He also had specific responsibilities for regional funding, such as the UN's Special Emergency Programme for the Horn of Africa (SEPHA).

The enormous geographical area we had to cover in a very short time, with only a small team, compared with other humanitarian relief aid reviews in countries in the region, confirmed that it was not feasible for us to travel together to the five countries that were to be covered. As a result we worked more as individuals, forming a loose net rather than a tight team. This was partly by choice, as it helped capture the widest range of issues on the basis of individual travel and access. However, it had an impact upon the nature of the output from the different countries.

Field methods   In terms of the preparation of field methods, our discussions in The Hague were quite limited. We agreed, on the basis of the Sida data analysis, that a sample of the organizations funded by Sida needed to be covered. This included all the major ones, and a purposively chosen representative sample of the smaller ones to include all the different types of partners. Beyond that it was recognized that the discussions would involve the most relevant people from these partners, usually the representatives, who had to deal with Sida, and the field staff, who had been involved with the implementation of the Sida-funded activities. Representatives of the beneficiary communities were also to be sought, and a geographical spread of projects was recognized as necessary. However, it was realized that travel conditions, time in the field and the historical nature of the activities studied would limit the identification of people for interview and that such decisions should be made in the field.

We had some considerable discussion about the issues that should be considered – impact, performance, and so on – and the criteria by which these might be judged. We agreed that impact was not measurable and that the focus would be more on the policies and programmes of Sida and its partners. We also recognized a number of problems with the quantification and quality/reliability of data. However, we agreed that we could cope with these, given the policy and programme focus. A checklist of questions to ask each partner organization about each project was produced initially by one of the team in an attempt to ensure that the data collected from the different countries were comparable. It was agreed that this would be used by us all, but that adaptation would be inevitable in order to cover the diversity of situations the projects had addressed. To some extent the items and criteria on the checklist were inferred from the details on the project outlines and their objectives (which the Sida data analysis had provided).

At the meeting in The Hague we agreed that, given the policy and programme focus, and the initial questions raised in Stockholm by Sida, we should spend more time in Stockholm focusing on the data, policy and management problems of the whole Sida relief programme. However, a request for this was refused by Sida. They replied that the evaluation had been agreed at senior level to be a field-oriented activity.

We did not discuss how to set about the fieldwork in each country. Each of us knew the place well and had our own contacts. Interviewing methods were left up to individuals. No requirements were made for us to circulate our notes during the fieldwork, and for the most part we were out of contact except for visits by the TL to two of us and a mid-fieldwork gathering in Nairobi. With better communications from Addis Ababa I was able to send weekly consolidated notes by fax to the TL based in Nairobi.

Team dynamics There were no conflicts or tensions in the initial meetings in The Hague and there was no development of camps or factions within the team. This was probably helped by the fact that three of us knew each other and I had worked with two of the team on previous occasions. However, to the three of us the TL was an unknown quantity and this was a potential source of concern. All of us had been TLs previously and so it was natural that we should react with some concern at working as a team member again, especially if the TL was particularly forceful and opinionated. In fact no such situation occurred, as the TL adopted a very open and participative approach, making no attempt to impose a prepared view of how the study should be undertaken. Indeed, a rather open and equitable discussion developed in The Hague at which there was a rapid achievement of a consensus on a number of points. No one tried to impose on anyone.

That being said, some of us did have concerns about the style of the Team Leader, perhaps because of our own team management styles or lack of experience. In particular it was questioned whether he was the right person given the complexity of the task and his accommodating personality.

While the discussions proved that he was an ideas person, the question remained until well into the study whether he could hold it all together and synthesize the diversity of material into a coherent report. In the end this was achieved not only without any problem, but in an inclusive and sensitive manner.

Field Process: Adjusting to Reality

Fieldwork The approach we took in the field was to try to talk with the representatives of as wide a range of relevant parties as possible. The main groups interviewed were officials in the NGOs that had been the field partners implementing the emergency relief activities that Sida funded. However, in addition we spoke with government staff involved with relief and rehabilitation, as well as policy and sectoral issues of relevance. Sida officials were interviewed in all countries, as were researchers concerned with relief and rehabilitation and staff in other agencies, especially UN agencies, in order to try to understand the overall context within which the Sida activities had operated.

The practicalities of the fieldwork were not a problem. Each of us was familiar with the country(ies) for which we were responsible and we quickly re-established our links with officials of different agencies, as well as transport and other services, in order to become operational. Local contacts proved to be of considerable importance and facilitated, but perhaps biased, the field visits and case studies we made.

Unfortunately the timing of the mission, in July and August, made it difficult for us to contact many of the senior representatives of international agencies as they were on leave. Also, because the study was being undertaken up to six years after particular relief expenditures had been made, it proved very difficult to speak with the individuals who had been involved in the actual field activities. Access to the field also proved a difficulty given the time of year, this being the rainy season, which meant that some roads were impassable and some flights were cancelled. In addition, the political situation deteriorated in Somalia at the time of the mission, and this made it impossible for the responsible team member to fly to Mogadishu as had been planned. Instead, he had to rely on speaking with contacts in Nairobi who had been involved in Somalia, although he did manage to visit Somaliland. Security conditions in Kenya also prevented the TL visiting refugee camps in the north of that country as had been originally envisaged. Access to southern Sudan was facilitated for the responsible team member because he could parachute and had undertaken Dutch national service. Somehow this meant that he was able to get a flight with one of the military crews servicing this area.

Individual approaches The approaches we each followed in our interviewing, and probing and exploration of the partners and their projects, were very different. This depended on our personalities (which affected how we approached people), the conditions in the countries (especially whom we were able to talk to and under what conditions) and our disciplines (affecting the areas where we had specific interests and skills for probing). As a result there was little standardization of the field data, despite the checklists that were used for guidance. To varying degrees and for different parts of our work we sought to be comprehensive, follow selected themes or achieve an overview.

Overall, despite the agreed view of the team that a policy and programme approach was necessary, once in the field we spent a lot of time also on the tangibles of individual projects. Considerable effort was expended on compiling details of individual projects and more so on the individual partners with whom Sida worked. We expected that a detailed country-by-country Volume Two was needed, and that it should form the basis from which the issues-oriented synthesis Volume One would be produced. However, in retrospect it appears that too much in-depth material was collected given the policy output that Sida accepted. (In the end Volume Two, although submitted by ISSAS to Sida, was never published, perhaps because it was too specific about some of the agencies or some issues.) This concern for detailed information was probably in part a result of the university background of the majority of the team, but was also probably a result of some of us being relatively naive evaluators who felt that without such information the study's conclusions would be rejected. Emphasis on detail may also have been sought to make up for problems of quality caused by the inability to talk to many beneficiaries and field staff.

It seems, on reflection, that this problem of excessively detailed findings might have been prevented if a clearer view of the final output had been achieved earlier in the evaluation process and the importance of Volume Two adjusted. It might also have helped if we had taken a different approach to the fieldwork, with the whole team visiting each country, as that would have reduced the country-specific emphases we each had.

Relations with persons interviewed The general experience of the team with the persons interviewed was extremely positive. There was little obvious evasion or discomfort, although in some cases there were tensions about who should be involved in interviews. For the most part the projects funded were already history, and that may account for the lack of concern on the part of the partners. There was a general welcoming of the evaluation by many partners. This was in part because they wished to tell the story of a task that had, on the whole, been successfully completed, and in part because they were genuinely pleased that despite the limited contacts with Sida, the organization was, on this one occasion, showing an interest in them. Also the partners welcomed an opportunity to provide an up-date on their policies and programmes in the area of relief, with the expectation that this might improve their prospects for future funding.

To some extent the fieldwork was facilitated by the perceptions of Sida by its partners. For the most part Sida was perceived as a benevolent and understanding organization, not one that was threatening, critical or over-concerned with detailed accountability-style evaluations. On the other hand the Scandinavian partner organizations, being familiar with the open government system in Sweden, were happy to be critical about Sida and felt free to make comments about how the emergency relief system could be improved. In addition, the open and constructive responses we obtained in general may have been in part a reflection of the characteristics of the team members, especially the fact that we were all known by name, if not in person, to many of their interviewees. Also our knowledge of the countries we were working in confirmed our credibility with the interviewees, putting them at ease. Perhaps as university researchers, for the most part, we were seen in a different light from a consultancy team, and possibly as less likely to be out 'to score points'.

Relations with Sida   Our relations with Sida in the field were variable. In Addis Ababa these were very good, and a great deal of help was provided both logistically and also professionally for this study. This situation stemmed in part from existing contacts I already had with Sida staff, but also in part because of the personality of the former Sida employee who was employed to assist the evaluation and was still based in the Sida office at the time of the evaluation. While relations with the Sida office were good, little specific interest was expressed in the study. No one with a specific relief responsibility remained in the office and the study had not been initiated with any input from this office.

In Nairobi the relationship was much more distant and there was a distinct lack of interest in the evaluation mission on the part of the Sida and Embassy staff. This may have been due to the study being undertaken during the 'leave season' when few staff remained. It may also have reflected the lack of interest by the Nairobi Embassy in the work of its other missions in the region and the management of relief funds, which at that time were distributed direct from Stockholm to partners, with little involvement of the in-country offices.

Nairobi meeting: coming to a team position   A critical stage in the fieldwork was the Nairobi meeting midway through the six weeks of fieldwork. We agreed the need for this meeting at our planning meeting in The Hague, it being seen as essential to get everyone together at some point given their independent field operations. As it turned out the meeting proved to be far more significant than had been originally envisaged.

The two-day meeting in Nairobi was important in the first place because it brought all of us back into contact. As a result we could learn from each other what our various experiences had been both of the methodology, which had been proposed at the outset, and the lessons that were being learned from the field experience. Second, and more importantly, it provided an opportunity for our field experiences to be reconsidered in the light of the conceptual framework we prepared in The Hague and for progress to be made towards building up a framework for the overall report. There is a major step of this sort required in all evaluations when at least some of the team members have to change gear in their thinking and consider what are the general lessons or broader conceptual issues. The Nairobi meeting provided the opportunity and catalyst for this. By the end of that meeting we had decided what would be the structure of the synthesis volume and who would be responsible for the first draft of the different sections in this.

At the meeting in Nairobi we reaffirmed the anticipated difficulty of project-level work, on the basis of actual experience, and the importance of addressing the work more on the basis of the policies and programmes of the different partners. At the same time a common framework for the presentation of project-level 'impressions' was agreed, to make for easy cross-reference or comparison and to facilitate the identification of illustrative cases of best, and worst, project practice.

Team dynamics There were no major conflicts within the team during the fieldwork. The reasons for this may be as much to do with the limited time the team spent together as in the personalities of the individual members! It should also be recognized that the individual team members did not tread on each other's territory and that individuals' views were respected and adhered to in the report, in all except the case of one project. The TL kept to his overview role and did not get involved with specific country work, except where asked to do so through visits to Eritrea and to Ethiopia. The latter of these visits was very important in terms of giving him contact with a number of local researchers working on the topic of emergency relief, as well as helping him have some first-hand experience of the research that was being undertaken by me and two local consultants.

Fortunately there were no major illnesses among the team and for the most part the field schedule was completed on time. A few extra days of field time were obtained for some of the team following a review of the situation and request to ISSAS after the Nairobi meeting. This was in view of logistical problems caused by the insecurity that affected the timing of some field visits.

Writing Up

This was an extremely protracted process, and it took some three months in all to achieve the final version of the report. The reporting was completed successfully only because of the unusual flexibility of the TL, who was not at that time required for teaching in his home university in Australia and so stayed on in The Hague to undertake the process, mostly at his own cost. The process was not helped by the dispersal of the team in three countries. Although two of the team were based in The Hague, one of these, the ISS staff member, was in fact travelling for much of the initial write-up period and was then involved in teaching. As a result he contributed little to the finalization of the report. The consultant, who was in France, was also heavily committed once he returned from the field and this delayed his writing and limited his contributions at the review stage.

The last meeting of the team as a whole occurred fairly soon after returning from the field. This completed a total of only five days that the team spent together during the evaluation. At this meeting the chapter headings and sub-headings were finalized for the synoptic overview volume. The main lines of the findings and the conclusions were also drawn out at this stage. We agreed how the writing would be finalized and determined the general nature of a two-day visit to international organizations in Geneva by two of the team, to complete the study.

In retrospect it was a mistake to have the meeting in The Hague so soon after we returned from the field, before all the data had been collected and the drafts completed and circulated for all the field visits (Volume Two). However, the Nairobi meeting had helped the team come to some common views. In fact, it seemed that some of the views being revisited in The Hague in August were the same as those that had been expressed in the planning meeting there two months earlier. As a result there were few problems in agreeing the emphases in the write-up. (Although, perhaps not noticed so clearly at the time, this seems in retrospect to raise questions about the influence of preconceived ideas on the fieldwork.)

In writing up the field material the team, with ISSAS approval, planned a report of two volumes. The second volume was to cover the field experience by country and by partner, with some project materials. The first volume was to summarize the issues and address the policy/programme aspects drawing the overall lessons from the work. It was planned that Volume Two would be completed first and that on the basis of this the issues would be drawn out for Volume One. In fact this proved difficult to achieve, as the two team members who had managed to collect the most in the way of field data found it a major task to write up. As a result Volume One had to be prepared before Volume Two was even 90 per cent complete.

The actual compiling of the report in pre-email days was laborious, with the circulation of partial drafts by fax followed up by extended phone discussions. (Fortunately there was typing support in The Hague when diskettes failed to arrive on time in the post!) In the end feedback and contributions in this process became a question of who was available, and only the TL and I were involved to the end.

This writing-up process did not involve an *aide-mémoire* and discussion of that with Sida. This might have been helpful in terms of clarifying the role of Volume Two and addressing some of the problems faced in balancing the global and the regional lessons. Certainly the team members drew different levels of generalization from their work, which left the TL with a considerable task in standardizing the conclusions from the different field areas. A team meeting after all first drafts were completed and with some feedback on an *aide-mémoire* would probably have been very useful.

Feedback and Finalization

The process of feedback and finalization can be very difficult. Being told where you have gone 'wrong' and fighting to keep your interpretations is very stressful. In this case it was not like that, and the reasons for this need exploring.

The final two-volume draft report was submitted to Sida in September 1994. It was followed by a visit to Stockholm by the TL and I. We verbally presented the report to a meeting of around ten Sida staff. This meeting was remarkably amicable and the general tone was to ask for further explanation of points made rather than to challenge conclusions. Whether this was because people had not read the report or because they agreed with the conclusions is hard to say. Certainly there seemed to be a view that no one around the table was being held responsible for any of the problematic issues raised, and in general the report seemed to be supportive of the way Sida's thinking was developing.

After the meeting three sets of written comments were produced by Sida. These were on the whole fairly brief and raised general questions. Interestingly, it was not from these comments that the major Sida input into the report came, but from the Sida official responsible for the emergency assistance statistics. He read the draft report extremely carefully and, whether on his own initiative or under instructions from above, spent a whole day in The Hague with two of us addressing virtually each paragraph in the report. Far from being a one-way process, with the team being told what corrections to make, this ended up as a most stimulating discussion, which led to a better understanding on the part of the two team members there and the Sida staff member of the reality of the relief process. The main recommendations are given in Box 3.2.

Dissemination

From an early stage in the evaluation, I had been concerned about the dissemination of the findings of the evaluation. Interestingly I was the team member who had been least involved with relief, and perhaps I pressed this point because much of the experience was new to me and I felt it to

---

Box 3.2 Summary of recommendations

Evaluation as a process The evaluation process should be continued through meetings with parties interested in relief in the region.

Administrative and institutional arrangements The best delivery and performance of relief can be achieved only by recognizing the comparative advantage of different channels, and developing government and community capacity.

Situational and structural responses Relief strategy must address both situational and structural aspects of emergencies. This will involve conceptual and operational linkages.

Sida policy Sida should develop further its relief policy, considering among other points being proactive, placing conditions on grants, developing specific criteria for decisions, including reference to partner agency records and considering the nature of the activities funded, especially their longer-term impact.

Sida administration Sida should consider improving the number and expertise in its Emergency and Relief Section, streamline its operations, and include disaster prevention, preparedness and mitigation in all country frames.

Making evaluation more inclusive The evaluation process should include policies and actions in Stockholm (Sida, Ministry of Foreign Affairs and NGOs) and multilateral partners.

---

be of greater value than the others did. This concern was also stimulated by comments from some of Sida's partners, who during the fieldwork expressed their concerns over the failure of previous evaluation studies to return any of their findings to the field. This view was strengthened by the recognition in the team that we were bringing together a uniquely broad range of experience, which we felt should not just end up in limited circulation in Sida's headquarters and in a few country offices. The whole team was supportive of the dissemination idea, although it seemed doubtful to them whether the idea would be accepted. However, I pursued the idea through ISSAS and, before the final report had been submitted, an agreement had been obtained from Sida that a summary of the ideas from the report should be prepared for wider circulation. It was also agreed that this should be used as the basis of a workshop with the field partners.

Consequently, this evaluation had another few months of life during which three of us worked together to produce a booklet exploring the emergency relief experience in complex emergencies and the relationship of this to development. Under the title 'Beyond relief', this booklet used the experience of the evaluation, but not just the material in the two volumes of the report, to explore general issues we felt needed consideration by those involved in the relief process (Wood 1996, 1999a, 1999b; Wood et al. 1996).

Reflections and Conclusions

There are eight ways in which the practicalities of this evaluation affected the nature of the report that was produced. These experiences are not unique and may have relevance in other evaluation studies.

The research nature of the team meant that its members were experienced and interested in the countries in which they were working. This facilitated fieldwork and the use of local contacts helped, and perhaps 'directed', some of that work. This expertise led three of the team to produce detailed country-specific reports of a publishable standard. Given that Volume Two, on the country-specific experiences, was never published by Sida, it appears that there was some unnecessary diversion of our resources from the main volume.

The preliminary visits to Sida's headquarters were essential. The first one allowed analysis of Sida's data to be put in place, which meant that the team had a clear picture of all the projects as well as their nature when we met for our planning meeting. This data analysis identified the partner agencies, Swedish, external and local, and the characteristics of their projects. This provided us with a basis for the selection of agencies with which we would seek interviews and specific projects for which we would seek data.

A particularly important output from the Stockholm meetings was the way in which the TOR began to evolve. In particular, it became clear that Sida wanted a study that would help them 'think about humanitarian assistance', rather than provide detailed reports of the activities of specific projects. This meant that the study moved from being an evaluation of projects to a policy-oriented study that focused more on partners and their programmes and capacities. This had significant implications for the field-work, making it much more manageable. However, Sida refused a request for the team to spend more time in Stockholm working with the emergencies system there, which the team felt was needed to answer the TORs properly. Instead the problems were seen to be 'out in the field'.

The initial team meeting achieved a high level of agreement about how to look at the phenomena we were to study. This was important as it ensured that we each had a common framework for our separate fieldwork. Allowing each of the team members so much freedom in the field could have been disastrous for the TL's task of producing a consensus report had it not been for that conceptual agreement from the outset.

Standardizing of field methods was attempted with the design, and redesign, of a checklist for use with each project and each partner. This proved of only limited use: individual personalities, as well as experience of the countries of study, influenced the way in which we each collected information. It proved impossible to enforce a standard methodology with each of us operating separately in the five countries in the region. To some extent the detail sought in these checklists was an unnecessary hangover from the original project-by-project view of the TOR.

The meeting in Nairobi, halfway through the fieldwork, was critical for making us raise our sights above the morass of the field data and focus on identifying issues for a final report. It also drew us together from our different field locations and provided an opportunity to exchange experiences and put our individual findings into perspective. As a result the remaining fieldwork was better attuned to the needs of the final report and the issues that were appearing across the five countries.

Writing up proved incredibly protracted. The conflicts of other responsibilities once team members returned to their separate bases, and the problems of getting people together to discuss the report and draft material in some consensus, meant that the TL was left with a mammoth task, which far outstripped the days allocated for this. A major burden was placed on him and team involvement in the final product was restricted. The final team meeting should have been later in the writing process and the team should have been together for more than one day after the fieldwork to reduce this burden on the TL.

Relations with the commissioning organization, Sida, proved extremely positive through the finalization stages. In addition to limited written comments and verbal responses to the presentation of a draft report, extremely useful feedback was provided by the person in charge of the emergency assistance statistics at the time. There was a unique experience when two team members had a day's discussion with him in a most open and challenging manner. This is not common, but the potential for such inputs, which ensure that the report is tuned to the thinking of the donor and the experience of the fieldwork, should always be looked for.

Notes

1. The author gratefully acknowledges the considerable input into this chapter by Raymond Apthorpe, the TL. Joint recall of experience was essential for the detailed observations that are made in it.

2. It was reported that the first study in this series was not what Sida wanted. Apparently it was more of an accountability study with too much detail, and did not generate many new ideas or broader conclusions for the ways of managing emergency assistance.

3. One, as a relatively new employee of ISS, had to support the commercial activities of his new institution, even though he would not receive much in the way of direct recompense. But this was traded off against his research interest in the Horn and his recent work in Somalia. For the professional consultant the evaluation was employment, and one with a new employer that might open up future opportunities for his relatively newly founded independent consultancy. He was especially keen to establish links with a Dutch institution and redevelop his network within his home country, having been based outside it for many years. But he was also interested in getting into Eritrea, an area with which he had had some contact through NGO work during the liberation struggle in the mid-1980s. For myself, the mission was an opportunity to get back to Ethiopia, where I had worked in the past and where I was trying to widen my range of research contacts. Despite working in Ethiopia for 20 years I had gained little direct involvement in emergency relief, and it seemed about time that I did get to know something about this rather central part of life in that country. For the TL, being involved in this mission was a case of coming home to the institution, ISS, where he had spent a large part of his academic life and where he still had many former colleagues. He too wanted to get to a field area, mainly to northern Kenya, where he had worked on a number of occasions.

4

Evaluating Sida's Complex Emergency Assistance in Cambodia: Conflicting Perceptions

Claes Lindahl

Anyone who has participated in an evaluation of a complex aid programme, such as emergency assistance, will have been challenged to think about the nature of the work they are doing and whether they are really confident about the conclusions they reach. I have faced this experience on a number of occasions and I find myself increasingly unhappy about this type of evaluation. Experience may help, but it also makes one more aware of all the problems there are with evaluation of humanitarian assistance in emergency situations. In this chapter I try to explore some of the concerns I have and to identify the issues I feel need to be considered more carefully than is usually the case.

The chapter is based on my experience of the evaluation of the Swedish International Development Agency (Sida) emergency aid to Cambodia (Map 4.1), carried out at the end of 1994 (Bernander et al. 1995). Added to this experience was a review on behalf of Sida of the methodology applied in two other major evaluations of emergency assistance in Africa's Horn (Apthorpe et al. 1995) and in southern Africa. Having worked with evaluations for a number of organizations during the last 20 years, I find it difficult to separate the lessons from the Cambodian case from my overall experience of such work. In this context it should be stressed that the Cambodia evaluation was neither worse nor better than most 'complex evaluations' I have experienced.

The Art and the Science of Evaluation

Evaluation of humanitarian assistance is both an art and a science. There are some 'hard' quantitative 'facts', but there are many impressionistic elements of such endeavours. There are several reasons for the uncertainty in these evaluations: the resources in terms of time and manpower spent on these evaluations are generally minuscule compared to the

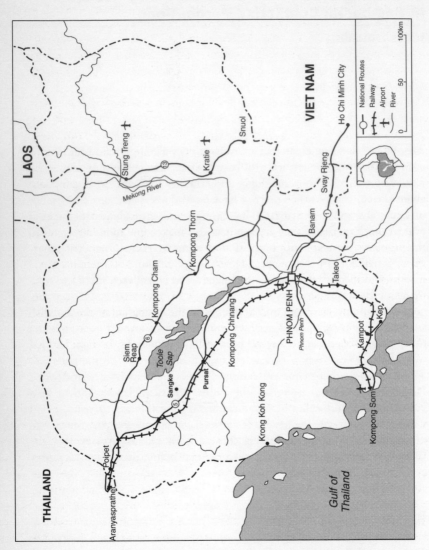

MAP 4.1 Cambodia

complexity of the disasters and the response by the donor community. Lack of benchmark data, poor monitoring systems of implementing agencies and underdeveloped or non-existent evaluation methodologies contribute to the impressionism. Furthermore, the crisis atmosphere in which the relief efforts often are carried out, and the urgency of life and death during the emergency, make evaluations of impact and effectiveness almost hearsay. Yet donors feel obliged to undertake periodic assessments of such emergency assistance programmes, partly because of the need to account for aid money spent and partly to learn from past operations in order to make the next response more effective.

The impressionistic nature of the evaluations makes the result as much dependent on the composition of the evaluation team as on the realities on the ground: send in another team, and the results are likely to be different. As a result, learning is less than that desired and attempts to determine impact and effectiveness are mostly guesswork. In particular, the cost-effectiveness of the interventions is generally left unexplained. Evaluation tends to be more of an art than a science.

There is a strong desire on the part of donor agencies and evaluators alike to change this state of affairs: to make evaluations more like science, providing similar results however the work is undertaken. There are clearly ways in which evaluations of complex processes, such as humanitarian assistance, can be made less impressionistic and more scientific. However, my own personal experience is that the art tends to dominate, and that the temperaments, judgements and perceptions of the evaluators in the end strongly influence the outcome of the process. The reasons for this will be discussed in this chapter, which also draws some conclusions that evaluators can make use of.

Origins of the Mission and Selection of the Team

Between 1979 and 1994 Sida contributed over SEK 500m for relief and rehabilitation in Cambodia. Although not a large amount over 15 years, it was provided in a context that made it politically significant in many areas and through a number of different agents. Consequently, when Sida was choosing country experience to include in its three case studies of its overall emergency assistance activities in the mid-1990s, Cambodia was selected. Unlike the other two studies, which were sub-contracted to consultancy organizations, this one was managed directly by Sida, which also recruited the team of consultants.

Five international consultants were selected to carry out this evaluation. The team included three people with extensive experience in development, of whom two had extensive experience in emergency relief operations.

The other two consultants had excellent knowledge of Cambodia and/or refugee issues. Knowledge of Cambodia was very well represented in the team, with three of the team members having been actively involved in Cambodia over an extended period of time. One had been involved from the time of the disaster relief operations in the 1980s, and one in a senior position during the United Nations Transitional Authority in Cambodia (UNTAC) period. The Team Leader (TL) had a long career in the United Nations and considerable experience in emergency assistance operations in the stage of rehabilitation and reconstruction, including in Cambodia. Thus the team members collectively represented quite a good mixture of competencies. Most of the team members did not know one another in advance.

Several issues emerged during the evaluation about the team composition and how this affected the team's operation. First, some of the team members could be considered stakeholders in the process, as they had been involved in the emergency relief operations in Cambodia in various capacities during the period under consideration. Such involvement provided very valuable information on the historical background to the conflict and to the process of the emergency operation, including the intricate process of decision-making in UNTAC. However, it also meant that the evaluation could not avoid vested interests. Such interests played themselves out in three different ways. First, an apologetic view existed of the behaviour of the aid system in Cambodia in general, and of the United Nations specifically. Second, there were some preconceived ideas of the value of various Sida-supported programmes, based more on personal affinities than on facts. Third, there was a tendency to look at programmes that Sida might continue to support in the future in an inherently positive way. In respect of the latter, the opportunities for future involvement by the team members concerned cannot be ruled out as a source of bias in the assessment.

A second issue is that in the Cambodian case Sida seemed to give priority to persons who had extensive knowledge of the country and then of emergency operations, while paying limited attention to knowledge of evaluation methodology and techniques. My broader experience, gained from other evaluations, is that those dominated by specialists risked being bogged down in technical aspects and often lost sight of the broader humanitarian or development issues and the context issues in which the assistance took place. In addition, specialists also appear to be notoriously weak in looking into cost-effectiveness.

Where local experience is sought there is also often a danger that the evaluators will have a personal interest in what is being evaluated or an interest in a continuous process of support, and therefore cannot be expected to be unbiased. This does not mean that such people should not be included in evaluation teams. However, they should not dominate and certainly should not lead such teams. At the time of the Cambodian evaluation, Sida was concerned with the limited knowledge of Cambodia in Sweden and this may have led to the emphasis on consultants with local knowledge. However, country specialists tend also to develop their own idiosyncrasies and become stakeholders in development aid. They are sometimes apologetic of dysfunctional aspects of development in their particular country of specialization.

This description is not intended to discredit any of the team members: we all took the task seriously, had good professional credentials, all had vested interests of one kind or another, and all probably put in more work than we were contracted for. The intention is to point out for aid organizations and Team Leaders how the team selection and the skills, experience and personalities of those selected can greatly influence how the team operates and the conclusions that are drawn. .

A third issue is that the Cambodian case, with its multitude of implementing agencies and generally long-term cooperation with Swedish aid, would have provided an excellent opportunity for institutional assessment, a key aspect of emergency relief operations and a constant problem for a funding agency such as Sida. The evaluation team was not well chosen for this task since we represented the implementing systems (United Nations and non-governmental organizations) with long-term careers in these systems, or had quite marginal experience of emergency operations and even less of the institutional set-up for such aid. As a result, the institutional assessment became biased and impressionistic, using different criteria depending on which team member happened to look at which organization.

Coping with the Terms of Reference

The Terms of Reference (TOR) are the sole governing guidelines for an evaluation. As such they are, or should be, important documents. In retrospect, I believe the TOR for the Cambodian evaluation had several weaknesses, which are not uncommon for 'complex evaluations' and should have been considered before the mission started. First, they required various assessments of the assistance (not specifying whether these impacts should be related to the overall assistance or just the Swedish inputs) such as: the impact on different ethnic, gender and age groups; the impact on special target groups such as refugees, internally displaced persons and demobilized soldiers; and the impact on the economy and various sectors. In addition, the TOR required an assessment of efficiency, effectiveness, sustainability, and so on. Requiring these types of assessment is legitimate. However, the demands were unrealistic given the time allowed for the evaluation, and the quality of the implementing agencies' information systems. Such a discrepancy between what is required by the TOR and what can be achieved given the resources available (time, systems and others) is not unique to the Cambodian case. The problem is that such gaps lead either to a mutual disregard of the TOR by the commissioning agency and by the team carrying out the evaluation, or to a false sense of accuracy and objectivity if an (over-)ambitious evaluation team tries to answer all of the questions raised without data of sufficient accuracy. In the Cambodian case it turned out to be a mixture of these two defects.

Second, in my opinion the TOR we were given made a mistake in limiting the evaluation to a narrow time frame, the period 1989–94, rather than looking at the full operation since 1979 when the humanitarian assistance was started. (No evaluation had ever been carried out previously by Sida.) The latter approach would have allowed a more contextual analysis, an assessment of the process of reconstruction and long-term performance by implementing agencies, as well as the politics of Swedish emergency assistance. In fact, I went outside the specific TOR to look at the historical record and the underlying factors, but this deviation led to various controversies within the evaluation team. A lesson that can be drawn in general from that work, I believe, is that decision-making in aid is strongly path-dependent, i.e. the actions this year are very much influenced by the actions and decisions last year, and so on. Hence the historical perspective is essential for understanding these processes.

Third, our TOR reflected a mixture of agendas by Sida, not uncommon in evaluations. The agency wanted lessons for its emergency assistance as a part of a broader thematic series of evaluations. Sida also wanted an 'aid audit' focusing on impact assessment in the particular case, reflecting the fact that there is hardly any feedback from these major aid programmes on what is achieved and whether the aid money is spent efficiently and effectively. A final need was for a forward-looking assessment to assist in programming, as Sida was in the process of making Cambodia a 'programme country'. While all four objectives can be justified in themselves, combining them in one (short) evaluation has serious drawbacks since they tend to compromise one another.

It would be fair to say that as a team we were poor in resolving these issues. While we recognized the breadth of the task, we did not negotiate the terms of reference and simply took them as written. We did not even discuss in the team whether we realistically could fulfil them, but rather tried to resolve this issue along the road individually. Individually we paid different attention to the various aspects of the TOR, especially the issue of future programming; some of the team members were more interested than others in the prospect of a Swedish programme country in Cambodia.

We went our own ways on the issue of the time period, some sticking to the stipulated period in the TOR, while others, including myself, wanted to put the programme in the broader historical context. In short, we made our own individual interpretation of the TOR and carried various conflicting views with us throughout the evaluation. As a team we never made the time to work them out before or during the fieldwork. Not until the report writing did all this surface as an open conflict. Limited time, a leadership style that emphasized getting on with the work rather than questioning the TOR, and the strong personalities of the team members created this situation.

Not Developing a Methodology

A second and related, but more important, gap in the preparations was that we failed to establish an agreed methodology for the evaluation. This was partly due to the time pressure we were under to start work in Cambodia. But it was also partly due to the lack of evaluation experience of the Team Leader, who, faced with excessively wide-ranging TOR, felt that getting on with the fieldwork was the most important task and the best use of scarce time. As a result, we each pursued substantially different approaches with no overall design. This led to problems in agreeing the overall conclusions of the evaluation at the end. With hindsight, I feel that the outcome of the evaluation was probably better than the lack of a shared and explicit team agreement on methodology would indicate. However, an agreed methodology could have led to more effective use of our field time and more productive discussions when drawing our conclusions.

The TOR did not help in this situation. They stressed the range of questions to be answered but failed to provide any guidance about the choice of methodology or the focus of the evaluation. From one perspective, the lack of an explicit methodology stimulated some creative tension as the team members' different perceptions, backgrounds and interests constantly engaged one another; but the outcome was too much of an *ad hoc* process. It is no coincidence that during the report writing, two conflicting views of the key results emerged, resulting in two different versions of a concluding chapter, one included in the main report, one attached as an appendix. I appreciate that complex cases, such as the Cambodian one, can easily give rise to different opinions, but a thorough discussion before the team undertakes the fieldwork on a methodology of what to assess, how to do it and what criteria should be used can reduce such controversy.

The Narrow Timeframe

The Cambodian evaluation also experienced another major constraint, one that is perhaps typical of most evaluations of humanitarian assistance. Each of the expatriate consultants was allowed a time input of six weeks, of which about four weeks were to be spent in Cambodia. Once the contract was signed with the evaluation team members, there was a period of three months in which the work had to be carried out.

One result was that, for the majority of the team, there was little preparatory time prior to the mission. There was insufficient time for reviewing available documents, and even less for agreeing on an approach. The expectation that evaluation should provide inputs for the agency's decision-making on new programmes added to the pressures to get to the field. While extending the time for the evaluation would have dealt with various problems of a practical nature, allowing time for the sufficient preparation and establishment of a commonly agreed methodology seems almost a precondition for the reduction of impressionism.

In contrast to Sida's normal procedures, no local consultants participated in this evaluation. This might have been the combined result of limited ownership by Cambodia of its development process at the time of the evaluation, the strong presence of expatriates at all levels, as well as the donor perception of a very weak local capacity.[1] While the latter might well have been true, I believe local research studies can contribute considerably to a good evaluation, through a more systematic collection of field data. This in turn creates better ownership of the evaluation process and adds to local capacity-building. My experience from other evaluations is that such local research studies should be incorporated into the evaluation rather than commissioned by the donor agency as a preparatory phase. The latter approach leads to results that are used to a very limited extent, if at all, in the final analysis.

Fieldwork

The way in which the fieldwork in Cambodia was arranged helped us 'resolve' the issue of lack of a common methodology. A division of labour among the team members on different aspects and subject matters was agreed, allowing us each to apply our own methods to the evaluation. This division was facilitated by the fact that Swedish humanitarian assistance to Cambodia was split among different external implementing agencies – the United Nations Children's Fund (UNICEF), the United Nations High Commissioner for Refugees (UNHCR), the Red Cross, de-mining non-governmental organizations (NGOs), Asian Development Bank (ADB), the World Bank, etc. – and line agencies, which specialized in certain subject matters such as education, infrastructure, repatriation of refugees, demining, etc. Each one of us applied our personal explicit or implicit methodology to the agencies whose work we were to evaluate.

The most important reason for the impressionism and conflicting perceptions in the Cambodia evaluation was the poor database on which to make assessments of the programme. Emergency assistance should of course not spend critical time and resources on establishing baselines and setting up systems to monitor progress and impact. However, much of the Cambodia experience was not really emergency assistance. It was more a long-term rehabilitation-cum-reconstruction phase undertaken in a generally non-crisis situation after 1981. Furthermore, it was a humanitarian assistance programme utilizing a large number of UN and other non-governmental organizations with well-established offices in the country, run almost entirely by foreigners. These organizations were running programmes over a considerable period of time, which would allow systematic follow-up and monitoring of achievements and impact. Some agencies even promised such monitoring in their agreements with Sida. However, we found little useful data, and the agency reporting tended to be non-analytical, more geared to argue for further support than to provide data based on results. Sida, in its turn, had neglected to follow up on its own conditions in terms of monitoring and reporting by its implementing agencies.

The availability of data is something an evaluation cannot know beforehand, and the hope that there will be adequate reporting is one excuse for accepting ambitious TOR. However, I think most evaluators have come across similar situations in almost all humanitarian programmes. In spite of years of arguing the need for systematic in-built monitoring and evaluation in assistance, the examples of this in fact taking place are rare.

Report Writing

Initially it was not very difficult to put together the final report as it was composed of the various agency/subject matter chapters. However, the crux came in drawing the broader conclusions. It could be argued that the report had a serious gap in this: there was no logical step or process (agreed or explicit) to move from findings to broader conclusions. As noted above, we had two rather different concluding chapters, one written by the Team Leader, with whom I disagreed, and one written by me, with which the team leader disagreed. Fortunately we respected one another and he had the courtesy to put in my conclusions as an annex.

Lessons for Humanitarian Assistance Evaluation

Much could be said on how an evaluation team should operate in order to reduce the impressionistic element of its work. There are six major points raised by the Cambodia experience that I would like to explore.

Terms of Reference The TOR for evaluation need to be more realistic, focusing on one main task. The evaluation team should continually refer back to these and be judged by them. To achieve this teams must ensure that donor agencies do not load evaluations with ambitious and unrealistic demands. This will require teams negotiating their TOR so that a level of realism and common understanding is established between them and the commissioning agency.

TOR can very easily become unrealistic because they require assessments, which must be based on long-term data collection, which often does not exist. For example, impact assessment and measuring efficiency and effectiveness are not *ad hoc* activities that an *ex-post* evaluation can carry out with any degree of validity and reliability, unless the programme under review has paid considerable attention to this already from its inception. This is rarely the case in any development cooperation programme, and even less so in humanitarian assistance.

How can we deal with such unrealistic demands? If a team is commissioned for an evaluation without a competitive bidding procedure, and if the Team Leader has sufficient standing and experience, he or she should in theory be able to negotiate the Terms of Reference with the agency, and scale down what is unlikely to be possible to assess. He or she might also persuade the commissioning agency to try to avoid too many agendas for an evaluation, and focus either on the analysis for learning, 'impact' assessment ('aid audit'), or the future programming after the emergency; but not combine the three. However, as donor agencies tend to have no other feedback mechanisms of the effectiveness of their support, and as they are often under pressure from their home constituency to show results and provide proof of their effectiveness, this is easier said than done. My own experience is that, rather than negotiating the Terms of Reference, there is a tacit understanding between the aid organization and the consultants that 'we understand that you have to ask more questions in the Terms of Reference than realistically can be answered, and we will try our best, but we assume that you won't hold us responsible for not being able to answer them all'. If this is to change, there is a need for courage by both commissioning agency and evaluation team.

If the evaluation is subject to competitive bidding, the evaluation team is in an awkward position. If it argues in its proposal that the TOR are unrealistic, there is a clear risk it will not be the winner of the bid. The same tacit understanding discussed above might therefore set in. One way out of this dilemma, in my own experience, is to undertake a thorough review of the Terms of Reference and to work out how various items can be assessed as a part of the proposal in bidding for evaluations. This is expensive, as it might mean a lot of unpaid work. But, if done in honesty, such a process reveals to everyone what might realistically be accomplished and what conditions are needed for accomplishing the task. Most importantly, it places the responsibility on the evaluation team.

Functioning teams It could be argued that when team members are selected by the donor agency, such as in the Cambodia case, the risks of internal conflicts and unresolved differences in perceptions are particularly great. Such conflicting views can always be blamed on the agency that forced together the group. In principle, team-building should be left to a consultancy company whose job it is to specialize in putting together teams of people whose skills and ability to work together in a complementary manner are known.

However, this might not always solve the problem. My experience is that a team put together by a consultancy company might turn out to have different perceptions and unresolvable conflicts, while a team composed by the donor agency can run quite smoothly. Evaluations of humanitarian assistance programmes require assessments of very complex issues in short periods of time by groups of professionals with different backgrounds. This requires amalgamating judgements of people with different professional skills, temperaments and perceptions into a consistent structure that is logical and practical enough to add to the client's way of doing humanitarian assistance. My own experience in creating consensus and common views in such complex situations has been to spend considerable time during the preparation for the evaluation fieldwork establishing a common frame of reference and a methodology that everyone can share, using, for example, seminars on methodology. While such efforts generally pay off, I have also learned that they are no panacea. A team might have considerable discussions on method and frame of reference in seminars and workshops during the start-up of an evaluation only to find that when the reality of the fieldwork sets in, the team members tend to follow their old tracks.

The *ex-ante* methodology discussions must be complemented by a way of doing the evaluation that involves considerable time being spent by the team members looking at the same thing and discussing what they see when the impressions are still fresh. It is during the discussions in the evening over dinner and drinks after long hours in the field that perceptions slowly approach one another, or, if they still are different, a structure to accom-modate them can be created. There is not much science in this, just a lot of time in personal interaction. Evaluators tend to be fairly seasoned people, not easily programmed to follow a certain track in a pre-programmed methodology. But as seasoned people, they also tend to be curious about the perceptions of other professionals and have an ability to understand dif-ferent viewpoints.

Methodological rigour and dealing with attribution　If an evaluation is to operate effectively in the field and not face major problems when it comes to drawing overall conclusions, time and effort must be put into developing an agreed understanding of what is being studied and a common, or at least complementary, methodology. This obviously has implications for the use of time at the start of the mission, but it is an investment that will pay dividends later in the process.

A second point here is the need for appropriate records. Methods can be far more effective if they have something to draw upon and use. The problem of lack of records in agencies working in non-emergency situations, with adequate staff and agreements requiring them to keep records, is explained in this case study. It is not unique. It is a routine problem faced by evaluation teams, especially in addressing humanitarian assistance.

A particular methodological dilemma in an evaluation is the issue of attribution, i.e. how much of a noticed change can be attributed to a specific aid programme. The problem is compounded by the fact that many agencies tend to operate in humanitarian assistance. Hence assessing impact by a specific aid agency is next to impossible. Evaluation of impact should theoretically assess 'with and without (aid)', i.e. counterfactuals, which by definition is poor science and in reality leads to guesswork and personal judgements. The best we can usually offer is a systematic judgement using the views of the stakeholders themselves, responding to questions such as: 'What would have happened if ... ?'

I believe that there is a general tendency to attribute too much to external assistance, and to underestimate the endogenous factors operating in the study locality. In assessing a particular programme we naturally focus on the contributions of this particular programme, wanting to be able to show results, or lack of results. This argues for a strong focus on the context of the humanitarian assistance, not only what others are doing, which might explain noticed 'impacts' or changes, but also, and possibly more important, non-aid factors – for example, the response by the popula-tion themselves in dealing with an emergency, or rebuilding their societies after the emergency.

I believe that too much of an emphasis on self-attribution in an attempt by an aid agency to show 'its' results is counter-productive. The issue is rather to determine whether the agency is reinforcing positive changes or possibly preventing them; whether a humanitarian assistance programme is moving in the 'right' direction, rather than putting a quantitative measure on its catalyst impact.

Standards in evaluations: dealing with half-full or half-empty glasses

In every evaluation, there is a question of what measuring-stick should be used, i.e. for finding the balance between faults and achievements. Some evaluators have a tendency to seek the faults and identify the problems, while others like to highlight the achievements. This is often more an issue of temperament and personality than of perceiving reality differently. An underlying factor determining the choice of views is that the humanitarian aid community is small and the number of evaluators of humanitarian programmes even smaller. We all know that a too critical review might put at risk the next job, while glowing praise tends to be appreciated by the client. Evaluators place different values on these risks and opportunities.

The potentially harmful effects and distortions of emergency relief operations are increasingly discussed, and should be an important element of the TOR for evaluations of aid in complex disasters. While the awareness of this is strong in the disaster relief phase, there are similar potential distortions in the rehabilitation and reconstruction phase due to a combination of factors: the magnitude of support versus the domestic resources of the country; the weakness of the host country administration; and the frequent lack of a country strategy due to the trauma of the disaster and to vested interest groups in the wake of the disaster. The potential effects of such distortions are massive corruption and other forms of rent-seeking, donor-driven agendas and the creation of aid dependency.

Too much criticism, however warranted, risks closing the ears of the commissioning agency unless the latter, for some reason, wants arguments to close down a particular programme. There is only a certain degree of intellectual freedom for an evaluation if it is to have any impact at all. Too much praise provides little learning, and too much criticism tends to create rejection. Finding the right tone within the degrees of freedom permitted, phrasing criticism in a constructive manner, and avoiding praise for the only reason of assuring the next job, is not science but art.

Dealing with cost-effectiveness

Cost-effectiveness considerations tend to be neglected in evaluations of bilateral programmes in general, and especially so in emergency relief operations. Donors appear to show little interest in the issue, and evaluators like to do other things than calculating costs. This is probably a result of the supply-driven nature of the aid, with little need for the agency to economize its resources. A result of this is that the real cost of a project is often not known. Even less is known about cost-effectiveness.[2] While it might be considered insensitive to look at the costs in operations concerning life and death, efforts to assess cost-effectiveness are essential for an aid agency to achieve the maximum with the funds available. This would improve the ability of agencies to meet the increasing demand for such operations with stagnant aid funds. While the TOR for evaluations routinely ask for assessments of cost-effectiveness, the reports equally routinely gloss over this issue with statements such as 'cost-effectiveness could not be assessed'.

At the same time, we should not fool ourselves into believing that we can undertake accurate cost-effectiveness assessments of most humanitarian assessments. First, effectiveness is very difficult to assess because objectives are difficult to quantify. And there is the problem of attribution. While cost-effectiveness assessments require good impact analysis, something can be done even when this is not available. Calculating unit costs is a first step: what is the cost of delivering a ton of food? What is the cost per beneficiary and year for a refugee operation? Of repatriation? Of rehabilitating a kilometre of road? Building such data might lead to more efficient choices of interventions, disguise dramatic inequalities in support (for example in the support directed to refugees versus that directed to internally displaced persons), or highlight any absurd relationships between what trickles down to beneficiaries and what is spent on overheads.

Time and resources for evaluation　A 30-person-week assignment, such as that for the Cambodia evaluation, is not a small undertaking and the budget for the evaluation was considerable. As an evaluation is one of the few available instruments for providing unbiased feedback on a humanitarian programme, and in the context of disaster relief is usually carried out very infrequently, the resources spent on evaluations should ideally be seen in the context of the size of the aid programme as a whole. The Cambodian evaluation corresponded to about 0.2 per cent of the total Swedish emergency assistance to that country. This is a very marginal effort for assessing impact and providing feedback.

Conclusions: More of a Science, but Still Mostly an Art

I have argued in this chapter that evaluations of humanitarian assistance tend to be highly impressionistic, more an art than a science, and as such highly dependent on the temperament of the artists. I have also argued that donor agencies commissioning such evaluations and the evaluators can jointly do a lot to make the result of the evaluations more independent of the people carrying them out. But the bottom line is that the art will probably continue to dominate, and that personal judgements of the evaluators will determine the conclusions and the recommendations. Development assistance is not an academic exercise, but a political activity. As such it is an art of the possible. This places a strong responsibility both on the commissioning agency in selecting the team and on the evaluators in being honest and showing integrity. In the end, evaluations must be a shared responsibility and a matter of trust between the parties. The commissioning agency must trust the evaluators, and listen to potentially critical views without partiality and with a preparedness to learn and change. The evaluators must appreciate under the conditions in which humanitarian assistance take place, and be constructive rather than scoring criticism for its own sake. Both must avoid the easy way out: of loading and receiving praise as a reason to do business as usual.

Notes

1. An expression of this is that when the team met with a major, supposedly local, NGO that was one of the channels for Swedish assistance, the NGO was represented by the two expatriates even if, as a formality, also by a Cambodian. This was a rather common feature.

2. The concept of supply-driven aid and its various consequences, such as neglect of the cost dimension, is discussed in J. Catterson and C. Lindahl (1999) *The Sustainability Enigma*, Ministry of Foreign Affairs, Stockholm.

5

Doing Study 3 of the Joint Evaluation of Emergency Assistance to Rwanda: The Team Leader's Perspective

John Borton

This chapter provides an account, from the Team Leader's (TL) perspective, of the unprecedented evaluation of the humanitarian operations mounted in the wake of the 1994 genocide and conflict in Rwanda, which resulted in massive population displacements affecting all the countries in the Great Lakes region of Africa (Map 5.1). The ensuing humanitarian operations were the largest undertaken during the last two decades and were primarily responsible for propelling global expenditures on humanitarian aid to their highest ever levels.

The evaluation of the humanitarian operations formed just one component of a larger unprecedented enterprise, initiated and led by bilateral donor organizations, to evaluate the effectiveness of the international community's entire response – in political, diplomatic, military, post-conflict rehabilitation and reconstruction assistance as well as the humanitarian operations themselves. In terms of the financial and human resources and time taken to undertake Study 3, 'Humanitarian Aid and Effects', it represents an undertaking quite different from most of the other evaluations considered in this volume and is closer to a commissioned multi-disciplinary research study than a conventional evaluation. Nevertheless the chapter provides valuable insights into the process of undertaking this ground-breaking study: the way the team was assembled; the difficulty of combining, within the role of Team Leader, responsibility for managing such a large team, as well as responsibility for 'content'; and the way in which defensive reactions by large humanitarian agencies were handled.

The crisis The 1994 genocide in Rwanda resulted in the killing of at least 800,000 people during a ten-week period. This represented 11 per cent of the country's 1991 population of 7.1 million. Those killed were predominantly members of the Tutsi ethnic group, but a significant number of Hutu who were considered politically moderate and/or sympathetic to

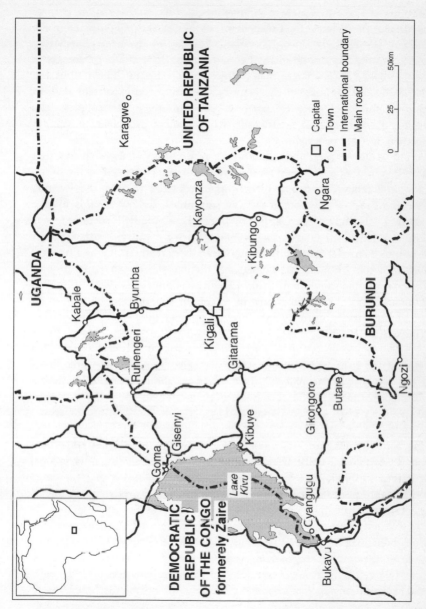

MAP 5.1 Rwanda

a political settlement with the Tutsi were also killed. The killings began on 6 April immediately after an aircraft carrying the Rwandan president was shot down. The initial spate of killings included ten soldiers in the Belgian contingent that formed the backbone of a UN peacekeeping mission in the country, the United Nations Assistance Mission in Rwanda (UNAMIR), and led to the withdrawal of the Belgian contingent and other elements of the UNAMIR force. There then followed an exodus of almost all of the non-Rwandan nationals in the country, including the expatriate staff of most of the relief agencies that had been working in the country. The exodus in effect cleared the way for the *génocidaires* to embark in earnest on their terrible programme.

The start of the killings prompted a resumption of the civil war that had been in uneasy abeyance for the previous year. Motivated by the desire to rescue fellow Tutsi and to oust the genocidal regime, the Rwanda Patriotic Front (RPF) fought its way southwards and westwards to take control of the bulk of the country by mid-July. As the RPF advanced, over 2 million Hutu fled as refugees into neighbouring countries, with a sudden flow into Tanzania (especially into Ngara District) in April and a massive flow into the areas around Goma and Bukavu in eastern Zaire in July. Perhaps a million more remained in Rwanda as internally displaced populations (IDPs) – many in camps in the south-west of the country in an area temporarily controlled by a French military intervention, Opération Turquoise.

The refugee and IDP crisis provoked a massive international relief effort that was in marked contrast to the pusillanimous military and diplomatic response to the genocide itself. Over the period April to December 1994 approximately US$1.4 billion was allocated to the relief response, 85 per cent from official sources and 15 per cent from private sources.

The Joint Evaluation   The enormity of these events led to an unprecedented international collaboration to learn the lessons from the international response – the Joint Evaluation of Emergency Assistance to Rwanda (JEEAR). The scale and ambition of the JEEAR dwarfs any previous or subsequent evaluation. An account of the process of carrying out the JEEAR and some of the issues that the process raised has been provided by the chair of the JEEAR Steering Committee (Dabelstein 1996). The scale of the undertaking is conveyed by some of the JEEAR's statistics: the Steering Committee was composed of the representatives of 38 agencies and organizations. Its total cost of US$1.7 million was met by contributions from 20 agencies and organizations. Overall 52 researchers and consultants were employed by the JEEAR. Their work was organized into four teams:

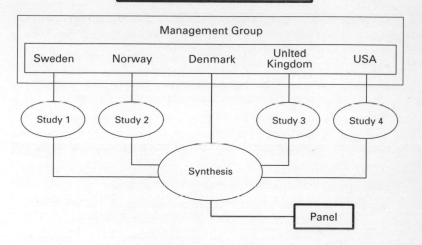

FIGURE 5.1 Organizational Structure of the JEEAR (*source*: Dabelstein 1996)

- Study 1, covering historical perspectives;
- Study 2, covering early warning and conflict management;
- Study 3, covering humanitarian aid; and
- Study 4, covering rehabilitation and reconstruction.

A separate synthesis report collated the main findings and recommendations from the different studies. The management structure for JEEAR is shown in Figure 5.1.

The Management Group was composed of the heads of evaluation within the donor organizations of Sweden, Norway, Denmark, the UK and the USA. The chair of the Management Group was also the chair of the Steering Committee to which the Management Group reported. Each of the five donor organizations took responsibility for managing the contracts in relation to one of the studies. Thus the Swedish International Development Agency (Sida) took responsibility for managing Study 1, the Norwegian Ministry of Foreign Affairs (MFA) for Study 2, the UK Overseas Development Administration (ODA) for Study 3, the United States Agency for International Development (USAID) for Study 4 and the Danish International Development Agency (Danida) for the Synthesis Study.

This chapter focuses on Study 3, 'Humanitarian Aid and Effects', which

---

Box 5.1 Study 3 timetable

1994

December	Interested organizations requested to prepare bids at beginning of month: Overseas Development Institute (ODI) awarded bid by end of month.

1995

January	Representatives of the four teams meet for the first time in Geneva together with the Management Group.
February	Formation of the Study 3 Team and development of the Analytical Framework.
April	Reconnaissance visit to region by six members of the team.
June–July	Bulk of fieldwork undertaken.
August	Technical Specialists prepare reports. TL begins writing the draft report. Team Workshop held in Wales.
September	External Workshop for representatives of selected agencies.
October	Draft Report completed and disseminated for comment to organizations represented on the Steering Committee.
November	Team presents review of the comments received and how it intends responding to them in the final report at a meeting of the Steering Committee.

1996

January	Final report finalized and submitted to printers.
March	JEEAR launched in Geneva, Nairobi and New York with special press briefing in London.

---

was the largest of the four studies. Its team was made up of 20 individuals with a combined input equivalent to more than four person-years; its eventual total cost at $580,000 represented 34 per cent of the total cost of the JEEAR. In common with the other studies the work commenced in January 1995 and its final report was published in March 1997 (see Box 5.1).

Landing the Contract

Within the JEEAR Management Group, ODA's Evaluation Department was responsible for overseeing the tendering procedure and ensuring the satisfactory completion of Study 3. Compared to the other four members of the Management Group, ODA arguably had the most experience in evaluating emergency aid programmes, having commissioned independent evaluations of the UK government's response to the African food crisis of 1984–86, the 1991 Bangladesh cyclone, the 1991–92 southern African drought and supported a geographical department in the commissioning of an evaluation of rehabilitation grants to British non-governmental organizations (NGOs) following the 1988 floods in Bangladesh. ODI personnel had been involved in undertaking three of ODA's four evaluations of UK emergency aid and were regularly used as specialist advisers on matters concerning emergency aid by ODA's Evaluation Department. If it chose to bid for Study 3 ODI clearly stood a strong chance of winning the contract.

ODA invited several international and UK institutions to bid. None of the non-UK institutions felt able to bid due to their existing work commitments. Only ODI and one other UK group submitted bids.

ODI's outline proposal, submitted in mid-December, proposed four named individuals and a number of other individuals we were in the process of contacting. A senior British professor with considerable consultancy experience in evaluation, based in Australia, was proposed as Team Leader for a period of nine months. My own role in the team was written as providing support on a part-time basis for a total of three months – my time being limited by other commitments as coordinator of ODI's Relief and Rehabilitation Network, which had been launched only nine months previously and was not fully staffed. Inputs of five months each were envisaged by a nutritionist, a coordination specialist with UN and Rwanda experience, a health specialist, a logistician, a water and sanitation specialist, and a refugee care/camp management specialist, with the individuals for these last four positions still needing to be identified. The rough estimated cost was £370,000 (approximately $590,000). Over the following two weeks additional individuals were identified as potential team members and the proposed Team Leader visited London and met with the head of ODA's Evaluation Department and the director of ODI. ODI was informed just before Christmas that its bid had been successful and this was confirmed at the next JEEAR Management Group meeting on 13 January, where a working budget of $450,000 was approved.

Losing the Team Leader and Starting Work

Following the Christmas break, contract negotiations between ODI and the proposed Team Leader broke down. Ostensibly the cause was the inadequate financial terms offered by ODI (which was itself constrained by the overall budget agreed by ODA) but possibly a more significant factor was the view of the (then) head of ODA's Evaluation Department and the (then) director of ODI that I should be pressed into giving up my other commitments and taking on the role of Team Leader. With the proposed Team Leader waiting in Sydney for ODI to improve its offer of financial terms I was obliged to represent the Study 3 team at the first meeting of Team Leaders held near Geneva on 22–24 January 1995. On arrival three members of the Management Group set about persuading me to take on the Team Leader role on a full-time basis. Each of my concerns was either downplayed or a course of action agreed. My weak French language ability, paralleled by my belief that the Team Leader had to speak fluent French to work in Rwanda and with the francophone agencies, was downplayed. Eventually I agreed to take on the role on the following conditions: that effective arrangements were made to carry on the work of Relief and Rehabilitation Network; that I be provided with language training; and that I be able to take a break with my family during July. Half an hour later I was being introduced to the other teams as the Team Leader of Study 3.

Two other members of the Study 3 team, the UN/Coordination specialist and the nutritionist, participated in the Team Leaders' meeting. The objective of the meeting was to review the TOR and clarify the schedules and also the relationships between the teams and between the teams and the Management Group. The three of us had agreed to undertake some initial consultations with key agencies in Rome, Amsterdam, Brussels, Paris and Geneva en route to the Team Leaders' meeting. These preliminary meetings were to prove useful, particularly during discussion of how the TOR should be interpreted. They also clearly revealed the degree to which many of the key personnel involved in the initial relief phases in Ngara in April 1994 and in Goma and Bukavu in July 1994 had already left to work elsewhere. The methodological implication was that we would need to put considerable effort into tracing and interviewing these individuals in other parts of the world.

On returning from Geneva, ODA requested the (nascent) team to prepare an Analytical Framework that would indicate the criteria and methods to be used in undertaking the study. A workshop was scheduled at ODA for mid-February at which the Analytical Framework would be presented to members of the Evaluation Department, the Emergency Aid Department and the relevant Geographical Departments. At a time when many of the key posts within the team still had to be filled and the budget worked out and negotiated the requirement to prepare the Analytical Framework within so short a timescale was not exactly welcomed by me. The UN/Coordination specialist on the team, who had begun a temporary contract in January, agreed to take the lead in preparing it. The process of developing the Analytical Framework led to differences emerging between the team and ODA's Evaluation Department on a number of issues relating to the Terms of Reference (TOR), the criteria to be used and the extent to which we should commit the report to make scoring-type judgements on overall performance using an 'Evaluation Success Ratings' matrix developed within ODA.

The TOR for all of the teams were very lengthy: having been obliged to take account of comments made by the 38 organizations represented on the Steering Committee; *par excellence* these were TOR that had been 'prepared by committee'. The text specifically relating to Study 3 consisted of four closely typed pages and read much more like a shopping list of points to be covered. Two key paragraphs encapsulated Study 3's objectives:

> The third study will assess mechanisms for and effectiveness of preparation and coordination of emergency assistance programming and the impact of emergency assistance. It will with due consideration of the complexity and dynamics of the emergency, concentrate on the effectiveness of coordinated action as well as timely and appropriate assistance through numerous channels to people in dire need. It will further assess contingency plans for possible and new emergency scenarios. (JEEAR 1995: paragraph 8)

> The objective of the study is to extract lessons of experience with regard to the organization and delivery of emergency aid by the international community. Emphasis will be on policy and operational issues, relating to the whole continuum of humanitarian response in the different scenarios and the volatility of the Rwanda emergency situation. Under each scenario the process and mechanisms created to secure humanitarian space, i.e. an acceptable basic humanitarian environment will be analysed and assessed. (JEEAR 1995: paragraph 36)

The team appreciated the difficulties faced by the Management Group in getting the TOR approved by the Steering Committee; broadly speaking we accepted the TOR as they stood. However, they were organized around an analytical framework that posed three possible scenarios, namely:

1. mass killings, mass movement and social collapse;

2. stabilization of mass displacement situations, authority vacuum, military offensive and new mass movements; and

3. consolidation, attempts at re-establishment of authority.

The team felt that this categorization was too simplistic and that if it were adopted by the team it would prove restrictive. An initial reading of the available accounts of the humanitarian response had revealed quite distinct phases to the response, which were both geographically and temporally distinct. The team felt that the overall response should be disaggregated into eleven 'episodes':

1. Rwanda: from RPF invasion in 1990 to April 1994;
2. Burundi: from October 1993 to late 1994;
3. Uganda-based operations: April to August 1994;
4. Burundi-based operations: April to September 1994;
5. protection and relief operations in Kigali: April to July 1994;
6. operations within the Humanitarian Protection Zone: end June to mid-August 1994;
7. refugee influx into Ngara and Karagwe districts, Tanzania: end April 1994 onwards;
8. refugee influx into Goma area, Zaire: July 1994 onwards;
9. refugee influx into Bukavu/Uvira area, Zaire: July 1994 onwards;
10. relief operations inside Rwanda: mid-July 1994 onwards; and
11. regional aspects of the response.

After some initial resistance, ODA's Evaluation Department agreed to the change. The disaggregation into the eleven 'episodes' was to prove a valuable modification, as it made the task of evaluating the overall humanitarian response significantly more manageable. Moreover, it increased the specificity of assessments of performance by situating such assessments within the particular context of that part of the response.

ODA wanted the team to use the standard Development Assistance Committee (DAC) evaluation criteria, but we were reluctant to adopt all the criteria in an unmodified form. While we had no problem with the criteria of appropriateness, effectiveness and impact, we felt that some criteria (e.g. sustainability) were not directly applicable and that none of the criteria specifically required examination of the extent to which the programmes had covered the needs of all the affected population. The team's Analytical Framework paper therefore proposed the use of the criteria of appropriateness, cost-effectiveness; coverage; coherence, connectedness and impact. The 'new' criteria of coverage, coherence and connectedness had been proposed by Larry Minear in a paper prepared for a meeting in Washington in September 1994 (Minear 1994) and were borrowed (with due accreditation) by the team. Eventually ODA accepted the criteria proposed by the team.

With regard to ODA's Evaluation Success Ratings[1] the team felt that they were entirely unsuitable for a system-wide evaluation of humanitarian assistance, and that anyhow it would not be appropriate for ODA to impose formats relating to its own aims and objectives on an evaluation that was being funded by as many as 20 other organizations. After several exchanges on the subject it was eventually agreed (but finally in the end not done) that the team would consider preparing a Success Ratings Table once the evaluation had been completed.

Assembling the Team

Out of a team of 20 only three of us were employed by ODI before January 1995, and the task of assembling the team was therefore particularly onerous. While the initial proposal to ODA had indicated a team of eight specialists the eventual team comprised a core team of three, an administrative support team of three (though only two were present at any given time) and a total of 14 technical specialists (see Box 5.2). While some of the technical specialists had only a minor input and one essentially served as a research assistant to another, there were several factors contributing to this expansion beyond the eight-person team originally envisaged.

One set of factors was the identification of new roles and the redefinition of what had been previously envisaged as single roles. One new role arose from recognition of the need for a military specialist who would be able to gain access to commanders of the French, Belgian, US, British and other military contingents that had been involved in protection and assistance activities. In addition I was keen to involve anthropologists in the team as a result of positive earlier evaluation experiences, and persuaded ODA's Evaluation Department of their potential value.

In some cases the redefinition of roles also resulted from consideration of the skills and availability of suitable individuals. For instance, only one logistician had been envisaged in the original proposal, but it became apparent that none of the candidates being considered could satisfactorily cover both bulk food logistics and airlift logistics – these required different skills. Consequently two were hired. One focused on WFP and ICRC's bulk food movements. The other concentrated on the massive airlift operation that had been mounted using a combination of civil and military assets. Another example was in the health sector, where I was keen to draw on the skills and data available in the US Centers for Disease Control, which had deployed epidemiologists in support of agencies in Goma and other areas during the response. In the event CDC were not in a position to allocate a specialist for a long period and we hired the services of an epidemiologist for a limited period.

One of the technical specialists was a Danish military medical doctor who was provided at no cost to Study 3 by Danida. Ostensibly the purpose of his secondment was to benefit Danish capacity in the field of humanitarian evaluations. Initially there was a suspicion that he was provided as some sort of check on the team's conduct, but this was not borne out by experience or subsequent discussions.

In assembling the team our approach was to identify several potentially suitable individuals for each post and then pick the one who was most suitable and available for the required periods. Potential candidates were identified through contacts from previous evaluations and work, and through requests to organizations represented on the Steering Committee for suggested names. CVs were then requested and once a number of CVs had been compared and further enquiries made about the suitability of the individuals, the preferred candidates were contacted and their interest and availability explored.

Box 5.2 Composition and inputs by the Study 3 team

Core team (ODI, London)	Total input
Team Leader (ODI research fellow)	210 days
UN/Coordination specialist (ODI research associate)	194 days
Economist (ODI research associate)	90 days

Administrative/secretarial support

Three, of whom two were involved at any time (one an ODI staff member and two on temporary contracts)	270 days

Technical specialists

Health specialist (freelance/Centre for International Child Health, London)	50 days
Anthropologist (School of Oriental and African Studies, London)	40 days
Anthropologist (Musée Royal de l'Afrique Centrale, Tervuren, Belgium)	30 days
Water and sanitation specialist (freelance, Botswana)	30 days
Nutritionist (London School of Hygiene and Tropical Medicine)	36 days
Epidemiologist (US Centers for Disease Control and Prevention, Atlanta)	15 days
Military/protection specialist (freelance/University of Lancaster)	36 days
Health/military specialist (Danish Armed Forces)	25 days
Field/airlift logistics specialist (EMMA Ltd, Ireland)	25 days
Transport economist (STEP International, Rome)	30 days
Environment/fuelwood specialist (ODI research fellow)	7 days
Media specialist (freelance/BBC, London)	20 days
Research assistant: media (London School of Economics)	10 days
Advisory/editorial assistance (University of Manchester)	4 days

Given the international nature of the activity, we were keen to create a multinational team and limit the number of British nationals, a stance that was encouraged by the JEEAR Management Group. The team as eventually constructed included eleven British and nine non-British members (two Belgian nationals, two French, one US, one Irish, one German, one Canadian and one Danish).

The fact that none of the team members was African was the cause of subsequent criticism of the team and the source of some embarrassment to members of the team. Significant efforts were made to identify and recruit African team members, but these were unsuccessful for a variety of reasons. A significant factor was the highly polarized nature of allegiances in the Great Lakes region and the need for the team to avoid accusations of bias towards either the Tutsi or Hutu communities (which had already been encountered by the Study 2 team). In selecting candidates we had to consider not only their views on, and any allegiances to, one side or the other, but also whether they might be perceived as being 'aligned' by one side or the other. Another factor was the very limited time available.

A condition imposed by the French government on their financial contribution to the JEEAR was that their funds be used to hire French nationals. We proposed that the costs of the UN/Coordination specialist be covered by French funding, but he was not considered appropriate by the French government as he was married to a British national and had been studying in London in the months prior to his recruitment.

Given the considerable expertise in the emergency health field in France I was keen to recruit a French national into the health specialist role. Several candidates were considered and one was selected who worked as a freelance emergency health evaluator in New York but had previously worked for Médecins Sans Frontières-France (MSF-F). Unfortunately, eight days into his contract while he and I were visiting CDC in Atlanta, he withdrew from the team as he felt the task could not be achieved in the 50 days allowed for his post in the budget. Fortunately the post was quickly filled by a younger and less experienced doctor/nutritionist of British nationality who had been considered, but passed over, several weeks earlier.

Although the UN/Coordination specialist, two of the administrators and I had been working on the study since January, it was not till the second week of March that the team really began assembling: the team economist and third member of the core team arrived from Mozambique and a series of working meetings were held with the military specialist, the Danish military-medic, the nutritionist and the two anthropologists. Work began on establishing a database of documentation that eventually was to exceed 2,500 catalogued items. Even though the appointment of several team members still had to be confirmed and their initial briefings take place, it finally felt as though the study was under way.

Back-up and Support Issues

The process of establishing such a large team and undertaking such a complex study would have placed strains on many institutions and organizational procedures. In ODI's case there were a number of problems.

A major problem was that the Institute did not receive its first tranche of funding until late April. The Institute was therefore obliged to cover the costs of the evaluation for the first four months of the process and during this period (i.e. the very time that contracts needed to be issued) ODI's Finance Unit was extremely reluctant to issue contracts. In some cases the issuing of contracts was delayed until after individuals had started their work, and in other cases the contracts were issued for only their initial inputs.

The fact that the whole of the Study 3 'project' was embodied in one contract was highly problematic. The nascent team was required to prepare a detailed budget with named researchers and consultants, their daily rates, and their travel and accommodation costs before we had developed very clear ideas about the issues that would require more detailed investigation and the realities of doing such work in the Great Lakes region. The need to prepare a detailed budget at such an early stage and in the knowledge that ODI would not receive any funding until it was finalized placed significant pressure on the nascent team at the same time as we were also having to prepare the Analytical Framework paper and assemble the team. In retrospect the JEEAR Management Group should have authorized a 'preliminary' and 'main' contract approach that would have enabled the core team to form and undertake an initial reconnaissance and prepare a 'scoping study' and then prepare the main contract.

Problems were encountered that stemmed from cultural difficulties involved in running a large consultancy activity within a research institute. The culture of the Institute in the mid-1990s was that of a research institute with a somewhat conservative and non-entrepreneurial management regime. Though the success of the bid for Study 3 was applauded by the director, very little effort was put into supporting the Team Leader and facilitating this unprecedented study. Three examples of this lack of support were:

• Delays in strengthening the secretarial and administrative support to the Team Leader and the nascent team during February and March, which resulted in overwork by the single administrator, who collapsed from exhaustion on two occasions.

- The two rooms allocated to the Study 3 team were on separate floors and at opposite ends of the building. Because the personal computers were not networked team members had to walk (or more often, run) between the two rooms many times a day. It was not until May that the team was provided with two adjacent rooms.
- ODI refused to relax its financial procedures requiring the lead researcher/research fellow on a project to approve all items of expenditure. I therefore had to check and sign (and sometimes negotiate) all claims by members of the team relating to days worked, travel and accommodation expenses, etc. But for the adherence to the financial procedures this could easily have been delegated to one of the administrative support team, and it added unnecessarily to my workload.

Fieldwork Methods

Fieldwork in the Great Lakes region was undertaken in two blocks. A 20-day reconnaissance mission to Kenya, Rwanda, Uganda, Zaire and Tanzania[2] was undertaken by me, with four other members of the team, during April and May. In Rwanda we were joined for a week by the military/security specialist. Our arrival in Kigali coincided with the killings of hundreds (if not thousands) of IDPs at Kibeho camp. The subsequent flurry of political, media and relief activity made it difficult to meet with key agency and government personnel and resulted in revisions to our schedule.

Logistical support for the mission was provided by the World Food Programme (WFP), the United Nations Rwanda Emergency Office (UNREO) and the United Nations High Commissioner for Refugees (UNHCR). The purpose of this first visit was to: interview those personnel involved in the emergency phase; collect documentation not readily available in Europe and North America; and initiate arrangements for subsequent visits by team members. Selected refugee camps were visited in Goma, Bukavu and Ngara. In several locations we gave short presentations on the evaluation at inter-agency coordination meetings. Although we travelled together, on arrival we would split up and interview key personnel in relation to our own areas of responsibility and also for team members who were not part of the reconnaissance mission – for instance, I interviewed several personnel on behalf of the nutritionist and the transport economist.

The reconnaissance mission was of enormous value. We gained a sense of the reality of the situation in Rwanda and in the main refugee areas; we introduced the evaluation to a large number of agency personnel (many of whom were not aware of the evaluation even where their agency was directly represented on the Steering Committee); we established contact with key individuals, which facilitated correspondence with team members and subsequent fieldwork; between us we gathered perhaps 20 kilograms of documentation; finally it gave us a 'feel' for some of the main issues, how these were perceived by different groups and agencies and how best to approach them in subsequent investigation. As well as placing the documents in the database on our return, we briefed other members of the team and wrote up the interviews with key personnel, then shared them with relevant members of the team.

The second block of fieldwork took place during June and July and involved seven members of the team (the transport economist, both anthropologists, the water and sanitation specialist, the health management specialist and myself). Our travel schedules were tailored to our own needs and, for the most part, we travelled separately or in pairs; for instance, the health management specialist and the water and sanitation specialists travelled together. Contact between the various team members as they moved about the region was limited due to their busy schedules and the difficulty of communications between the different locations.

Apart from the two anthropologists, all other members of the team used secondary data. For the most part this involved data collected by the agencies involved in the response, but data drawn from surveys and studies undertaken by other researchers were also used.

The anthropologists worked separately: one was based in Bukavu for several weeks and the other spent periods in Goma and Ngara and also revisited Rwanda in an attempt to conduct interviews with beneficiaries of assistance and affected populations in the south of the country.[3] The anthropologists had previously prepared a questionnaire covering all the points that could usefully be asked of beneficiaries, local officials and agency personnel during their fieldwork. In practice, however, the questionnaire served more as a checklist of points to be covered in discussion rather than as a formal survey. This resulted from the tendency for interviews with beneficiaries in the refugee camps and in Rwanda to draw a wider audience than the selected interviewee, with associated problems of confidentiality and thus accuracy of responses. For the most part, interviews with beneficiaries were conducted without agency personnel or government officials present, but this was not always possible. Indeed, the attempt to conduct interviews with IDPs and host communities in the south of Rwanda was largely unsuccessful due to the extreme sensitivity of the situation at that time and the anthropologist being unable to conduct interviews without government officials being present.[4]

Fieldwork in the region was complemented by extensive visits by different members of the team to collect documentation and undertake face-to-face interviews with key personnel involved in the response in France,

Belgium, Italy, Germany, the Netherlands, Denmark, Switzerland, the UK, the USA and Canada. In some cases, the same individual was interviewed by different members of the team on different occasions, with the content of the discussion reflecting the different interests of the team member undertaking the interview. Team members were encouraged to write up their interview notes in order to share the information. In June, a pack of 130 pages of interview notes was disseminated among team members. This was followed by the dissemination of further interview notes with key individuals, as they became available. The proportion of interviews that were written up and shared within the team declined during the second block of fieldwork, partly because everyone was busy pursuing their investigations in their own areas and also because on return they were immediately preoccupied with preparing their reports.

In all, the team interviewed a total of 620 individuals of whom 235 were in the Great Lakes region, 245 were in donor countries and 140 were beneficiaries interviewed either individually or in groups.

As well as the interviews and assembling of documentation, special investigations were undertaken. One that was to absorb a substantial proportion of the team economist's time was the compilation of a database of resource allocations during 1994. This involved modifying and complementing the Department for Humanitarian Affairs (DHA) Financial Tracking System (FTS) dataset for 1994 through correspondence with the principal official donors and attempting to reconcile any substantial discrepancies between the information provided to the team by donor organizations, UN agencies and NGOs and that contained within the DHA FTS. It also involved adding information on onward allocations by the main intermediary agencies, such as UNHCR and Caritas, linking resources to the location of final use, and attempting to capture as much of the private flows as possible through correspondence with the organizations, mostly NGOs, involved in administering public appeals.

The resultant database enabled analysis that would not have been possible using the DHA FTS alone and gave the team a greater level of confidence in the quality of the data and an understanding of those areas where coverage and accuracy were poor. The combined scale of undercounted private flows and the costs of the military contingents and support operations can only be guessed at, but could well have been in the region of $400–500 million.

As a separate exercise, an attempt was made to contact all of the NGOs that appeared to have been involved in the response inside Rwanda itself and to obtain information on their activities. Using the various lists prepared between July 1994 and April 1995 by UNREO and the Ministry of Rehabilitation, and one prepared by the US military in August 1994, it appeared that over two hundred organizations had programmes in Rwanda during this period. Contact details for the head offices of these organizations could be obtained for only 177 of these organizations. A short questionnaire was faxed to this group. Responses were received from 61 by mid-September 1995.

Two research papers were commissioned. One, undertaken in support of the work of the media specialist, examined in detail the content of British TV news coverage over a six-day period in July 1994, which included the influx into Goma and the installation of the new government in Kigali (Glasgow Media Group 1995). The other, commissioned from the French epidemiological research group Epicentre, involved the analysis of its datasets to establish the incidence and characteristics of dysentery epidemics in Rwanda and the refugee camps (Paquet 1995).

Preparing the Draft Report

From the outset I felt that I should write the main report using the material contained in the reports submitted by the various technical specialists. My view stemmed from unsatisfactory experiences in earlier evaluations where different team members had written different sections of the report and it had proved difficult to iron out inconsistencies in the style and lines of argument.

While some of the reports by the technical specialists were submitted during July, in most cases they were submitted in the week before the team workshop in mid-August. In a couple of cases the reports submitted were first drafts only, and the final reports were not submitted until early October.

The team workshop was held over three days at a pleasant rural location in Wales. As well as the whole team we were joined by an ODI research fellow who ably facilitated some of the sessions and by the Study 3 contact person in ODA's Evaluation Department. By the start of the workshop I had prepared the first two and a half chapters of the report (i.e. Methods, Overview and part of the Security/Military chapter) and had notes for the remaining five chapters, but this was substantially less than had been planned in the original schedule. Ideally the workshop would have had a rough draft to review, as it would have provided a more effective focus for the discussions. However, the schedules of nearly all members of the team, including the delivery of their reports to me, had slipped.

While all the technical specialists were familiar to the core team and the administrative support team, for some of the technical specialists it was their first time they had met other team members face to face. Several members of the team had tended to work independently up to that point and had not been involved in earlier meetings involving parts of the team. In contrast, some other members of the team had been working closely together or had known each other well before joining the team.

Despite the potential for differences of opinion about events and defensiveness about one's own work, the workshop was stimulating, productive and enjoyable. We worked through each chapter and the relevant technical specialists presented the results of their work and were subjected to questioning by other members. A session to identify the key recommendations was held towards the end of the workshop and this led to the identification of the five Principal Recommendations of the draft report. However, not all the recommendations were unanimously supported. Some of the team members felt that they were not qualified to hold a view on issues that lay outside their particular technical area. In the case of the issue of co-ordination within the UN system we developed the concept of the 'hollow core' to convey the weakness of DHA in relation to WFP, UNHCR and UNICEF. But the recommendation that logically flowed from this (the need to consolidate the emergency response functions of the principal UN humanitarian agencies and DHA within one organization) was not accepted by the UN/Coordination specialist. Differences over this particular recommendation were not resolved at the workshop and were to resurface later.

The issues that produced the sharpest disagreements within the team concerned the role of UNAMIR and subsequent military contingents in failing to prevent or limit the genocide and in undertaking humanitarian assistance activities that would normally be undertaken by NGOs. In part this was a clash between the different professions and cultures represented on the team, but it also reflected a very real point of contention in the overall response.

Following the team workshop I had eight weeks before the draft report had to be submitted to the Management Group. This period also required my involvement in the preparation for and participation in: a one-day 'Study 3 external workshop' for selected agency representatives; a three day Team Leaders' Management Group meeting in Washington; and a two-day ODI 'retreat' not connected with the evaluation.

The 'external workshop' had been added to Study 3's schedule in July following discussion with the Management Group. Its objective was to give the key agencies an early indication of the main findings emerging from Study 3. Key UN agencies, the International Committee of the Red Cross (ICRC), the International Federation of Red Cross and Red Crescent Societies (IFRC) and key NGOs were invited. A short paper summarizing the main points was sent to participants three days ahead of the workshop. However UNHCR, whose performance in preparing for the Goma refugee crisis was strongly criticized by the team, claimed not to have received the paper before leaving for the meeting. Their representative at the meeting did not react to the criticisms and a strong reaction was received only several days later. (The 'UNHCR issue' grew in significance following the dissemination of the draft report and will be discussed in more detail later.) Core team colleagues and I felt that the workshop was 'happening too soon' and ideally we would have had more time to prepare the summary paper. Nevertheless, the workshop was useful and apart from the 'UNHCR issue' helped us sharpen some of our points.

The process of writing the main report was a tortuously slow and difficult process for me as a result of the need to prepare for and participate in the various JEEAR meetings and deal with the significant administrative burden resulting from the study, such as authorizing payments. Some reports were much fuller and more detailed than others and so, when writing particular sections, discussion with team members was necessary for clarifying certain points. In some cases additional work by them was required to 'dig out' particular statistics from the raw notes or to bring further clarification.

This process was made more difficult by the fact that the contracts of all the technical specialists ended with the end of the team workshop. Time put in after this date was mostly at the technical specialists' own expense. In some cases they had moved on to other consultancies or started new full-time jobs, making them either unavailable to give any more time to the evaluation, or difficult to contact. Shortly after the team workshop the team economist (the third member of the core team) returned to Mozambique for several weeks and so was absent for much of this draft report stage – although he did take responsibility for preparing a particular chapter on his subsequent return.

Problems caused by incompatibilities in software used by different members of the team were not insignificant. All the graphs prepared by the transport economist had to be redone in the software used by ODI. The nutritionist's report, generated by the ODI software, was missing several pages – a fact that only became apparent some weeks later when I came to the relevant chapter and made some critical, but unfair, comments on the quality of his work.

The pressures on me and the long hours worked began to take their toll on my health; a minor infection developed into a more serious infection of my lung lining, which required several weeks of treatment with antibiotics.

In September the team economist returned to the UK and I decided to delegate responsibility for preparing the draft of Chapter 7, 'Taking account of the views of beneficiaries and mitigating the impact on host communities'. The team economist had gathered material on the impact of the refugees on host communities during the study, and it seemed logical for him to build on this. In addition I have to admit that there was an element of delegating a task that I was finding difficult. The two anthropologists on the team had submitted lengthy reports. Though rich in terms of insight into the structure and functioning of the camps and on the issue of the perceptions of the refugees of the relief agencies and the situation in Rwanda, they had much more to say on the situation at the time of the fieldwork (June July 1995) than of the situation eight to twelve months previously when the relief operations were at their peak – the period that was the focus of Study 3. Consequently both the team economist and I found it difficult to draw material from the reports that could be used in assessing the effectiveness of the relief efforts during the relief phase of the response. The result of efforts by the team economist and myself was a short chapter of six pages. Both the anthropologists felt their work had not been properly utilized in the report, and one has subsequently referred implicitly to this in a recent paper (Pottier 1999).[5]

The way I handled two other issues during this period was also to prove somewhat contentious within the team.

One concerned my differences with the UN/Coordination specialist on the issue of UN coordination and developing the 'consolidated agency' recommendation. My view was that Study 3 had revealed unsatisfactory performance by UN agencies at different stages of the operation, a low regard by key UN agencies for both UNREO and DHA, which were responsible for coordination, and that the experience highlighted the inadequacy of the numerous efforts over the previous decade or so to address the humanitarian coordination issue. The UN/Coordination specialist's views were more moderate and nuanced and he believed that the performance of the UN system could be improved through alterations to committee structures and ways of working. I found this unconvincing and felt that his four years working in different parts of the UN had reduced his ability to be critical of it; a view that was shared by several other members of the team. Furthermore I felt that the unprecedented nature of the JEEAR presented an opportunity to 'add our voice to those calling from a radical reform' of the UN's arrangements for providing and coordinating humanitarian assistance. This sense of the 'strategic opportunity' presented by the JEEAR was increased through my discussion with members of the Management Group.

In preparing the relevant chapter of the draft report, I drew on material in the specialist's reports, but also worked in material that he had not used from the reports by other team members, together with points of my own. I stuck with the 'consolidated agency' recommendation that I had proposed at the team workshop but which, though supported by many team members, was not unanimously supported. For me the experience raised two questions, both of which remain highly debatable. First, what constitutes an appropriate balance between consultation and leadership within a team, where the Team Leader's input and responsibilities are significantly greater than any other member of the team? Second, is it acceptable for evaluations to make recommendations that, while they may be desirable in the long term, are not feasible in the short and medium terms?

The other issue that was somewhat contentious was my lack of consultation with members of the team over some of the 'second order' recommendations made in the draft report. The report contained five 'principal recommendations' that were developed at the team workshop and 13 'other recommendations' that had not been discussed at the workshop. Many of these other recommendations had been suggested by the technical specialists in their own reports but had been considered to be too detailed or sector-specific to warrant substantive discussion at the workshop. While I was aware that they would need to be included in the draft report, I was preoccupied with other issues until the day before the draft report was finalized and sent off to the Management Group. The team preparing the synthesis report had just indicated that if Study 3 did not get all its recommendations into the draft report they would not be eligible for inclusion in the synthesis report which, of all the reports, would be the one to have the widest circulation and readership. The day before the draft report was sent to the Management Group (it was already eight days late) I added the 'other recommendations'. During this process I realized that not all of the technical specialists had made specific recommendations and that certain additional recommendations could be developed on the basis of points made in their reports and on the basis of the text developed in the main report. I therefore added several 'new' recommendations to the list of other recommendations.

The draft report was submitted to the Management Group on 17 October and immediately relayed to members of the Steering Committee. In the case of some of the NGO umbrella groups represented on the Steering Committee – International Council for Voluntary Agencies (ICVA), Voluntary Organizations in Cooperation in Emergencies (VOICE), Steering Committee for Humanitarian Response (SCHR), InterAction – the draft report was sent directly to their key member agencies whose programmes had been commented upon by the team. Comments were requested for 10 November so that the team would be able to collate and reflect upon them in time for the final Steering Committee meeting on 17 November.

In the week following the dissemination of the draft report, copies were sent to all members of the team together with a covering letter informing team members of some of the events and decisions over the preceding weeks. Attention was drawn to the 13 'other recommendations' and members were asked to comment on the wording of them. To the best of my memory none of the team suggested any alteration to the recommendations with the exception of further discussions around the recommendation relating to 'UN consolidation'.

Preparing the Final Report

The final meeting of the Steering Committee   In all Study 3 received 123 pages of comments from 19 organizations.[6] A striking aspect of some of these comments was the extent to which agencies simply wanted their names added to those sections where we had indicated some of the principal agencies working in a particular area or sector, leading us to refer to their viewing the evaluation as a 'brochure'.

The team economist and I participated in the Steering Committee Meeting in Copenhagen on 17 November at which each of the teams presented their response to the comments received. We organized the comments received on Study 3 into those we accepted outright, those to be given further consideration and those we rejected. Our presentation dealt with two issues in some detail because of their importance and the need to explain Study 3's position. One related to the recommendation on 'UN consolidation' – which was dealt with by introducing the idea of recommended options. The other concerned our strong criticism of UNHCR for its lack of preparedness for the refugee influx into Goma in July 1994. How this last issue was handled over the next four weeks was to test severely our resoluteness and credibility as well as 'smoke out' the balance between lesson-learning and accountability in the JEEAR process. It is therefore to be discussed in some detail.

'The UNHCR Goma issue'   From the start of the evaluation it was apparent that the issue of preparedness for the huge refugee influx into Goma in July 1994 would be a critical one, for this single event had resulted in the loss of 30,000 lives as a result of cholera, dysentery, dehydration and violence. While the international community's failure to prevent or mitigate the genocide that resulted in the death of approximately 850,000 people was a much, much greater failing, within the remit of the Study 3, the appalling loss of life in Goma ranked as by far the most serious of the failings within the international humanitarian system *per se*.

During his time with UNREO, the UN/Coordination specialist had been responsible for facilitating a contingency planning exercise in relation to the build-up of displaced Rwandans in the western part of the country during May and June 1994. Among the possible scenarios that had been considered was the extraordinarily prescient one of a movement of approximately 1.5 million people westwards from Rwanda into eastern Zaire. I asked him to prepare a chronology of this process and to take responsibility within the team for focusing on the 'Goma preparedness' issue. In retrospect this was a poor judgement on my part as his objectivity as an evaluator was at risk of being compromised by his involvement in the actual process being evaluated. Using his old files and material collected from visits to UNHCR in Geneva he developed the chronology. The picture that emerged was that UNHCR had not taken the UNREO-led process seriously and had persisted in using its own planning figure of only 50,000 refugees rather than a more realistic, substantially higher, figure. Most members of the team felt strongly that this issue and UNHCR's role should be highlighted in the report as a means of encouraging greater accountability for its poor performance.

Following Study 3's External Workshop in September, UNHCR had disputed our finding that their preparedness could and should have been much better. We did not alter our position and the draft report contained the following: 'Given the massive scale of the influx, many deaths were likely. However, the lack of preparedness for the influx was remarkable and UNHCR should bear the principal responsibility for this situation' (Borton et al. 1995).

At the Steering Committee meeting in November UNHCR's representatives reacted strongly when I indicated that Study 3 was standing its ground on this issue. Faced with an impasse the Management Group insisted that one of the UNHCR representatives present (a member of the Evaluation and Inspection Service) and I should lunch alone together. While our perspectives on the Goma preparedness story remained far apart, we at least managed to establish a working relationship and open a dialogue.

The following week the stakes were raised significantly when the High Commissioner for Refugees wrote to the UK Minister of Overseas Development and to the Danish Minister of Foreign Affairs complaining about Study 3's conduct. The head of evaluation in ODA requested the Team Leader to 'at least visit Geneva to ensure that your facts are correct'. I made the visit in the second week of December, but due to staff changes then taking place in ODA's Evaluation Department was not accompanied by an ODA representative to monitor the discussions and represent the Management Group's interest in the way the discussions were handled.

The visit commenced with a confrontational meeting with a dozen UNHCR senior staff. The fact that much of the work on preparedness had been carried out by someone who had been closely involved in the contingency planning process was seized upon to assert that our analysis was not objective. It emerged that the sequence of events was more complex than that indicated by Study 3's account.[7] This initial meeting was followed by individual meetings with key personnel involved in the events of 1994 and photocopying relevant documents from files that had apparently not been made available to the Study 3 team earlier.

On my return I began preparing a fuller chronology of the period between UNHCR's initial response in Goma in April and the influx in July. On the basis of this, I prepared a draft background paper over the Christmas period. It emerged that ICRC and Oxfam had played an important role in the events, and telephone interviews were conducted with personnel of these two agencies. A revised draft copy of the background paper was sent to UNHCR, Oxfam and ICRC on 11 January (Borton 1996). Time was extremely tight, as the deadline for the final report to be submitted to the JEEAR editor was 18 January. While the background paper was being prepared I was also involved in contributing to the synthesis study and to the overall JEEAR recommendations, as well as finalizing the rest of the Study 3 report. The process for resolving the dispute with UNHCR was now clearly at odds with the schedule for producing Study 3's final report. Yet the Management Group insisted that we adhere to the deadlines because the whole JEEAR was locked into them.

On the basis of the background paper and feedback received from the three agencies the relevant sections of Study 3 and the synthesis report were amended. UNHCR requested to see the amended version and this resulted in more discussions, disagreements and further amendments. During this process I had discussions with the chair of the Management Group/Steering Committee over the extent to which the JEEAR was concerned with 'accountability' as opposed to 'learning'. While the text of the final report makes it clear that UNHCR's performance in preparing for the influx was very poor, the text stops short of attributing blame for the significant number of deaths to the organization. Two years later I was informed by a senior UNHCR official (in a regretful rather than a crowing tone) that a memo had been circulated within UNHCR in January 1996 to the effect that the organization had 'seen off' Study 3.[8] Four years later I still have very mixed feelings about these events and their outcome. Had I been manipulated into letting off the hook an agency whose poor performance I believed had contributed to the loss of thousands of lives? Did the agreed final wording make it sufficiently clear to readers that the team considered UNHCR's performance to have been sadly lacking?

As a result of my working closely with the synthesis team in the weeks before the submission of all the reports to the printers, the five 'principal recommendations' of the draft report were moulded into recommendations within the synthesis report that were structured and phrased differently to their rather crude presentation in the draft report. In order to ensure consistency between Study 3 and the synthesis reports I used the text contained in the synthesis report as the basis for a reworking of the 'Findings and recommendations' chapter in Study 3. Consequently the text in the final report was better structured and more clearly explained than that in the draft report.

The published report was launched at simultaneous events in Geneva, New York and Nairobi on 12 March. A press briefing was held the previous day in London. In all 6,000 'boxed sets' containing the four studies and the synthesis report were produced and disseminated through the Steering Committee and a special Africa distribution effort undertaken by Oxfam and by commercial sales managed by ODI. (The full report is available on Danida's website <www.um.dk>.)

Follow-up

Following the launch of the final report several follow-up events were organized at which I presented Study 3 and in which some of the team members participated. There were also discussions between the Team Leaders and the Management Group about forming a group to facilitate further follow-up and to monitor the progress of the system in responding to the 64 recommendations contained in the synthesis report. At the final meeting of the Steering Committee in November there had been agreement that the Steering Committee should meet again one year after publication to review the impact of JEEAR. This created an opportunity, and a certain obligation, to establish a formal follow-up group.

What emerged was the Joint Evaluation Follow-up, Monitoring and Facilitation Network (JEFF). It was a network of eleven individuals representative of the Management Group, study teams and the principal types of organization that comprised the Steering Committee. A Secretariat was established in ODI – consisting of myself and an administrator on a part-time basis, with finance and capacity support provided by the Canadian International Development Agency (CIDA), Danida, Sida and USAID. Over the next 15 months, members of JEFF participated in 73 'events' on or relevant to the JEEAR (meetings, presentations, media interviews and conferences). A draft report was produced by three members (the leader of the synthesis team, a former member of the Management Group and myself) which was presented to the JEEAR Steering Committee in February 1997 and a revised version was published in June that took account of the outcome of two important processes that were ongoing earlier in the year (JEFF 1997). After publication of the final JEFF report the network was wound up.

Some Concluding Comments

What are the main points I would draw from the experience?

First, Study 3 was a veritable Rolls Royce of humanitarian evaluation with unprecedented scope and unprecedented resources available to it, and this made it a privileged and professionally extremely rewarding process.

The level of resources available meant we were able to afford what other evaluation teams would regard as luxuries: a large multidisciplinary team of very high-calibre individuals; an approach that at times bore a closer resemblance to research than to conventional consultancy; a reconnaissance mission by several members undertaken several weeks ahead of the main period of fieldwork; a catalogued document collection; a three-day team workshop at a pleasant rural location; and a funded follow-up process that enabled some of those involved in the team to 'sell' the report and its key messages within the humanitarian system as well as to monitor and comment upon the reactions to the report and its recommendations by the principal humanitarian agencies.

The broad scope of Study 3 and its location as part of a larger evaluation also covering political, diplomatic, military and rehabilitation responses by the international community enabled it to raise issues that had not been raised before, or at least not in so convincing a manner. For instance, it was able to show that humanitarian aid had been used, in this particular case, as a substitute for more effective political and military action to confront the *génocidaires*; that the UN system for providing and coordinating international humanitarian assistance was structurally flawed; and that the accountability mechanisms within the international humanitarian system were extremely weak. As such it has had considerable impact. By 1995–96 pressure was building for important changes in the way in which the international humanitarian system operated. While innovations such as the Sphere Project, the Ombudsman Project and the increased use of the evaluation mechanism in relation to humanitarian programmes would probably have happened anyway in due course, many observers would agree that Study 3 and JEEAR gave a substantial fillip to such innovations and developments. Its impact has been significant.

The second point I would draw from the experience concerns the problems I encountered in managing a large team. I took on a Team Leader role that combined responsibility for managing a large team with responsibility for the 'content' and as a consequence was overloaded and my management skills exceeded. Indeed, some of the major difficulties that emerged resulted from my own decisions. Were I ever to undertake a study of such scope again I would think very carefully before assembling such a large team. A small number of, say, four effective generalist evaluators working closely together able to draw upon the knowledge of a reference panel of technical specialists would be an attractive formation. If a large multidisciplinary team were unavoidable then I would make sure that the team included a manager, or at least had a stronger management capacity than was available within Study 3.

The third point is that the task of managing such a large evaluation would have been easier and more rational if we had had a two-stage rather than a single contract. It is very difficult to anticipate the issues that will emerge during a humanitarian evaluation and it cannot be rational or effective to tie the team into a single contract before they have been able to undertake adequate scoping work – including an initial reconnaissance. Ideally 'scoping' contracts should be completed and the results considered before the 'main' contract is drawn up. Fortunately, this point has subsequently been included in the DAC Guidance (OECD 1999).

A final point concerns the value of JEEAR's structure, in which the Management Group formed an intermediary body between the evaluation team and the agencies being evaluated. By virtue of its role in selecting the teams to undertake the studies, approving the teams' contracts, having regular meetings with the teams to discuss the progress of their work and their emerging findings, and approving their final payments, the Management Group played an important quality control function that was not dependent upon the wider Steering Committee, which was made up of many of the agencies being evaluated. The Management Group was therefore able to act as referee between the teams and the agencies being evaluated and in several instances effectively shielded the teams from undue pressure from the agencies and governments. This was an extremely valuable arrangement for, while it maintained a pressure on the teams to be rigorous in their analysis and in providing supporting evidence, it simultaneously kept the agencies 'in their place'. The fact that the members of the Management Group were all heads of evaluation departments in bilateral donor organizations was helpful in this regard, for they combined the status of being within donor organizations with a strong tradition of objectivity.

Given the merits of the structure it was unfortunate that it did not work better in relation to UNHCR's dispute with the Study 3 team. The timing and nature of the dispute resulted in the team (represented by myself alone) negotiating directly with UNHCR personnel over the text relating to the agency's lack of preparedness in Goma. Ideally the Management Group would have interceded in these negotiations, or at least more closely monitored and refereed them. The result was that our final report analysed UNHCR's poor performance in preparing for the Goma influx, but we withdrew from attributing blame to the agency for the tens of thousands of deaths that followed.

Given the many and often acknowledged benefits of evaluations taking a system-wide perspective it is remarkable that evaluations on this scale have not been repeated since the JEEAR, even in relation to natural disasters such as Hurricane Mitch. Some would argue that the enormity of the events that galvanized the international community into launching the JEEAR have not been repeated since. Some would argue that the system found the results of the JEEAR too difficult to want to repeat the experience. Having been part of this unique process I firmly believe in its value and am working to encourage periodic system-wide evaluations. I hope that this frank assessment of the process of undertaking Study 3 will assist those involved in undertaking similar studies in future.

Notes

1. The ODA's Evaluation Success Ratings took the form of a five-level rating (A+ being 'highly successful', A being 'successful', etc., with D being 'unsuccessful'), applied to a list of project performance criteria such as enhancement of productive capacity, promotion of good governance, alleviation of poverty, promotion of status of women, and impact on the environment. The idea was that the respective ratings could be combined to give an overall success rating for the project.

2. It had been planned to include Bujumbura (Burundi) on the itinerary, but this visit was cancelled largely for security reasons.

3. This anthropologist subsequently published two accounts of his methods and findings in the camps (Pottier 1996a, 1996b).

4. While the new government was keen to present the country as being stable and secure, the reality was that killings were continuing as populations sought to return to their villages of origin.

5. 'With hindsight, the data I collected in 1995 revealed several important political dimensions, but these were insufficiently highlighted and insufficiently used (or shall I say ignored?) in subsequent policy recommendations. This should not have happened … What can I do to ensure that policy makers move beyond the habit of selecting only those bits of information that fall neatly within their own (scientific) categories? How can I make them move beyond what they expect me to do, which is to have neat (apolitical) questions and bring back neat (apolitical) answers?' (Pottier 1999: 124).

6. UNICEF had been unable to edit the raw comments from various members of staff and so had simply stapled them together and forwarded them. In all, 41 pages of comments had been received from UNICEF.

7. For instance, our accusation that UNHCR had not taken the contingency planning process seriously was contradicted by UNHCR's charter of two aircraft to ensure that the most appropriate personnel were present at a key meeting of the contingency planning process, and it was claimed that it was the behaviour of other UN agencies at the meeting (some of which refused to allow the meeting to carry over to a Saturday and interfere with their weekend) that had led UNHCR to conclude that the process was not worth taking seriously.

8. Jeff Crisp, personal communication, June 1998.

6

Mission Possible: Six Years of WFP Emergency Food Aid in West Africa

Raymond Apthorpe

This account of a humanitarian aid evaluation is one of personal reflection. It narrates some of the crucial issues that arose in actually doing the three-month evaluation of the United Nations World Food Programme's (WFP) six years of 'prolonged' emergency aid in a West African sub-region comprising Liberia, Sierra Leone, Guinea and Côte d'Ivoire (Map 6.1). None of the evaluation team members kept personal diaries of events at the time. These are, therefore, recollections only, and, unfortunately, by just one of our number.[1]

Initiated in 1990, the programme involved colossal quantities of food aid (well over half a million tonnes) at a cost of around US$110 million. It also involved other agencies such as the United Nations High Commissioner for Refugees (UNHCR), various WFP partners and distribution channels, some local and new, some old and church-affiliated, and two or three with strong bilateral links to particular donor governments. In all, around thirty non-governmental organizations (NGOs), mostly international NGOs (INGOs) with a huge variety of activities had been contracted to take care of one or other aspect of the programme, in different locales (Apthorpe et al. 1996: Annex 3).

But why the decision to evaluate then? Was it tied into supply issues at a time when the predominantly US source of food aid was drying up? Was the diminishing supply a reflection of more generalized donor fatigue in the face of a conflict that continued to be given little or no prominence in the media? Whatever the reasons, the evaluation team's task was to carry out the first 'independent' evaluation of this WFP programme, then already in its sixth year.

Our Terms of Reference (TOR) provided us with an eleven-week period in which to complete the evaluation, of which eight were to be spent in the sub-region, and three for the Team Leader (TL), myself, to write the final report. By an aid agency's standards, eight weeks in the field for an

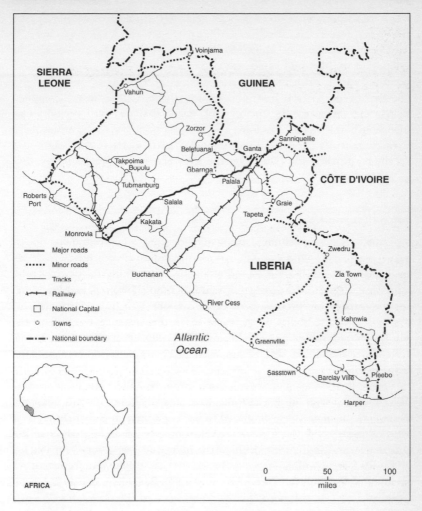

MAP 6.1 West Africa

evaluation is very long. That four countries had to be visited, and six years
of humanitarian aid reviewed, was the reason. In this particular case it
acknowledged the breadth of the work in terms of the number of countries
we had to visit, and the length of the period under review. However, even
then it meant just two weeks (or less) in each of the four countries.

Obviously management consultancy of this kind is very far from social
research, even though it may (and in this case did) draw on research and
on research skills. For university-based consultants, such consultancy has

the inestimable virtue of bestowing relatively hassle-free access to 'the field'.

These consultancies, known as 'missions' – a word familiar also in military, evangelist and espionage parlance – offer those who undertake them the adventure of the chase after a big important quarry, shadowy and elusive on the surface, yet solid and permanent underneath. Another motivating factor can be the pull of the drama (or even melodrama): inclusion in the plot as it unfolds and in a cast that, where the atmosphere is right, provides support and camaraderie, particularly in the long hours on the road, when you cannot get the ferry across, run out of petrol, and so forth.

Team Composition

Usually the composition of a consultancy team is far from being one of your own making (and the TL may be the last to be recruited, as I was in this case). Availability is all too often the determining factor, driven by a perception of overriding urgency and failure to allow sufficient lead-time for the recruitment process. This threatens – or actually undermines – at the outset the credibility of the exercise. In this instance, too much time was given to developing the TOR, and too little to everything else. Is this really how something that is supposed to be taken seriously should be managed?

Our evaluation team of six (plus one 'accompanying') was composed by WFP's headquarters in Rome (otherwise termed 'Rome' in this chapter). Four 'core' members were employed to work and travel together throughout the evaluation. One was the WFP Evaluation Section staffer, who had the primary responsibility for recruiting the team, and was also responsible for administrative coordination (mainly for our travelling requirements). A second member of the core team was an independent consultant with personal research in Liberia. She was registered at the time for a Ph.D. in economic history, and her contract described her tasks as social anthropological. The third, an agricultural economist from the United Nations Food and Agriculture Organization (FAO), considered that he had only a specialist, sectoral, contribution to make – which, though travelling with us throughout, he believed he could best undertake by working alone. The fourth was myself, on unpaid leave from my university, contracted by search as a 'senior public administration specialist' to serve as TL. The specifics of my own TOR were that I should 'lead the team', with the additional, standard, TL responsibility for structuring and writing the final evaluation report. My Africa-wide experience was extensive and varied. It included some work with a peace process (Biafra/Nigeria) and familiarity over 30 years with a sometime WFP-aided humanitarian project in northern Kenya. I had no previous knowledge, however, of any of the team members appointed. Such, in my experience, is more or less usual in consultancy teams, in contrast to research teams.

A fifth member of the team was a WFP staff logistics officer who was to work and travel independently of the core team. We met with him in the region for only a day or two. He, like the FAO member, failed to respond to anything that I circulated for comment and advice, whether during the fieldwork or the writing-up phase.

The sixth member, an independent nutritionist, was recruited by WFP for Sierra Leone and Liberia only. Happily, she worked closely with the core team both there and in Rome, during a debriefing, and later from London when, along with the economic historian, she helped to copy-edit and improve parts of the final report.

A seventh 'member' who formally just 'accompanied' the team in Sierra Leone, represented the principal food aid donor. Reportedly, that a donor was thus involved at all was initially strongly opposed by WFP. His quiet contribution was hugely valued, especially by me when he helped with the greatly needed team personnel management support I needed badly at the outset. Then, when we were ending our (curtailed) Sierra Leone stay, and feeling that the task we had taken on might prove simply to be impossible, he cheered us on with some complimentary words about the 'sound team process' he had witnessed and his certainty that we would come through with the goods in the end. To him I can only express my thanks.

From time to time, we were also joined by various WFP country staffers, particularly for the second half of our time in Guinea, and more or less throughout our time in Côte d'Ivoire.

Such, then, was 'the team'. Not a research team, not a self-selected and closely functioning cohesive group, with everyone working in unison, just a contractual, administrative, expression. Also, it did not greatly contribute to team morale and credibility that two of the UN staffers frequently declared themselves to be 'really development not emergency people'. One even claimed at one point never even to have come across the expression 'complex emergency', despite, as he had to be reminded, it being in his TOR.

Team Dynamics

Our initial briefing, thin in the extreme, provided the first occasion for all the team to meet. The WFP evaluation staffer reported that all her efforts to acquire comments on our (then draft) TOR and other materials from the four country offices in the Liberian sub-region had been in vain.

As a result, and through no fault of her own, she was herself ill-informed, and so were we.

A problem, which could have been a major one, arose in fact at the very outset because of – how innocuous it can sound, but not in the world of diplomacy and peace talks – 'seating arrangements'. When we checked in at the airport in Rome for the flight to Freetown, it emerged that, while the TL and the two other independent consultant members would travel economy, the WFP and FAO staffers, also the donor's representative, were booked into business class. (The latter discovered this to his chagrin only in mid-flight, when he thought to use some of the travel time for an initial meeting with me.) That this crass discrimination did not contribute to an immediate evaporation of our team spirit is a credit to those involved, particularly those who sat at the back. WFP's response, when I formally complained about it, was: 'Don't carp, it is our policy.'[2]

Early on in the field, concerns about my suitability as TL were openly voiced. One UN team member questioned (not unreasonably) how I, 'know[ing] nothing about the WFP – or the FAO – could possibly lead a team whose recommendations were to be specifically directed to these organizations'. Another went to considerable lengths to verify her anxieties that I – or any other non-UN staffer on the team – might go off on irresponsible tangents when interviewing alone. But on return from her (at first secret) mini-mission to some UN and EU people whom I had interviewed alone, she reported to all of the team, with visible relief, that they had assured her 'the UN need have no worry on that score'. Thereafter the team atmosphere started, jerkily, to improve.

Team solidarity was crucial to staying the course of two months, travelling in four countries, where security risks were high. We had a huge amount of work to get through urgently (at least one institute earlier approached by WFP to undertake this mission had turned down the offer, saying that twice as much time as that allowed would still scarcely be enough). We travelled, interviewed, saw for ourselves some appalling conditions, read, learned, got tired, took an evening or two off. At times, each of us fell mildly ill, recovered, doubted whether what we had set out to do was possible after all, then resolved that it was. Throughout fortune smiled on us, however. Somehow it was always either the day before, or the day after that security incidents occurred or ferries stopped operating – never, it seemed, on the day of our visit.

Around our halfway point in Liberia, elements of team solidarity were clearly setting in. This was because to travel outside (and inside) Monrovia presented many problems, and virtually *required* some solidarity. I had decided against us having an armed escort. Nevertheless, escorting of some sort was necessary if we were to have the best chance of crossing the borderlines, bristling with AK47s, of the various rebel territories we wished to visit. Clearly there was every need for caution. Eventually, three political escorts were found for us, from some of the different political factions dominant in the country – but on the big day, after we had already set out from Monrovia, it transpired that it was also their first time too to go to the zones concerned.

It was our drivers and the young Sudanese WFP country office staffer who accompanied us in the field in Liberia who – in our opinion heroically – *were* familiar with all the terrain. It was their decision at borderline gates whether or not to press through, after only the most perfunctory of stops to negotiate a bit to avoid a looming difficulty. At one frontier, we were presented with an ultimatum and consented to provide an 'admission charge', as it was called. We had been carrying some 'stationery' for precisely such purposes: some plain and thin paper in which the militias smoked their drugs, which they could otherwise not obtain.

If any one of the team revealed any of their anxiety about security or any other issue, the others responded by shedding a little of their own, and becoming undemonstrably but palpably supportive as a result. Also, as each of the four core team members travelling together fell ill, for some reason never simultaneously, there was more rallying round.

When, unexpectedly, my French language abilities initially failed on arrival in Guinea (broken fragments of Chinese came out instead), our trilingual WFP evaluation staffer graciously stepped in to play my role on those occasions. Retiringly she declined my sincere invitation to act as TL for that period.

The result of these experiences was that, by the time we reached Abidjan, the core team had moved beyond being just an administrative expression. Of course, what is involved in team life and politics are personal traits as well as official allegiances, professional interests, backgrounds, biographies and micro-demography, all of which are perceived and managed differently. Good fortune on a mission helps, but also the pressure of outside circumstances, and the evolving creation of mutual respect and 'team space' within. And this, to judge from a chance remark that was made long afterwards, is perhaps how in this case all team members saw it.

Terms of Reference and Field Reality

From the outset we noted the difficulties of dealing seriously with the broad variations that typified the WFP programme, from activity to activity, agency to agency, and year to year. We had six years of food aid in four countries over a 'prolonged' humanitarian emergency to evaluate, with only two weeks in each country, and an effective team of only three in two of them. Our sense of foreboding was multiplied when, arriving at Freetown airport on the date agreed, the country representative politely informed us that, because things were so busy, it would have been better if we had not come! After a night holed up at the airport, our briefing the next day in Freetown included information about the ship standing offshore ready for 'evacuation'. What, in such entirely unfavourable circumstances could we, with any credibility, hope to achieve?

Our answer: the evaluation would for the most part necessarily have to be issue-oriented and thematic, lifting its horizons above individual activities. It had to go for 'the bigger issues, the broader picture' (Apthorpe et al. 1996: 8), and focus on matters of institutional design, if it was to go anywhere. But varying the interpretation of our TOR in that direction was a process within the team in itself. Externally, from Rome, came no difficulty either then or later, perhaps because I saw no reason to consult Rome on the matter. With the country directors, however, we talked freely all the time, and perhaps there was some communication on the matter between the WFP staffers and Rome outside the team. If there was, I learned nothing of it.

Sierra Leone: getting going On already our third or fourth day in Sierra Leone, the speculative view we reached, about which we became very sure in Liberia, was that WFP's 'joint food needs assessments' were locally – and nationally – seen as neither joint nor food needs. The numbers of the affected populations were not known with even a fair degree of certainty, and we could not see that any, even acceptably adequate, food needs survey had been carried out. To attempt to get such data from nutrition information alone was defective methodology anyway (Apthorpe et al. 1996: 26). Food security data were virtually entirely missing. Those organizations supposedly party to the joint assessments told us openly that they did not consider themselves bound in any way by what they saw as only WFP-led assessment decisions.

To the TOR question as to 'whether WFP's emergency response in its food-aid operations had been "appropriate" or "efficient"' I was forced to rule that we were unable to make a credible judgement. So much for what was in some respects the major part of our TOR.

Nevertheless, we came to believe (and reported back) that there was a relatively unsatisfactory track record regarding final distribution and accountability. We attributed this to ineffective institutional and organizational arrangements on the part of WFP, and lack of a proactive policy dialogue with UNHCR to look for a solution. (Or perhaps 'the other side' simply did not want a solution.) There were numerous communication problems between these two UN agencies. To some of us these appeared to relate closely to a badly judged Memorandum of Understanding between the agencies.

This was how our mission in the field started – and how our time in the region could have ended. It was hardly a promising start to the mission as a whole or a particularly promising end to that first stage. Our message in our debriefing by the country director was that we were unable to conclude anything in particular with any certainty. Understandably, this was not well received. He had anticipated an endorsement of past and present operations, perhaps with some added lesson-learning pointers for the future. In his view our position could be misread as being over-critical of a programme that was running 'as-well-as-could-be-expected-given-the-difficult-circum-stances'. The personal slight he felt was probably increased by the fact that he was aware of our respect for his highly disciplined programme adminis-tration, as well as his keen intellect and commitment. Our criticism was in fact directed principally at the (so-called) 'joint assessments', for which it appeared Rome had the greater responsibility. If it had not been established, how could it be determined if it had been met or not?

In respect of the numbers and best estimates of refugees and internally dislocated people and others in need, we were unable to go along with any given to us, by any party. It seemed to us that each of the INGOs, international agencies or governments was putting its own interests – and policies – to the fore, and preferring the numbers that supported these. The agencies, which had limited resources that they wanted to deliver and distribute as effectively as possible, said that the 'real numbers' were 'far lower than' those the government was giving out. The government, to strengthen and expand its case for aid, said: 'Of course, as usual agencies greatly underestimate everything.'

Our mission to Sierra Leone was cut short for reasons beyond our control. We left noting the unhappy divergence that had emerged with the country director, and concluding that interests and policy were determining the numbers given to us.

Our methodology at this point could be described as being based less on scientific than on philosophical principles as to what was likely to be the case, and what we could say about it. Policy analysis orientations were already well on the way to crowding out anything more project-linked. However, at this early stage – still more or less week one – we did not express such concerns explicitly. Instead, at this point I think we were in a way as disappointed and worried as the country director was with the way things were going. We were starved of time and data and it seemed we had no opportunity to do much about it, other than just prepare to move on to the next country and see what we could find, and do, there. That was also the week of heavy team divisions and uncertainties.

Liberia: becoming certain that policy was the only credibly evaluable issue Arriving in a small Russian aeroplane at what was left of Monrovia's airport we were met with the news that the Country Office's operational data were 'gone' following a recent raid in which the computers had been looted. Whatever doubts we had felt earlier about our purpose, this additional revelation, so to say, clinched the point. There was only one credible way forward for us: to focus on policy, not operations, as the only evaluable issue, while taking operational 'soundings' wherever feasible (Apthorpe et al. 1996: 8–9). Nothing remotely like a scientific sampling of (even highly selected) operations would be possible, nothing exact, nothing really that was greatly worth adding to the puzzle of which operations achieved what.

Understandably, some team members initially found this very hard to countenance. In the early and mid-1990s, 'humanitarian evaluations' meant 'emergency response evaluations' primarily, and then looking 'out' to conditions and problems in the field, not 'up' to those at headquarters.[3] It is scarcely any wonder that bureau chiefs often asked whether humanitarian aid were evaluable at all, or even worth evaluating, given that circumstances in the headquarters as regards emergency assistance were apparently no more structured than those in the field.

An additional complication was that, in Rome, 'evaluation' and 'policy' were housed in different departments with, it appeared, little love lost between them. Our core WFP staff member was from the former. We had no one from the latter. Also, while our TOR did touch on policy, as well as on operations, it was by no means clear what had been meant by the term 'policy'. Our UN team members were emphatic that, whatever this was, it was something for head office only. They feared that if the mission transgressed into such a protected area they would be placed squarely in the firing-line on their return, after 'the independents' had left.[4]

Getting towards the end of our fieldwork, it became clear that the degree of devolution of power from Rome to the region that, *inter alia*, we were going to propose in our report was the same recommendation that was emerging from a special review body set up and working in Rome. Only then did our UN staff members finally relax on this matter.

A year earlier, the situation faced by the team (of which I was also the TL) undertaking the evaluation of Swedish emergency relief experience in the Horn of Africa (see Chapter 3) had led to precisely the same conclusion: policy themes, the general programme, and relations with partners were the only seriously evaluable issues, not operations. The team in that case, made up solely of independent consultants, had been able to reach that conclusion from the outset. In this West African case, with a core team that included staffers, reaching it was a more tortuous affair.

The fact that both these evaluation teams had been asked to provide advice on how humanitarian programme evaluation ought to be done,[5] as well as to deliver such, was an indication of how new and controversial the idea of humanitarian evaluation was in the early and mid-1990s.

Relations with our Client's Country Directors

In each of the four countries, we naturally sought to interact as closely as we could with our client's country directors and their staffs, one of whom served also as WFP's Regional Representative. They helped us unstintingly.

Before setting out from Rome, all we had been supplied with from the region was a February 1995 Addis Ababa African Regional Seminar paper on the whole programme. This, we were informed, had been written by a WFP staffer then – and still – in West Africa. It claimed to give a balanced description of the whole sub-regional policy and operation on the basis of first-hand management experience of it. It portrayed the programme as a perfect model for replication.

Evaluators, as well as researchers, university teachers and others interested in development and relief, frequently have to deal with such entirely uncritical, self-congratulatory *ad nauseam*, official documents. They are sometimes written by self-serving, and highly PR-conscious, managers, or by hack, and equally self-serving, evaluators. This was a particularly archetypal specimen, strident, self-contradictory in places, but virtually data-less anyway, and without either balance or qualification. To any autonomous reader it was entirely unconvincing.

The team considered that it was at its most misleading where it spoke of 'a model of ideal UN interagency, Donor and NGO collaboration, with a clear cut and cost-effective division of labour ... the joint partnership participation ... as full mission members ... in joint food needs assessments'. The realities of the situation as we had found them in one week must have been known to WFP long before we appeared on the scene. Aspects of WFP–UNHCR relations in the region were freely described to us by members of both agencies as 'mini-complex emergencies within the larger complex emergency'. Stand-offs between them and the resulting further tensions were manifest, and, at times, experienced directly by us (in Guinea and Côte d'Ivoire particularly).

Halfway through our mission, we met – and worked with – the suspected author. Whether he was aware of our suspicion we never knew. Neither we, nor he, ever referred to this paper directly. Also, he proved to be an unflinchingly considerate host and seemed not at all averse to my taking him on frankly. Our most protracted and calculated head-to-head exchange was on the subject of ethnicity (see below), subtly brokered by the WFP team member while travelling to and across Guinea's border with Côte d'Ivoire.

On the road and during our evenings together, travelling-companion conviviality was maintained, diplomatic distance partly dissolved, and many topics pursued. That Rome should devolve more power to the region was one on which everyone agreed.

Three-quarters of the core team felt that nothing had been lost by such 'open exchange'. On the contrary, much had been gained, for instance in exploring such matters as: relief and development issues; WFP's food-for-work (which I preferred to call work-for-food) schemes; aid complementary to food aid; lack of mandates for internally displaced populations who did not qualify for refugee status; and so forth.

Fighting False Socio-political Assumptions and the Limitations of 'Consultancy'

As 'an old Africa hand', as he called himself, the suspected author of the Addis Ababa Regional Seminar paper claimed an in-depth understanding of issues of African ethnicity. This included *his* view, which had appeared in WFP official documents, that, in situations where refugees crossed national borders and were hosted by families, this was on the basis of 'common ethnicity, same tribe' bonds. *My* view was that this could not possibly be the case. 'Common humanity' might well be a good part of what was involved in such humanitarian hosting, or even some sort of historical/particular relationship or networking,[6] but to put such arrangements down to just 'tribalism' was preposterous, prejudicial, and just plain wrong.

My view was that to reduce real people to notional cardboard cut-outs betrayed the lack of social and cultural understanding about beneficiary populations that is typical in the 'foreign aid-land', constructed and inhabited by international agency staff and their 'partners' – a floating layer of virtual reality, with only token roots in the actual, domestic, reality of the land beneath.

In Abidjan, the official Ivoirean discourse turned out to be just as full of 'our brothers they are not refugees' and '*même ethnie*' as WFP's perspective, if for different reasons, as I will relate later. I felt I was beginning to burst. Such discourse had to be wrong. If I didn't confront it what would be left of me as a social analyst? As a team we were keenly aware of the limitations of a consultancy that wasn't also a research mission, with never enough time, or sufficient resources, or region-knowledgeable people on some of the most crucial issues of all. However, I was so sure that such hostings were complex and varied that I asked our *de facto* social anthropologist if she could come up with any 'factual findings' at all in support of this position – which she shared anyway, on the basis of *her* personal social experience.

It was not easy convincing all the team just how this quasi-research task might be carried out. But, with a hired local assistant, the social anthropologist worked intensively on the issue and within just a few days had results that amply confirmed our beliefs.[7] With earlier evidence, drawn from household surveys held on file in Conakry, that only 30 per cent and 50 per cent of the refugee populations in Guinea and Côte d'Ivoire respectively had access to land, we were able to challenge several of WFP's assumptions about local–refugee social and economic relations. Sometimes they were economic relations, sometimes not. Sometimes they provided access to land, sometimes not.

Thus, while WFP food aid policy in the sub-region had for long been one of gradually phasing out food aid, with the laudable aim of promoting food self-sufficiency among the conflict-affected populations, we questioned the assumptions about local–refugee social and economic relations on which this was based. How anyone in any agency working in Africa could neglect serious assessments of land, in whichever of its various concepts and meanings, sociologically, economically or politically, beggars belief. We asked also whether the (spurious) assumptions were simply a smokescreen for a caving in to the reduction in the available food aid for the region, a supply-driven factor that is one of the common characteristics of aid practice everywhere.

The team's last interview in Abidjan was with a very senior Ivoirean civil servant who, besides being a very reputable administrator, was, I had been briefed, also an intellectual, a scholar and 'very open'. Towards the end of our interview it seemed worth the risk of saying (by now my French was getting going again) that 'surely you must know yourself' that what you have been repeating to us is 'very unlikely to be the case'. This (sociologically incorrect) leading question was of course put softly. Nevertheless, the tightrope atmosphere typical of such encounters with very senior interlocutors in their offices tautened a bit more before it slackened. Either side could have lost its footing, but neither did. Then urbanely, half-smilingly, straightforwardly he agreed with the proposition. Africans, he said, of course are not the stereotypes that colonialists, 'who, as you have seen, are still with us', stupidly imagine, but, it 'is not entirely in our national interest now' to say so.

Thus, at the very end of our voyage, our social critique came to enjoy the baptism of not just a drop, but a little fountain, of vindication; but, to what effect? Why would WFP want to accept this bit of informed social learning when it believed it faced no crisis, had nothing to be particularly defensive about or to look hard to find? A senior manager's reputation, an organization's official discourse and standing could be needlessly damaged if care were not taken to keep the independent flies off the elephant's back, with their fidgety and, to the elephant, insignificant social facts. Why this particular piece of social learning ought to have been received, deserved to make a difference, and yet didn't, is another matter. Organizational learning involves much more than just hired hands. It is an internal social process, though in rare cases it may be triggered by an external intervention.

Getting from Evidential Findings to Conclusions and then Policy Recommendations

Report writing was an ongoing activity throughout the mission. Before even the end of week one, I had begun structuring the material I wanted to present by, sometimes weekly, iterations of proposed lists of contents, often down to sub-paragraph heads.

One team member found that this helped her to see the possibility that we would have to be very directly concerned with that elixir 'policy'. I had learned through my experience as TL for the Swedish International Development Agency's (Sida) Horn of Africa evaluation (see Chapter 3) that such an iterative process would be better started earlier than later. However, perhaps in Liberia I went into too much detail. Certainly I wondered myself sometimes whether an earlier proposed outline was not better than a later one, and if such an exercise was really to anyone's benefit other than mine. Was this why only one of my colleagues ever actually directly said much to me about it? But my experience is that it is usually difficult to engage colleagues with specialist TOR in the generalist horizons needed for an evaluation's final report, particularly where they take these latter to be just the TL's responsibility.

In looking for a structure for the report as a whole, I was guided as much by the particularities of this assignment as by a search for the systematics.

From evidential findings to conclusions On the road, frank exchanges, whether within the team or between the team and a WFP country staffer, were usually at the rarefied level of first principles, and images and experience about which one had already come to a firm conclusion elsewhere (i.e. before this mission even started). It could scarcely have been otherwise. The 'elsewheres' chosen were, I hope, relevant ones that had been seriously studied with research techniques rather than just consultancy experience. Seldom do humanitarian evaluations have the luxuries of reliable (or any) baselines, reasonable needs assessments, up-and-running surveillance systems, and so forth.

I suspect that where evaluation reports do produce such basic evidential findings, rather than offering definitive statements of what is, they are often just impressions of what probably is not the case. Exceptions may occur where external evaluators are greatly helped by insiders (as we were, particularly in Guinea), or where they are able to draw on their direct experience of the case, acquired in roles other than those of consultants and validated through a peer review of some sort. The process, conventionally seen as one that leads from evidential findings to conclusions, is often in actual practice more like the reverse, with evaluators in effect looking for evidential findings to confirm and illustrate their best expectations. While it involves a change of frame and discourse, the process relies heavily on (usually implicit) contrasts and comparisons made with programmes and situations and structures elsewhere.

Evaluators report mainly on the basis of what they see as normative in the situation concerned. Drawing interpretative conclusions is often closer to drawing a picture than drawing a bucket of water from a well. Matters of style, school of thought, university discipline, gender, cultural background, and so forth are as important as – perhaps more important than – forensic logic that provides a solely a-technical, a-social and apolitical skill.

In reaching conclusions, sensory skills in the divination of programme intent and effect account for much. This evaluation was no exception. In addition (at the risk of sounding trite) are needed an open mind, an agile way with conversation, a readiness to seize every opportunity to learn and exchange (whether formally or informally), and a constant awareness of the likelihood of reasonable (and unreasonable) rebuttal of what you think are, or are becoming, clear and sure. And, oh yes, an obsessive grind and a lateral relentlessness to be ready to receive and act on flashes of insight and inspiration as they come are also required.

In this respect, evaluators would do well to consider their role to be closer to one of investigating juries than of sentencing judges, more like that of expert witnesses called to represent and uphold what ought to be normal practice, than line actors with the job of implementation. If evaluators recognized and made explicit in their report that they aimed to follow this practice, approaches to evaluation could be greatly strengthened.

Thus my own views about evaluative argumentation closely resemble some of those held by Michael Scriven, author of the indispensable *Evaluation Thesaurus*. He states that, usually,

the tools [for evaluation] ... are analogies, examples, counter-examples, counter-explanations, contrasts, more often than they are exact rules ... [which like] 'rules of grammar' are only rough guides to the truth, that is hints and heuristics rather than exact laws [with] certain modifiers – like *prima facie*, balance of proof, and *ceteris paribus* – sometimes probably – [used] to flag the qualifications involved. (Scriven 1991: 221)

From conclusions to policy recommendations Moving credibly from conclusions to recommendations involves another change of frame and discourse. Some of the standard criteria available for humanitarian evaluation – such as appropriateness, efficiency, etc. – are much less appropriate for policy than they are for operations analysis (for which they were originally devised). In formulating recommendations, careful account must be given to how they are likely to be judged by the commissioning organization. Recommendations, say about targeting, exiting and so forth, are expected to be sensible (not true or false), feasible (not relative or absolute), realistic (not idealistic or worse). If these are the main grounds for their likely rebuttal, they should also be some of the grounds on which recommendations are made.

Most evaluators fight shy of admitting to their methodology – *mea culpa* as well – much as programme managers and others often appear uncomfortable when asked to come up with their mission statements. What you can find in most evaluation reports about the methodology the team adopted usually borders on the banal. Just a mission timetable, a list of persons interviewed, little else. My own are not exceptions. Indeed, while it was easy to put to myself the question above about how evaluators come to their findings, conclusions and recommendations, I found – and still find – it difficult to answer. This attempt is only better than no attempt.

We found WFP's programme (and for the most part its reputation) to be strong in the logistics of actually getting the food (including in this case through local purchase) and moving it up to the points of distribution, even allowing for defects in the available commodity-tracking data. On these matters country directors and the team shared closely similar views. In contrast, however, where the team found substantial weakness was in the programme's

> lack of socio-economic assessment and monitoring ... [for example] self-settling and local community support for refugees and other displaced persons was seen by the various actors [themselves] as a highly positive, and unique, response to the war. But no serious attempt was made to analyse the phenomenon or to probe the reality of the relationships between refugees and displaced and local population. (Apthorpe et al. 1996: 24)

In this instance, we recommended that WFP introduce to its humanitarian programmes a new category of professional staff, 'socio-economic-nutrition assessors', with the necessary room for manoeuvre to carry out their work efficiently. We saw it as a way of ensuring that the status and needs of different categories of people would be better identified and served with, as a result, the overall programme being better informed and more able to reach the goals it had set for itself.

In respect of food targeting, some members of the mission had witnessed some incidents where it had increased existing levels of turbulence and violence, so we cautioned strongly against expecting too much from a strategy encapsulated by social ignorance. But we also argued, on principle, that as 'the humanitarian rationale for food aid' is normally for an approach using a general food ration, both operations and policy should focus on this more than targeting accordingly. (See Box 6.1 for selected recommendations.)

Briefing and Debriefings in Rome and in-country

Only a token amount of time (less than a day in each case) was made available for our briefing and debriefing in Rome. Usually more importance is given by commissioning agencies to final reports than to debriefings (or briefings). That I chose to write the final report there, at my own accomodation expense, and not at home in Sydney or London, was my decision. I needed to learn more about our client. Having a client is much better than not having a client if you want to make a difference to policy.

As already related, our initial briefing in Rome was thin in the extreme. This may partly explain why the policy-not-operations issue had not arisen seriously at that stage. I have also already noted our first in-country debriefing, in Freetown. The second, in Liberia, was less eventful, and was virtually called off anyway at the last minute for circumstantial reasons. Key people simply couldn't come, and the country director was less sure than his counterpart in Sierra Leone had been about the need for one anyway. No country debriefing took place in Guinea, mainly because we were accompanied almost throughout by WFP's deputy country director, so were continually engaged in exchanging ideas. However, let it be noted that, on arriving in Conakry, two core members of the team expressed the view that a better mission timetable would have provided for some sort of break, after Liberia and before Guinea, to allowed for reflection and for example a peer review process, at mid-point. Unfortunately this excellent idea occurred to none of us earlier, let alone when starting in Rome.

Our final in-country debriefing in Abidjan – which, like the others, excluded for example government representatives and was conceived of as an in-house event only – was intended as a regional affair (in the event I think only one of the other country directors attended). It was intended to allow the team to present the results of its endeavours in depth, and so it did. While of course we found ourselves being corrected on various points of detail and emphasis, our presentation was welcomed as having read things well. And exactly the same happened when we presented the broad – and Abidjan debriefing-corrected – outline of our work on arrival at Rome almost immediately afterwards. That too turned out to be warmly congratulatory. No issue was raised at all, for example, to query our wisdom – necessity – in having gone for principally a policy focus. On the other hand, no one at that small meeting felt responsible for the problems we reported about the joint needs assessments, so there was no embarrassing accountability issue to address there.

But further, neither meeting provided any intimation whatsoever of what much later was to happen. Indeed, with all this appreciation and approval, the job of writing the report was approached with less foreboding than might otherwise have been the case.

What, to complete this story, months later did transpire was a very different episode. I had been asked to be in Rome to attend a WFP Executive Board meeting (in October 1996), along with the WFP staffer who had been a core team member. The significance of what happened there remains a puzzle to me. One of the West African country directors

---

Box 6.1 Selected recommendations of the study

Leading principles for humanitarian aid

a) The rationale for food aid in complex emergencies should be primarily humanitarian, with general distribution as the paramount mode.

b) Linkages between relief, rehabilitation and development should be sought through 'productive relief', but not to the extent of subordinating the urgent and the immediate to what is important in the longer run.

Phasing in and phasing out of general distribution

a) Phasing in and phasing out of general distribution should be governed by humanitarian monitoring, assessment and decision-making.

b) The way of ending general distribution should be decided from the moment it is started, and made known to all concerned from the outset.

Delivery and distribution

a) Among other things, a comprehensive commodity and tracking and reporting system is needed to provide timely information for WFP's own management purposes and donor reporting.

b) WFP's logistics and operational responsibilities should be expanded to include, besides delivery up to the final delivery point, distribution from this point.

(the one the team suspected had written the Addis Ababa seminar paper mentioned above) was also at the meeting, being then in Rome on leave. Having had the floor secured for him by the then head of WFP's Evaluation Section, he then proceeded simply to rubbish our report from beginning to end (as, to be even-handed, the team had done – but privately and with good reason! – with what we suspected was his Addis Ababa seminar paper). Neither I nor our WFP Evaluation Section staff team member, who was as frustrated as I was, was given the floor. We thus had no opportunity to defend the report. Instead we sat wondering why we were there at all. Having had no intimation that this was what could happen, I had done no corridor lobbying beforehand.

Despite assurance that our report would be published, it was not. Neither did the Abidjan workshop take place. Whether or not its other recommendations were accepted and implemented in the terms in which we made them (or any other for that matter) is unknown to me. Our sense

---

Regionalization

a) The 'regional approach' should be improved and strengthened.

b) Data need to be reconciled at the end of each Protracted Relief Operations (PRO) phase, preferably through an internal audit.

c) For socio-economic-nutritional assessment and monitoring, a major change is required, i.e. the creation of a new kind of recurring short-term WFP staff position.

d) Ways and means must be found to improve the resources and capacity of the joint WFP/UNHCR/donor/NGO food needs assessments.

Policy instruments

a) With regard to policy dialogue, advocacy, coordination and communication, there should be focal points or lead agencies at every point in the process and chain.

b) Programme policy evaluation should be a regularly scheduled activity, as distinct from operations evaluations, by teams that are mixed in composition, including internal as well as external evaluators with emergency-specific competence, and donor participation.

Follow-up

a) A follow-up workshop should be held in Abidjan with the purpose of qualifying the mission's findings.

b) A post of social-economic-nutritional assessment and monitoring officer should be established.

was that, for example, any devolution that might occur would relate to the policy review mentioned above, not our report.

An Independent Evaluation?

Our assignment had been commissioned as an 'independent' evaluation. We were, however, a mixed rather than an independent team, made up of both outsiders and insiders, selected and paid (probably the FAO staffer was seconded) by the commissioning organization. We travelled in WFP vehicles, usually with its field staff, reported to no other body, and evaluated no other organization's programme. Arguably we were not mixed enough, having no UNHCR member, no one from the region, no donor member (apart from the principal donor representative who 'accompanied' us in Sierra Leone), yet mixed we were, and where team management difficulties arose, in my view this was largely because of this volatility of composition.

On the other hand, being a mixed team made for the possibility (and in this case actuality) of a more competent piece of work, in terms of relevance and appropriateness and the like to the client, than if we had been composed of outsiders only. I was persuaded by this team experience that the merits far exceeded the downside of a mixed team.

We were, so to say, authorized by WFP to be independent, without being independent in any other way. Our independent report is usually referred to in the humanitarian literature as 'WFP's evaluation', or sometimes even as 'an internal evaluation' only. Agencies' marks of ownership, through such labelling, be these projects or evaluations of projects and government, or partner, excuted or not, are the norm in foreign aid-land.

Responsible evaluators believe that, if only in an appointed tribune-like way, they should be accountable not only to the supplier of humanitarian assistance but also to its recipients. Responsible humanitarian assistance workers are no different. But quite *how* either can do this effectively appears at the time of writing these reflections, and despite new steps being under way, to be as elusive as ever.

A Final Proposition

Where an independent evaluation is needed, arguably this could best be done under the auspices of an independent body, not the client organization. Perhaps the client might receive privileged report-back rights at certain stages before the final report goes to the independent, and, it is to be hoped, public body. An advantage of this approach would be that multi-agency evaluations could be commissioned more readily, and economies of finance could apply. TOR could be designed to include some specifically comparative dimensions – for example, between one agency or programme and another. Other beneficial features could include a broader or more specific composition of the evaluation team, depending on the case. Selection processes could be trialed, with more disaggregated TOR and reporting requirements tailored to a range of purposes. Economies of financing could apply.

But one size does not fit all. While such an institutionalization could well suit evaluation with particular reference to 'accountability', it may not equally well serve evaluation with 'lesson-learning' purposes. Indeed, whether evaluations – rather than suitably composed seminars or workshops – offer the best route for policy lesson-learning, as distinct from policy lessons-to-be-learned, is another matter to be explored.

Notes

1. For reasons of circumstances, unfortunately this chapter couldn't be a team effort, as I had first thought would be possible. It is meant not to be an essay in self-justification (even if in part it is), but a sort of document of record.

2. Obviously I can't vouch for the accuracy of these or any other actual words recollected after five years.

3. This may, to an extent, still be the case. For example, while the current European Commission Humanitarian Office (ECHO) manual (ECHO 1999) for consultants evaluating humanitarian aid tells them how to proceed in the field in no uncertain terms, it is completely silent on what consultants should ask in Head Office. It reads, therefore, as if they have no role to inquire there at all.

4. My repeated efforts to have a formal meeting or two with the 'policy people' in Rome came to nothing. On one day, however, occasions presented themselves in the shuttle-bus going from FAO to WFP and back again to talk to one of them informally. Among other things he ventured that he had calculated that 'it would have been cheaper for us to have sent money rather than food'.

5. In both cases accordingly a special effort was made to structure and write the final reports at once both generically and particularistically. Also, shortly after the Horn study, Adrian Wood ensured some follow-up in Stockholm and Addis Ababa, and shortly after the West African evaluation, I organized a two-day training workshop in Rome. So far as I know, the follow-up seminar in Abidjan we recommended never took place (for reasons unknown to me, but presumably not financial, if the donor's offer made to me in Abidjan to fund this was confirmed).

6. It is striking just how similarly varied and complex such 'hosting' was for example in 1999 in Macedonia, where also most refugees were not in camps, to what we had divined in West Africa. In this Balkans case, because rents were commonly part of the deal, some agencies eventually used the term 'private accommodation' instead of 'host families' (Wiles et al: 2000).

7. For further illustration see my earlier personal account of actually doing consultancy (Apthorpe 1998: 77–8). Doubtless Philippa Atkinson will take such matters up again in her own forthcoming work.

7

Review of the International Federation of Red Cross and Red Crescent Societies' Tajikistan Programme

Peter Wiles

Tajikistan, a Central Asian state, became independent from the former Soviet Union in 1991. Political conflict between an opposition coalition of nationalist, democratic and Islamic forces and the ruling Communist Party developed into a violent civil war in 1992. Between 1992 and 1993 an estimated 60,000 people were killed, 75,000 fled to Afghanistan and probably more than 500,000 people were internally displaced (Jawad and Tadjbakhsh 1995).

By the time of our review in 1996 the war was continuing as a low-intensity, but violent, conflict mainly confined to the Garm area, with sporadic incidents elsewhere in the country.

Apart from the internal conflict, Tajikistan, already one of the poorest former Soviet republics, suffered a chronic humanitarian crisis due to a precipitous economic decline after independence in 1991 and the attendant loss of Soviet subsidies and support.

Tajikistan's geo-political situation on the Central Asian fault line between Europe and Asia, bordered by China, Afghanistan, Uzbekistan and Kyrgyzstan, added a further dimension of instability (Map 7.1). Western governments and Moscow have focused on Tajikistan's possible role in the spread of Islamic fundamentalism and as a conduit for illegal drugs.

The International Federation of Red Cross and Red Crescent Societies (the Federation) started relief operations in Tajikistan in 1993 in the aftermath of the civil war, working with the Tajikistan Red Crescent Society (TRCS). The International Committee of the Red Cross (ICRC) had been the lead Red Cross/Red Crescent Movement agency in Tajikistan during the civil war and by 1996 retained that role for provinces still affected by the conflict. The Federation and the ICRC, together with the TRCS, were important players in providing humanitarian relief to vulnerable populations throughout the country.

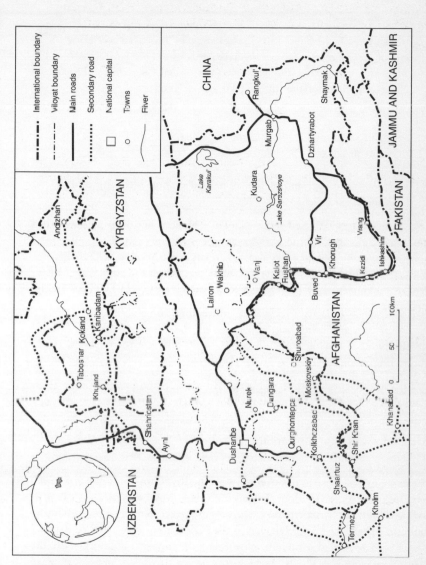

MAP 7.1 Tajikistan

Legend:
- International boundary
- Viloyat boundary
- Main roads
- Secondary road
- National capital
- Towns
- River

UZBEKISTAN

KYRGYZSTAN

CHINA

AFGHANISTAN

PAKISTAN

JAMMU AND KASHMIR

Andizhan
Kokand
Taboshar
Kanibadam
Khujand
Shahristan
Ayni
Dushanbe
Nurek
Dangara
Shuroabad
Moskovskiy
Qurghonteppa
Kolkhozabac
Khanabad
Shaartuz
Shir Khan
Kholm
Termez
Lairon
Wakhio
Vanj
Kudara
Lake Karakul
Lake Sarezskoye
Rangkul'
Murgab
Dzhartyrabot
Shaymak
Kalot
Rushan
Buved
Khorugh
Vir
Vrang
Kizidi
Ishkashim

0   50   100km

Context for the Review

In the light of the continuing chronic humanitarian crisis in Tajikistan, the Federation commissioned an external review of its programme in 1996. The overall aim of the review was:

> to ensure the Federation/TRCS programme in Tajikistan is offering a high level of service meeting the immediate needs of the most vulnerable people and is identifying and building on Red Cross/Red Crescent and beneficiary (client) capacities for the future. (Wiles et al. 1996)

The TOR focused on five main areas:

- health programmes, including medical distribution;
- nutrition programmes, including food distribution;
- logistics;
- general relief programmes (i.e. non-food or non-medical); and
- developmental relief.

The review was also asked to consider the broader and longer-term issues of disaster prevention and the development of the TRCS.

The areas of developmental relief related specifically to the nine key factors identified for developmental relief practice in the 1995 Copenhagen workshop convened by the Danish Red Cross, IFRC and ECHO, namely:

- building on capacities as well as addressing vulnerabilities;
- identifying the needs and capacities of the diverse group of disaster survivors;
- participation;
- accountability;
- strategies based on the reality of the disaster faced;
- decentralised control;
- demonstrating a concern for sustaining livelihoods;
- building on local institutions; and
- setting sustainable standards of services (Danish Red Cross 1995).

To some extent these issues overlap with the Red Cross/non-governmental organization (NGO) Code of Conduct, but they emphasize, *inter alia*, capacity-building, participation, accountability to beneficiaries and future sustainability. These were relevant to the Federation's mandated role within the Red Cross/Red Crescent movement of capacity-building with the national society, the TRCS. As such this review was really an assessment of performance for planning future programmes and capacity-building, rather than a rigorous evaluation of the impact and effectiveness of past activities.

The Terms of Reference (TOR) gave detailed guidance about the topics on which we should report. However, they omitted study of Federation management and structural issues, which proved, as often happens, to be important. We did, in fact, comment on management arrangements for the Federation sub-delegation in Dushanbe, in part so that it could better support the TRCS. The TOR did not require us to look at management issues within the TRCS, partly because the society was just emerging from a major governance crisis and it would have been inopportune to focus on this area at that stage. In fact, we were able to talk openly with staff of the TRCS about a wide range of issues and there were no bars on discussion topics.

Setting up the Review

The review was managed by the Central Asia desk officer in the Federation Secretariat in Geneva. The way in which the review was set up reflected the multiple stakeholders involved in the Red Cross/Red Crescent movement and the role of the Federation secretariat in Geneva, which acts as a coordinator, fundraiser, facilitator and monitor of programme standards. The Federation secretariat is not an autonomous operational agency and it does not possess its own independent funds. Funding for programmes comes from the donating Participating National Red Cross societies (PNS in Red Cross terminology). The in-country partner is always the Operating National Red Cross/Red Crescent society (ONS) – in this case the TRCS.

The TOR for the review were drawn up by the desk officer in consultation with Federation staff in the country and region, the TRCS and donor Red Cross societies that had an interest in the programme. The TOR were not discussed with any of us on the team before they were finalized. There were no apparent major divergences of view among stakeholders about the TOR.

The review team was assembled by the desk officer in consultation with staff within the Federation and the TRCS and involved staff from the PNS that were supporting the TRCS programme. The funding for the review was dependent on PNS contributions of money and human resources. Our team composition therefore reflected the interests and choices of the PNS involved, particularly the American and British Red Cross societies.

The core review team was constituted as follows:

- Team Leader – myself, an independent external consultant identified and funded by the British Red Cross, with previous evaluation experience of Red Cross work;
- an external public health and emergency medicine expert from the US Centers for Disease Control and Prevention (CDC) Atlanta, identified and funded by the American Red Cross Society using funds from an external grant;

- a public health and nutrition specialist seconded by the American Red Cross Society from its headquarters staff; and
- a logistics expert – a Federation secretariat staff member.

None of us in the core team had direct experience of Tajikistan, but some of the members had carried out work in other former states of the Soviet Union and I knew neighbouring Afghanistan.

In addition, the president of one of the branches of the TRCS and the head of the Federation's sub-delegation in Dushanbe were seconded to the team. The participation of the senior staff member of the TRCS was very important, not only for grounding the review but also for internal TRCS political reasons, as it underlined the unity of the society in a divided country. All of the team members were male, except for the American Red Cross Society's public health and nutrition specialist. This was despite the TOR requiring efforts to be made to ensure a gender-balanced team.

Preparations before the Fieldwork

The team members external to the Federation were briefed by their respective sponsoring Red Cross societies before arriving in Geneva. The core team of three, myself and two American-funded health experts, assembled in Geneva for three days of briefing, interviewing and looking at the documentation before going to the region. I asked for three days in Geneva, against a shorter time suggested by the Federation. The list of whom to see was reached by agreement with team members, and there was no controversy about this.

The Federation secretariat staff team member was not available during that period, except for a brief meeting, and the branch president and Federation sub-delegation head from Tajikistan were not able to attend the Geneva briefings.

There was little opportunity in Geneva for discussion about the TOR and methodology before the work began of interviewing staff in the secretariat and looking at documents. Methods of working in the field were discussed while we were *en route* for Tajikistan. The sectoral responsibilities within the team were fairly clear, with the two health-orientated team members working closely together. As Team Leader, I addressed areas not covered by the technical specialists on the team, such as management, TRCS–Federation relations and some parts of the relief operations. The team members from the Federation and the TRCS did not have specific areas assigned but acted as general advisers to the core team.

Identifying and tracking down key documents proved to be problematic and time-consuming in this preparation stage. As often happens, no one location (headquarters, regional office, country office) had an easily located full set of programme documents. We received a half-day briefing at the Federation's regional delegation in Almaty, Kazakhstan, *en route* to Tajikistan and we spent four days in Dushanbe before fieldwork started. In retrospect it might have been useful to have had one or two more days in Geneva, although we felt reasonably well briefed by the time we had been in Dushanbe for two or three days.

The Fieldwork

The fieldwork, lasting 20 days, primarily involved interviews with key Federation delegates in Almaty, Dushanbe, Osh and Khodjent, some past delegates who were interviewed by email, staff of TRCS and informants in the government of Tajikistan and international agencies. A limited number of projects and TRCS branches were visited. Beneficiary interviewing was limited and opportunistic. The schedule sometimes underestimated the time needed for interviews and meetings where there was a need for translation. Independent translators were not hired. This would have been time-consuming and would not necessarily have resulted in a better standard of work, as they were likely to be unfamiliar with the subject matter and the people being interviewed. Our feeling was that the translations provided were adequate.

In retrospect, it would probably have been useful to have allowed an additional day in each physical location visited, but the overall time-frame for the review did not allow for this. However, we went to considerable lengths to ensure that most stakeholders had an opportunity to give their views to us, including the Federation's locally recruited staff and staff other than senior management. This interviewing was done on the basis of looking at staff lists and organograms and deciding who were the key people to talk to. We looked at all the major projects within the Federation's programme, thereby covering the main activities and areas of expenditure. In addition, we looked at whether the collection of projects constituted a coherent programme, corresponding to the major humanitarian needs that fell within the Federation's mandate.

Staff security and relationships between the various Federation delegations were among the management issues we considered in Tajikistan. We each used checklists as a basis for semi-structured interviews. Interviews were a mixture of one-to-one and group meetings.

Functioning of the Team

There were three main issues relating to the way we functioned as a team:

- The Federation had originally nominated a senior field delegate and senior representative of the TRCS as team members. These members did not start their participation in the review with the rest of us in Geneva, probably due to cost considerations, and were not involved in report writing up. In fact, these people participated as facilitators, informants and contributors to the review, but not as completely full members of the team.

- Some of the team members brought approaches to the work that related to their employer's agendas, rather than specifically to the TOR. For example, one team member was piloting a health assessment format for the American Red Cross. Another used the opportunity of the review to carry out a standard internal review of Federation logistics procedures in the region.

- Because of other work priorities, two of the four core team members could not participate in the full period of the fieldwork. One had to leave just over half-way through the mission and the other carried out a limited mission on a separate timetable, only meeting once briefly with the rest of us while in the field.

As a result of these practicalities we hardly acted as a team, and the opportunities to discuss and develop ideas throughout the fieldwork as a result of progressive reflection and discussion were very much constrained. This left the responsibility with me, as Team Leader, and the one other team member who completed the itinerary with me. We became the core of the inner team. Despite the fragmentation of the team timewise, morale and relations between us were generally good and the position of the Team Leader was respected. We had no serious disagreements and had generally reached headline conclusions by the time that we disbanded and some of our members had returned to Geneva.

Debriefing

We provided some initial feedback to Federation and TRCS staff in Dushanbe and Almaty before leaving the region. The response to this was generally positive, although there was some disagreement about our analysis of the relationship between the Dushanbe and Almaty delegations. The two of us who were the inner core of the team returned to the Federation's headquarters in Geneva after the fieldwork for a second round of interviews and also gave a debriefing to secretariat staff on the preliminary findings of the review.

Writing the Report

After the team split up, each us in the core team drafted our sectoral sections of the report, bearing in mind the overall conclusions that we had reached in the field. I was responsible for pulling the contributions together and writing other sections. The main issues during this process, as often happens, were:

- different writing styles;
- a tendency by specialists to write at length in too much technical detail; and
- a tendency by specialists sometimes to be preoccupied with their sectoral issues without grounding them in the reality of the work being reviewed.

In spite of these difficulties, there were no major divergences of view among us concerning our recommendations.

The draft report was circulated to key staff in the Federation at both Geneva and Tajikistan levels and to the TRCS for comment. The main feedback came from the commissioning desk officer in the Federation secretariat in Geneva. His comments were mainly relatively minor, factual corrections. The report was finalized without any major disagreements, either within the team or with the key stakeholders. The report contained a short appendix on lessons learned about the review process.

The TOR specifically asked us to look at the extent to which the programme addressed the principles for developmental relief outlined in the 1995 Copenhagen workshop. In fact, we included a chapter that commented on the programme in relation to both the Copenhagen principles and the Red Cross/NGO Code of Conduct. The programmes had not been established with these principles in mind, nor had staff received any training in them.

The Report and its Follow-up

The report made two overall recommendations and nine specific points (Wiles et al. 1996) (see Box 7.1). In addition, detailed recommendations were made in relation to sectoral programmes and management issues.

The timing of the review meant that it was being undertaken at the same time as the Federation secretariat was preparing its funding appeal plans for the following financial year. This meant that the secretariat and the TRCS had little time to look at the report and internalize its findings before plans for the following year were finalized.

Box 7.1 Review recommendations

Federation programmes in Tajikistan should be guided by two main aims:

- to improve the long-term situation of the most vulnerable in Tajikistan; and
- to strengthen the capacity of the TRCS in order to become a strong and resourceful national society.

In programme planning, the following factors and issues should be taken into account:

1. All Federation initiatives should be planned and executed in close cooperation with the TRCS. All programmes should contain elements of capacity-building, including training, for the TRCS that fit with the TRCS's strategic priorities.

2. Institutional development work with the TRCS should be developed as an overall integrated programme into which individual programmes, be they relief or development, should fit.

3. The speed and scale of programme development should be carefully tailored to both Federation and TRCS capacities, while recognizing that the TRCS must be seen by public and government as delivering much-needed services to the vulnerable in Tajikistan.

4. Programmes should shift where possible to a more developmental approach.

5. Every effort should be made to exploit the potential of national (and regional) resources. There should be a move to increased local purchase of materials. (Efforts in this direction will be time-consuming and frustrating, and the Federation will need to have procurement procedures and capacity in place.)

6. Federation planning and operations should recognize the unity of Tajikistan as a country.

7. The Federation should work on a five- to ten-year planning span and individual programmes should be planned and funded on a two- to five-year span.

8. Programme planning should bear in mind the possibility of disruption due to conflict and the Federation should continue to help strengthen the TRCS's disaster preparedness and response capacities.

9. In programme planning, consideration should be given to programme exit strategies.

One of our recommendations was that there should be a structured follow-up process to the review for the implementation of its recommendations and that a senior manager should be designated to manage the process. While this did not happen, it was stated that our report was taken seriously by both the Federation secretariat and the TRCS. The report was widely distributed and it was referred to in Federation delegate mission instructions as a key document to consult. Some, perhaps 50 per cent, of the report's recommendations were subsequently implemented.

Reflections

A number of points can be made from the experience of this review:

1. The team should, if at all possible, be together for the duration of the work.
2. The inclusion of staff and national society persons in an evaluation needs to be carefully thought through, and they should have clearly defined roles. The arrangements for this review worked well but were of an *ad hoc* nature.
3. Problems can arise if team members are bringing into the work agendas from their employing or funding agencies that are not explicit in the TOR.
4. Excessive expectations should not be raised about the evaluation, as occurred in this case where the Ministry of Health and the World Health Organization (WHO) in Dushanbe were led to believe the evaluation was a joint Federation–WHO mission.
5. Documentation was a problem on this mission, with incomplete materials in Dushanbe and little time for studying them in Almaty, where the best set was available. Advance collection of documents and provision of appropriate time to study them is essential. In addition, teams need to have the basic documents copied, which, in the Federation's case, are not limited to the Appeals but have to include applications to donors, contracts and final reports.
6. Overall time allowance has to be made for translation.
7. The TOR should have been reviewed since they were somewhat over-ambitious.
8. The review's gender analysis should have been stronger, although our report did recommend that the Federation and the TRCS had to do much more work in that area. The presence of an experienced female Tajik fieldworker on the team would have been greatly benefited the review.
9. As often happens, management and organizational development issues proved to be as important as programme issues. These should be included in the TOR.

Despite these various problems, from the Federation's perspective the report apparently met its objectives of providing an independent review of its work so far and guidance on future programme development. In addition, an important recommendation to upgrade the status, in management terms, of the delegation in Dushanbe was accepted and implemented.

8

A Self-evaluation of my Experience Reviewing Australia's Official Assistance in Response to the 1997–98 Papua New Guinea Drought

David A. M. Lea

The 1997–98 drought in Papua New Guinea (PNG) was probably the most severe and prolonged in the last 100 years (Allen et al. 1989: 300–3; Allen and Bourke 1997a). The unusual set of circumstances in 1997 included widespread garden failure; fires in forests and dried-out swamps; serious shortages of water; a rise in morbidity; severe and repeated frosts in highland valleys; and destruction of houses, and in some cases hamlets, by fire.

The serious situation in 1997 was aggravated by declining rural services; rapidly increasing populations; a rise in lawlessness; declining rural self-sufficiency; many, but highly exaggerated, reports of deaths and starvation; and strong local political pressures for relief. By September 1997, there was a perception within the Australian High Commission (AHC), the PNG and Australian media, many NGOs and some sections within the PNG government (GOPNG) that the effects of drought had exceeded the capacity of many rural Papua New Guineans to cope.

In September 1997, the GOPNG requested international relief aid. The government of Australia (GOA), the main donor, immediately responded and over the following nine months about $A30 million of aid was provided. The aid was to assist with drought relief in remote areas without access to road or sea transport that the GOPNG would have great difficulty in accessing,[1] and included food aid, various forms of technical assistance, separate NGO funding, and assistance with rehabilitation. The GOA appointed its Agency for International Development (AusAID), as the lead agency. It immediately commissioned a team of agricultural experts to undertake an assessment. Between October 1997 and April 1998 3,203 tonnes of relief, mainly food, were delivered by Australian Defence Force (ADF) aeroplanes and helicopters.

Setting up the Evaluation and Team Formation

In January 1998, AusAID sought 'expressions of interests' from several Australian-based consultancy firms to undertake a review[2] of Australia's relief operation. In April 1998 AusAID contracted ANUTECH Pty Ltd, a free-standing commercial operation of the Australian National University, to undertake the work.

In March 1998, ANUTECH, following some discussions with AusAID about some individuals and team composition, chose six team members from its own network and contacts. In selecting the team, ANUTECH was guided by the Terms of Reference (TOR), which specified that the team should consist of five to six people with the following types of experience:

* familiarity with PNG, preferably with experience of emergencies in PNG or the wider South Pacific Region;
* cost-benefit analysis of development activity;
* emergency situation food delivery mechanisms/rapid appraisal techniques;
* logistics/emergency assistance administration;
* sociological survey (including gender analysis);
* health/nutrition;
* crop science/rural development in affected areas of PNG; and
* environmental analysis.

As Team Leader (TL), I had undertaken many evaluations and had extensive field experience in PNG but no experience with emergency relief. The other five team members included one person with considerable experience with humanitarian relief operations in Africa, but not in Papua New Guinea; an ex-Australian Army officer logistician; an agricultural research scientist with experience of social and environmental impact assessments; an epidemiologist with experience of project evaluation in health and demographic issues; and a transport economist. The only team member with extensive field experience of famine and emergency relief, but not in PNG, and myself formed the core team.

Initially, the proposal was to undertake the Review during the last of the food deliveries. At the request of AusAID staff at the Australian High Commission in PNG (otherwise known as the Post),[3] the Review was delayed until the relief effort was finished. This was unfortunate because the delay meant that not all the team members could adjust their schedules to be together for the full period of the consultancy and no team member saw the actual process of food delivery, apart from some deliveries by NGOs. It also had implications for mission logistics in the field as the team had to organize its own transportation. While the team was completely independent of ADF delivery schedules and able to work to its own agendas and timetables, it would have been more valuable for the review to have started its work while the food distributions were ongoing.

Contracts

ANUTECH first made approaches to team members in early March 1998. Within a week all team members had expressed interest. Within a few days, ANUTECH had been awarded the consultancy and informed team members that, if they were interested, a briefing in Canberra in late March would be followed immediately by fieldwork to witness final food deliveries by the ADF.

While all team members were prepared to undertake the Review immediately after the briefing, AusAID delayed departure until 20 April. The team, acting in good faith, did a considerable amount of work without pay or even a contract.[4] AusAID and ANUTECH signed a formal contract only on 17 April 1998. Team members signed contracts with ANUTECH in late April or early May 1998, well into the fieldwork of the Review.

When finally presented with a contract similar to ANUTECH's contract with AusAID, I was concerned that the findings of this independent review could be altered by AusAID to suit their interests and requirements. While no one could object to a commissioning agency rejecting material that was unprofessional, poorly written, or with little analysis, it appeared that the commissioning agency could force the contractor to 'correct' rejected material even if it was factually correct or a legitimate interpretation.[5] It also concerned me that the clauses on confidentiality and copyright were too restrictive and that the commissioning agency might be attempting to 'own the brain' of consultants (see Trigger et al. 1998).[6] As it happened in this case, confidentiality and copyright never became issues, but I think they should have been given more airing and discussion.

Terms of Reference

As the Review progressed, some changes to the TOR were negotiated. Some were made with the knowledge and consent of the team and ANUTECH. Others were changed unilaterally by AusAID. Many of the changes were cosmetic, but there was no formal signing of some important changes.[7] Both the original and final TOR were brief (about 1,300 words) and very similar in most respects. They consisted of five sections.

Objectives   The Review was to 'assess the effectiveness of Australia's ...

drought relief effort'; to 'identify lessons which will enhance Australia's ability to respond to emergency situations in PNG and elsewhere in our region'; and to 'draw general lessons from Australia's drought relief effort which have implications for Australia's broader development cooperation relationship with PNG'.[8]

Background This section consisted of a brief description of the drought and Australia's role in the relief operation. One sentence stated that '[u]nderpinning the findings of the Review will be a recognition of Australia's "special relationship" with PNG'. This led to misunderstandings between the team and AusAID. The team read this to mean 'tactful treatment' of issues involving GOPNG and the bilateral relationship. In contrast AusAID and DFAT (the Department of Foreign Affairs and Trade) expected the team to avoid any critical mention of GOPNG agencies or policy initiatives of either GOPNG or GOA.

Scope This section outlined the following topics AusAID wanted the team to assess and make recommendations about:

1. the adequacy of the assessments;
2. the logistics of the actual emergency relief delivery;
3. the effectiveness of the relief assistance;
4. the implications of emergency assistance for long-term (non-drought) development;
5. the ongoing GOA and GOPNG working relationship;
6. relationships with other donors; and
7. AusAID's management of public relationships.

Method This section listed the skills required by the team; the approximate timeframe of the Review; and the barest lineaments of method requiring an initial 'desk study' in Canberra and field visit to a 'sample of remote regions, where AusAID has provided assistance'. It gave the team enough scope to develop its own field methodology and to be independent in data collection and analysis, requiring a draft report to be written before the team left PNG and the contents discussed with the Post.[9]

AusAID appointed a task manager from its Performance Information and Assessment (PIA) Section, within the Office of Programme Review and Evaluation, to act as a liaison person between the team and AusAID. A Review Advisory Group (RAG) was set up to 'play a central role in guiding the review process and commenting on the Review report'. The RAG consisted of the head of the Task Force – a group in Canberra responsible for the coordination of the relief programme – and six representatives of the three major sections of AusAID[10] and the three other Australian organizations[11] most involved in the operation. A chief technical adviser (CTA) was also appointed to be available to advise the team as necessary.

Reporting   The report was always intended to be an internal AusAID document, with a draft circulated to stakeholders before being finalized. An edited version was later to be made available to the public.

The mix of objectives in the TOR led to some conflict about whether the team were undertaking:

• a conventional and independent *evaluation* of the objectives, planning, and strategies of the operation; the need for, and effectiveness of, the initial assessments and drought relief operation; the timing and performance of personnel; the accountability of resources invested in the operation; and, in general, what actually happened 'on the ground'; or
• a more general, *ex-post*, high-level, reflective review[12] looking at policy response to the drought; learning institutional lessons for all stakeholders; and looking at the implications of the operation for the bilateral and multilateral relationships; or
• as the team attempted, a combination of an 'evaluation' and a 'review'.

Briefings

After the first introductory team meeting at ANUTECH, the remaining three and a half days of the preparations in Canberra were not effectively used. Briefings by AusAID lacked preparation and there was very little information available. There were no maps available, no lists of staff and key people to meet in order of priority to observe protocols, no briefing papers and no basic statistical data.[13]

We wasted time trying to find out very basic information and to understand relationships, procedures and structures. In spite of repeated requests, the team was not given access to key cables, ministerial directives and many drought-related reports (including AusAID commissioned reports) until our fieldwork was completed. Other requests for data were not met until the fieldwork had started in PNG. We were not invited to meet a number of key staff who had been or were actively engaged in the drought relief effort in Canberra. Nor were we aware of the role of these people until fieldwork in PNG was well under way.

During that initial briefing in Canberra, the team met with about a dozen people in AusAID and the non-AusAID members of RAG. In the light of these meetings we planned the fieldwork, discussed contacts, divided the workload according to a preliminary table of contents, and developed a work plan and the Review method. The 'desk study' period in Canberra was far too short, and the time spent in developing a work plan left insufficient time for key interviews and the proper study of files.

Developing Methodology

From our reading of the literature, one team member's experience in Africa, and our knowledge of the ADF and AusAID, we correctly suspected that the delivery of food relief to distribution points would be efficient and effective. As frequently happens in emergency operations, the final distribution to people living in outlying villages and hamlets is the really critical issue and is far more problematic. Thus, from the beginning we worked on the premise that *a humanitarian relief operation must be judged by the level of effectiveness achieved in the final distribution*. Who, of the target population, got what, how, when and where?

Four of the team felt strongly that this could be done only by undertaking fieldwork in target areas. As a result they made a deliberate decision (which was clearly articulated in the work plan) to devote the greater proportion of time in PNG to qualitative fieldwork in the target areas with the purpose of evaluating the targeted recipients' perceptions of satisfaction and displeasure, successes and failures. The two other team members, who concentrated on logistics, the performance of Australian NGOs, and cost-effectiveness of various delivery alternatives, were less field-oriented. They were content to consult files and to interview key players in national and regional centres. While there were no disagreements about conclusions, the majority of the team sought their primary insights from the field, using Rapid Rural Appraisal methods and assessing the perceptions of the recipients about the aid.

The methodology of the Review, decided upon in a brief team meeting in Canberra, can be summarized as follows:

* to study files in Canberra, to hold interviews with key players in Canberra, and to hold phone interviews and face-to-face interviews where possible with key people outside Canberra;
* on arrival in Port Moresby, to set up an 'operations room' in a hotel so that all team members had access to a telephone, computers, printers, relevant files and papers, maps, and a standing display of cards showing the structure of the report, issues, problems, queries and subjects to be covered in each section of the report;
* to hold interviews with key informants in Port Moresby and provincial centres;

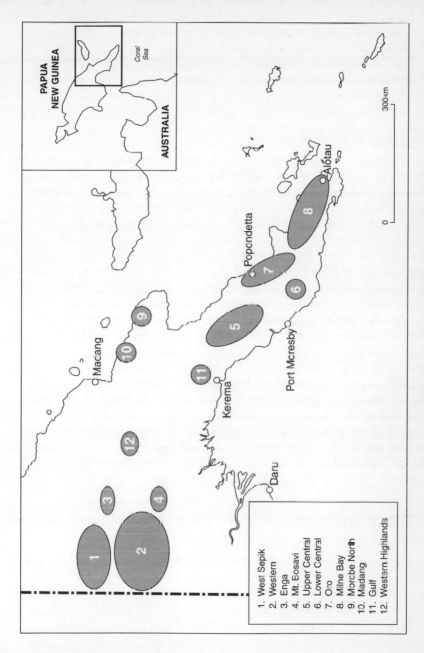

MAP 8.1 Papua New Guinea

1. West Sepik
2. Western
3. Enga
4. Mt. Eosavi
5. Upper Central
6. Lower Central
7. Oro
8. Milne Bay
9. Morobe North
10. Madang
11. Gulf
12. Western Highlands

- to undertake fieldwork in selected operational areas;
- to undertake a cost-effectiveness analysis of using the ADF rather than commercial operators as a food delivery mechanism;
- to hold workshops and discuss ideas and experiences in the field and in Port Moresby and to dedicate the final week in Port Moresby to writing a preliminary draft to be discussed with staff at the Post in Port Moresby and GOPNG.

Selection of Study Areas

Australian aid was delivered by air[14] to twelve focal areas over a five-month period (see Map 8.1). Six[15] of the focal areas were relatively minor, each receiving less than 100 tonnes of food aid in only one or two months. Three focal areas had to be eliminated: it was impossible to mount cost-effective fieldwork in the time available because of distance from Port Moresby.[16] Of the remaining three areas, we felt it was critical to visit the Goilala (Upeer Central) area (5) which received 40 per cent of all Australian aid delivered by air. Of either the Raba Raba (Milne Bay) area (8) or the Kiantiba (Gulf) area (11), we chose Raba Raba because it received eight times as much aid as Kiantiba over a longer period, had four times the population, was more densely populated and suitable aircraft and helicopters were available to allow fieldwork in the time available. Quick visits were made by one or two team members to provincial centres or isolated villages in focal areas 2, 3, 11 and 12.

We visited all delivery points (DPs) in the Raba Raba area and all DPs in the Woitape area (roughly the eastern third of the Goilala area) (see Map 8.2 for all delivery points). We attempted to visit at least three villages around each DP — one close, one as far away as possible and one in about the middle. Villages were arbitrarily selected from maps (and sometimes aerial inspection) on the basis of maximizing helicopter use and time in villages.

Undertaking Fieldwork

The fieldwork in PNG was carried out from 20 April until 23 May 1998. Three team members had to carry a strenuous burden of fieldwork, interviews in Port Moresby, and administration[17] in the first half of the consultancy due to the late arrival of other team members. Because only I and one other team member could speak Tok Pisin, the major lingua franca in PNG, there was little flexibility in the way in which field teams were formed.[18]

The initial work programme was followed, with minor changes.[19] Each

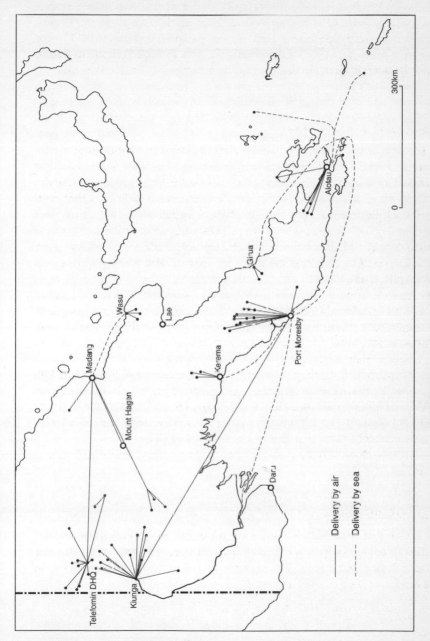

Delivery by air ———
Delivery by sea – – –

MAP 8.2 Papua New Guinea delivery points

field group typed detailed field notes[20] every evening in the field so that facts, problems and impressions could be documented and shared as soon as possible with other team members. Two of us trained the PNG field assistants[21] so that they could hold discussions and interviews with different groups in villages. Often the team deliberately formed groupings of male and female villagers for this purpose.

In all, one or two team members visited 37 regional centres, research stations and DPs and 48 remote villages[22] by helicopter, foot and road in about 45 'person-days' spent in the field. The major part of the fieldwork involved basing two team members and assistants in a regional centre near DPs or at a hub where food supplies were pre-positioned. Visits (usually of two to three hours) were made by helicopter, road and foot to DPs and arbitrarily selected target villages served by the DPs. People were asked a whole range of questions about the drought and how it affected them; what coping mechanisms they used; how, when and what relief they received; how the distributions were managed; what problems they had with supply and distribution; health, livestock, trade stores and markets; garden rehabilitation; and their perceptions of the whole drought and drought relief efforts.

Team members also visited a number of seriously affected villages in the PNG Highlands outside the AusAID target areas to study how these communities, Australian-sponsored NGOs and GOPNG coped with drought and frost.

Team members attended seminars and workshops relevant to the drought in the provinces and Port Moresby. They also examined files in regional centres; examined whatever scanty documentary evidence was available in DPs and villages; and interviewed key people in NGOs, provincial governments, missions and private enterprises while away from Port Moresby.

Team Coherence

The team met for the first time in late March 1998 during five days of briefings and meetings in Canberra. While we had few conflicts or even disagreements, we never functioned as a coherent, well-integrated group. This was serious because it led to problems of spreading workloads, allocating tasks, formulating methods, drafting and getting the balance right in the final report. The reasons for this lack of coherence were as follows:

• None of us had worked with any other team member before.
• The delayed start of the Review made it impossible to get everyone together in Canberra for more than a few hours during the pre-field

briefing session. Later during the fieldwork in PNG the whole team was together for only a single three to four hour meeting.

- The skills and other commitments of each team member, as well as their workloads, were very uneven; the cost-effectiveness study required only five or six days of data collection in Australia and PNG; the logistician chose to collect his data from within Australia and Port Moresby and provincial centres; and the other two team members were available for only just over half the field period of 33 days in PNG.
- The team came from, and returned after the fieldwork to, a widely dispersed area. We were linked by email and so all drafts were circulated for comment. All communications with AusAID and ANUTECH were shared, and all major problems raised. Because AusAID was willing to pay only for myself and one other team member to meet for post-fieldwork discussions and redraftings in Canberra, our ideas dominated the final report. Certainly the other four-team members were marginalized once fieldwork was completed. They often expressed frustration about having no ownership of the Review process once the fieldwork was completed.
- The period of fieldwork was limited, so we had to constantly divide into smaller groups to get a reasonable geographic coverage of the study areas.
- I and one other team member carried the Review in the early days of fieldwork. We also did much of the fieldwork and the fine-tuning of methodology, and most of the writing. We became the core of the team and AusAID and ANUTECH treated us as such.

Relations with the Commissioning Agents

The Review was managed by a member of the PIA Section of AusAID, who was able to join us in some of the early fieldwork in PNG. We established a good relationship with him, although he made it clear that he thought we were too direct in our critical comments. We had no formal and very few informal contacts with anyone else in Canberra after the limited initial briefings. We also had no contact with RAG or CTA until the final stages of the consultancy, although individual team members interviewed some non-AusAID RAG individuals before fieldwork started and the TL met briefly at the outset twice with the CTA.

Relationships with the Post were good initially, although it was short-staffed and very busy. It was only when drafts were submitted to the Post towards the end of our field period that some staff became critical of us and our report. We certainly got the impression that AusAID staff did not expect any criticisms of the relief effort. They seemed affronted that outsiders should come in at the end of the exercise and make any comments that did not support the Australian political and bureaucratic opinion that the whole exercise had been a great success (a view not shared by many international agencies operating within PNG or by PNG officials). Dealing with AusAID's responses to the Review's comments and criticism became the team's major problem, as discussed below.

Writing the Report

We wrote seven drafts. The first draft of 20 May was a very preliminary draft presented to the Post in Port Moresby a few days prior to departure for Australia. It was intended merely to show the lineaments of our thinking, and received very useful factual feedback from Post staff. The second draft of 22 May was written while most of the team were still in Port Moresby and was intended to take on board many of the Post's comments. The third, and first complete draft (Lea et al. 1998a) was written under pressure to meet the contractual requirement of producing a report for submission to RAG within three days of our return from PNG. We thought we were submitting the draft to RAG so that comments from them and AusAID staff could be considered when writing the final draft. This was not the case.

This third draft generated great heat and little light within the section of AusAID mainly responsible for the relief operation, which refused to send it on to RAG. Acting as a gatekeeper, this section deemed this report to be in great need of refining. We accepted that this draft was inevitably rough, written while the team was splitting up and some members were still completing their own field studies. But we were upset that there was no acknowledgement that such constraints existed. Further, many criticisms were made about the qualitative approach and the lack of hard quantitative data, which directly ignored the field conditions in which we had worked and the field methods approved by the commissioning agency before we left for the field. There was also no acknowledgement that we had provided, without being asked, nine comprehensive sets of field notes, which were impressionistic, interpretative, speculative and largely qualitative (as all field notes are), but included details of what people said and did, fairly rough – but quantitative – details of aid received by villagers, and evidence of what team members actually saw.[23] To us refusal to send the report on to RAG was not only a breach of contract but meant that there could be no independent feedback at this key stage from the group formed to 'guide' the Review process and advise the team.

To help 'correct' the report we were given three annotated drafts of the report with some 579 comments from six to nine people in the form of marginalia and some 21 pages of notes written by three or four people. I and the team member with specialist experience of emergency relief were asked to rewrite the report bearing in mind these comments, notes and marginalia before the report could be handed on to the RAG.

While many comments were useful, in that they pointed out poor wording, inadequate or ambiguous explanation, or minor errors, most of the comments dealt with matters of 'tone', 'balance' or 'emphasis' and there was no serious questioning of the main conclusions. Some comments contradicted each other. Other comments reflected careless reading, excessive defensiveness, ignorance of PNG conditions, complained of too much or too little detail, or questioned our use of anecdotal information or examples to make points that were well supported in end notes and in the supplementary field notes.

When the two of us agreed to rewrite the report prior to a draft going to RAG, we were informed in writing that there was no need to change main findings and conclusions. The team was to dwell more on the 'positive attributes' of the relief effort; delete all names; delete most of the end notes that provided examples and detailed justification; delete comments that 'denigrated' AusAID; and 'make the criticisms more palatable'.

Between June and August we prepared three further drafts before AusAID agreed to forward the sixth draft on to RAG for comment.[24] These drafts amplified comments and tightened up the conclusions and recommendations, but no substantial changes were made to the original recommendations and conclusions. CTA was brought in by ANUTECH at this stage and assisted the two writers to address the various points. All team members were irritated by the process and thought that the redrafting resulted in too many compromises and the omission of some key criticisms, explanations and caveats. The seventh draft was a further revision following the first and only meeting with RAG, which involved only the two of us who were undertaking the rewriting. This was in September 1998 (Lea et al. 1998b).

That first meeting with the RAG[25] proved very useful as there was some helpful debate and a clarification of those areas that were troubling senior officers within AusAID. We were also able to explain our position, and DFAT suggested more careful wording in places that touched on the bilateral relationship.[26] ADF was generally very supportive of the whole report and EMA (Emergency Management Australia) had nothing to add or to criticize. It was a pity that meeting had not taken place earlier!

After the meeting with RAG, we wrote the final draft. AusAID was responsible for the final report and made a number of changes, most of which were minor.[27] However, one change did concern me. All the team's drafts referred to 'serious inefficiencies and structural deficiencies within the National Disaster and Emergency Services (NDES) of PNG'. AusAID considered that such statements could harm the bilateral relationship even although no one in PNG would have said anything else and, indeed, nearly all officers within NDES were sacked towards the end of the emergency on grounds of ineffectiveness. Many of the actions of the Post and our recommendations were only understandable in the light of the problems within NDES.

The final report is available only on a 'restricted' basis within AusAID. Subsequently an abbreviated report (Lea et al. 1999) was rewritten by a media consultant who retained in a gentler form the original meaning and intent of the team members. Criticisms were muted and the 'positives' of the operation highlighted. This became the version for distribution within AusAID and it is available to stakeholders and anyone else who requests it. A summary of the findings is provided in Box 8.1.

Box 8.1 A summary of the Review's findings

On the basis of fieldwork, the Review Team did not find a target village or hamlet that received nothing at all. At least some food relief was disbursed right out to the periphery. This represents a very considerable success. In summary, other very positive aspects of AusAID/ADF's work were that:

- Between November 1997 and April 1998 some 100,000 people (about 60,000 each month) living in isolated areas, usually neglected by government and difficult to reach, were saved from greater hunger and associated sickness and, in a few cases, starvation may have been averted.

- Just over 3,200 tonnes of aid – mainly food aid – were procured and delivered efficiently and on schedule to about sixty DPs in six months.

- The first national assessment called for immediate food relief. Within weeks of the report being published, AusAID and ADF were supplying food to the target areas. This was a remarkable achievement, reflecting a good response capability.

- The operational planning undertaken by AusAID and ADF was well documented, transparent and very effective.

- The tasking of the ADF to deliver aid was a sensible initial decision and the relationship between ADF and AusAID was professional and productive.

- Coordination between Canberra and the Post was good. A specially established Drought Task Force was established in Canberra, to

---

coordinate the activities of AusAID and other key departments involved. The Task Force had access to daily updates and cables from PNG. In return, the Task Force informed the Post promptly of any developments in Australia.

Critical points identified in the Review were:

*   The monitoring system established was inadequate and this led to an over-response to the emergency (see Broughton and Lea 1999). The assessments, made under incredible pressure, were taken at face value and treated somewhat inflexibly (especially in regard to traditional and modern coping mechanisms) rather than made subject to continuous re-evaluation and modification.
*   While the national assessments commissioned by AusAID (Allen and Bourke 1997a, 1997b; Wayi 1998) were professional, expeditious and cost-effective, the assessment teams were largely made up of PNG agricultural experts and lacked people with emergency relief experience. They focused on food availability in gardens and therefore underestimated traditional coping mechanisms and people's ability to access non-garden food and assistance from others.
*   The final distribution from the DP's to people living in outlying villages and hamlets was, as is frequently the case in emergency relief operations (Apthorpe 1997), problematic and less effective than it could have been.

Other important problems were that: (1) while operational planning was good, there was little strategic planning, definition of clear objectives, review of risks and assumptions, or development of exit strategies; (2) there were conflicts of interest in AusAID because it was donor, coordinator and implementer; (3) there was inadequate communication with the provincial authorities and a partial failure to involve local institutions adequately; (4) the choice of food ration was reasonable in terms of calorific value but more acceptable alternatives could have been explored in consultation with local nutritionists; (5) the rehabilitation programmes were too late and often inappropriate; and (6) there should have been better coordination of NGO activity in both Australia and PNG.

Unlike most international emergency relief operations, this relief effort took place in a fairly safe and secure environment. There were few, if any, deaths by starvation. The response was premature and probably excessive, rather than late and insufficient.

Reflections on the Review Process

In considering the Review process, my attention focuses on the response by AusAID to the third draft. The whole team were surprised that AusAID did not react more openly and positively to it. I feel that this draft would have formed a good basis for a reasoned and coordinated response from both AusAID and RAG, with preferably a day-long seminar to discuss main differences of opinion before the writing of the final report with, as the original contract specified, a dissenting statement from AusAID or RAG if they thought it necessary. It concerned us that there was a reluctance (with one or two notable exceptions) to accept that there were shortcomings in the aid process and lessons to learn from the Review experience.[28] Was this due to an excessive defensiveness by bureaucrats, remote from the scene of operations, who had been misled by the hyperbole about the success of the operation put out by their own public relations? Was it that AusAID would be blamed for inadequacies of assessment reports and other commissioned 'experts'? Was our report too 'academic'?[29] Were we naive about bureaucratic, political and strategic realities? Was the problem one of excessive detail in end notes, appendices and field notes, which tended to confuse or annoy people with little inclination or time to plough through them?

While I consider that the Review was undertaken in a professional manner, in hindsight, the following actions, if undertaken by both the team and AusAID, would probably have led to better results and a more harmonious, productive and efficacious relationship between the consultants and the commissioning agency.

TOR issues

- AusAID could have followed a two-stage evaluation, with an independent team commissioned to undertake a field-based evaluation of the actual operation and later another smaller team established with a mix of fairly high-level AusAID and independent people to undertake a more reflective, long-term *ex-post* review of the drought relief effort (using, preferably, the work of the independent evaluation) concentrating on lessons learned, policy formulation and structures.
- A process of exploring and negotiating the TOR would have helped ensure that all players were aware of the precise meaning of the TOR, as well as the changing rules and emerging problems.
- The structures involving communication between the team and the commissioning agency should have been made more effective by giving RAG a more central role and opening up communication between the consultants and key players in the relief operation.

- The objectives of the Review should have been more specific and the TOR should have defined carefully what the agency expected and the limits on what could be reported.

Timing issues

- The evaluation process should have been started earlier so that the evaluation team could have seen the operation in progress.
- The timeframes should have been relaxed so that there was more time for briefing, consultation, team formation, planning and preparation of fieldwork, and drafting of a report. The submission of the full draft report only three days after returning from a hectic field schedule was almost guaranteed to set up a perfect situation for anyone wanting to undermine the report.

Team issues

- The evaluation team could have been smaller (three to five people), but it should have been together for the full consultancy period (including debriefing and the writing of the first draft).
- Less emphasis could be placed on sectoral competence among the team members, with more emphasis on recruiting good, senior generalists who collectively have both good country experience and experience of emergency aid.
- The Team Leader should have some say on team membership, including the need to include representatives from the aid-receiving country and from the commissioning organization.[30]

Reporting issues

- Evaluation and review teams should give debriefing seminars, oral presentations or workshops following fieldwork and prior to a draft report being submitted.
- The commissioning agency should make an integrated and formal response to the draft report before the final report is written and, if they have problems with the final report, write a supplementary report or add an annex to the published report explaining their reservations or disagreements.
- The final report should be published so that it is freely available. Consultants and their clients are quick to recommend that governance and so forth should be transparent and accountable. But to whom is a consultancy transparent if its final report is confidential to the client only? (Apthorpe 1998: 81).

Issues of linkages between the team and the commissioning agency

• It is not enough for consultancy teams to work hard and be professional, independent, and concerned about accountability, transparency and learning lessons. Teams must also have an understanding of political and bureaucratic sensitivities within their commissioning agency and have the skills to communicate effectively and sympathetically with senior aid administrators.

Of all these interrelated issues, I believe that the most important relate to structures set up by the TOR among the various actors (i.e. the team, RAG, CTA, Post, task manager etc.) and the poor communications between the team and AusAID. Better trust and cooperation could have been built up if there had been more creative and constant communication between the team and AusAID from the start. It was significant that when two of us (Broughton and Lea 1999) gave an extremely well attended and interactive seminar at AusAID at the end of the consultancy many of the problems of the Review seemed to disappear or were at least better understood by both AusAID and the team.

Notes

1. Providing relief for such areas meant that AusAID could mount an almost 'stand-alone' relief effort with some cooperation with provincial and national authorities and relatively few security risks. These remote areas represented about 5–17 per cent of the total rural population the assessments considered to be 'at risk'.

2. The consultancy cost about $A250,000 and was both a review and an evaluation. It is described henceforth as the 'Review' with a capital R, although it was really a fairly conventional evaluation.

3. 'The Post' is shorthand for AusAID staff based in the AHC in Port Moresby. They felt they were too busy to handle a review while deliveries were being made and there were problems in obtaining formal clearances for the Review from the GOPNG.

4. ANUTECH recognized the problem and signed an interim agreement on 3 April 1998 to confirm that the team was working on the project, even though ANUTECH had no contract with either AusAID or the members of the team.

5. Clause 5.1 reads: 'The Commonwealth reserves the right, at any time, to alter, qualify or reject … any report, statement, design, conclusion or recommendation made by the Contractor under this contract which is not to the Commonwealth's satisfaction but the Commonwealth shall not exercise its discretion unreasonably. Rejected Contract Material shall be corrected at the Contractor's expense.'

6. Here I do not go into the issue of the work of fieldworkers who may collect data from people who 'own' that information.

7. In this regard both ANUTECH and the team had to face the dilemma of interacting professionally with AusAID on the one hand and wanting to get on with the job and not appearing too bureaucratic and legalistic on the other.

8. The objectives also stated that at 'a later stage, the Review findings may also form the basis of an accountability report'.

9. One clause of the original TOR stated that, prior to the team's return to Australia, the content of a draft Review Report had to be 'agreed with the AusAID Post and the GOPNG in Port Moresby'. The team perceived that this could be well nigh impossible and negotiated a change.

10. These sections dealt with PNG, humanitarian and emergency aid, and evaluations and programme review.

11. Emergency Management Australia (EMA), the Department of Foreign Affairs and Trade (DFAT), and the Australian Defence Force (ADF). One of EMA's tasks is to prepare and administer the Australian government's contingency plan for the coordination of physical and technical assistance to overseas countries during emergencies and disasters.

12. The planning, development and aid literature is not clear about how the terms 'evaluation' and 'review' should be used. Often 'review' is used as an internal mid-term process somewhere between 'monitoring' and 'evaluation' (e.g. Broughton and Hampshire 1997: 20). I use 'review' mainly in the *Oxford English Dictionary* sense of 'to survey in retrospection', 'to write a criticism', 'to look back upon'.

13. Later, in Port Moresby, AusAID staff at the Post were more open, better prepared, and much more cooperative about briefing the team in spite of the fact that very few extra AusAID staff had been recruited for the operation and Post staff were trying to wind down the drought relief operation while catching up on their other duties. They gave the team unrestricted access to files, suggested contacts and helped with the recruitment of field assistants.

14. About 550 tonnes were also delivered by the Royal Australian Navy and civil shipping.

15. Enga (3), Mount Bosavi (4), Oro (7), Lower Central (6), Madang (10) and the Western Highlands (12)

16. Ok Tedi (1), Kiunga (2) and the Kabwun area (9).

17. Setting up interviews, organizing aeroplane and helicopter tickets and charters, correspondence, filing, booking accommodation on fieldwork, setting up operations room/office, and writing up of field notes. Fortunately ANUTECH sent an experienced field officer to Port Moresby for about a week to help with these tasks.

18. As it happened, many people in the areas visited preferred speaking another lingua franca Police Motu.

19. Two debriefing sessions were held with Post staff in Port Moresby but no debriefing sessions were held with officers of GOPNG because, I suspect, staff at AHC questioned many of the team's conclusions and recommendations and saw the report as 'unhelpful' to the bilateral relationship between PNG and Australia.

20. Nine typed reports totalling 158 pages.

21. Two male graduates in geography from the University of Papua New Guinea, one female local staff member from the Australian High Commission who spoke Police Motu (the lingua franca not spoken by any team member), a female professional research worker from the Institute of National Research, and a female indigenous former employee of ANUTECH in PNG. In addition, the consultancy recruited one PNG graduate and very experienced fieldworker for a week. He had published on drought, frost and traditional coping mechanisms in PNG (Goie 1986; Wohlt et al. 1982) and could have been a very useful team member.

22. Ten of about 60 AusAID/ADF DPs were visited and 30 villages around each of these DPs.

23. With hindsight it was probably a mistake to make these field notes available, because AusAID staff seemed to be uncomfortable with qualitative narratives.

24. Even as late as August before the Review team's first meeting with RAG, I, as Team Leader, received eleven pages of criticisms from three senior AusAID staff. These reactions were not coordinated by a responsible person within AusAID and the Review team just got everything given to the task manager. Only two or three comments in all those pages provided a reason to change anything in the draft and those changes all related to wording rather than substance.

25. AusAID did not want the full team to attend and would not agree even to have Canberra residents present. In the end only myself as Team Leader and the team member assisting in rewriting the report attended.

26. Some of these seemed supersensitive to the Review team. For example, the team was not allowed to mention that PNG was a former colony of Australia, and we were not permitted to be explicit about several shortcomings with the PNG bureaucracy that everyone involved in the drought relief programme in PNG was aware of. These short-comings were central to many of the comments and criticisms the Review report made of AusAID's performance and explained a number of the inadequacies raised.

27. Some 'defensive' footnotes were inserted, a number of key footnotes explaining or documenting critical comments were deleted, and critical comments about some the reports commissioned by AusAID were deleted.

28. The professional literature on emergency relief abounds with similar findings made by other evaluators (see, for example, Apthorpe 1997).

29. In fact only two of the six team members were academics: one was retired and the other was an academic who had been involved in many secondments to non-academic agencies. Both had undertaken many evaluations and other consultancies for national and international agencies.

30. As Apthorpe (1999: 4) notes, at least one AusAID insider would have been useful so that 'credibility is not lost and organizational ownership ... gained'.

9

An Experimental and Inclusive Approach to Evaluation as a Lesson-learning Tool: Groupe URD's Work on the Post-Hurricane Mitch Emergency

François Grunewald, Claire Pirotte and Véronique de Geoffroy

In the immediate aftermath of the disaster created by Hurricane Mitch, our inter-NGO network specializing in humanitarian research and evaluation, Groupe URD, started to receive questions from its members in the field. These were very much related to our main research themes: tools for diagnosis, food security, partnerships in turbulence, moving from handout to cost recovery schemes, coordination of the macro, micro and meso levels of interventions, and the relations between state and private humanitarian assistance. In response Groupe URD[1] proposed a field evaluation and collective learning process following an integrated approach. By the end of November 1998, we had drafted a project and it had been circulated among the French NGOs and state actors, especially from the French Ministry of Foreign Affairs, who had been involved in the post-Mitch humanitarian response.

Initiation of the Programme

The objective was 'evaluation, capitalization and collective learning'. The initial reactions were generally positive, but often cautious, both features reflecting the typical reluctance of NGOs, especially the smallest, which had not been following the current trends in evaluation thinking and emphasis from accountability to lesson-learning. It took us some time and effort to persuade them that behind the 'the challenges and risks involved in evaluation work' there is a dramatic potential for improvement.

Groupe URD did not propose the project in the usual way. During the course of December 1998, the initial concept of a field-oriented learning process was elaborated through interactions with the headquarters staff of a number of NGOs within a coordination entity called Commission Coopération Développement (CCD). This is composed of representatives

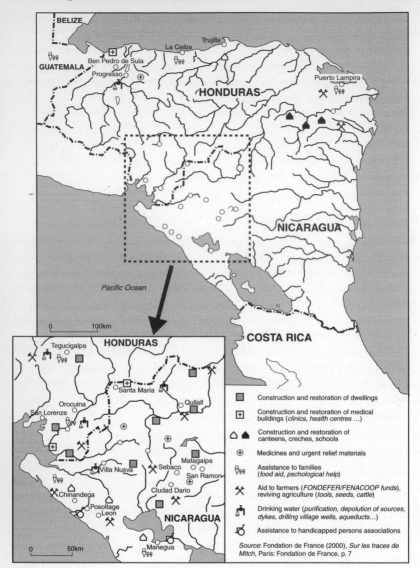

MAP 9.1 Central America

from NGO and government bodies. CCD assisted URD to develop its proposal on Mitch from a purely NGO focus to one that would consider an inter-NGO–government framework. As a result the Mitch Evaluation Task Force, which was to be influential in the following phases of the process, was established.

Another important player in the development of this evaluation was the Fondation de France (FDF). During the weeks after Hurricane Mitch, fundraising for the French NGOs was coordinated by FDF, a private foundation that became the main donor. FDF gave a very positive response to the request by Groupe URD to fund the evaluation and it became one of the leading actors on the Task Force. They were interested in the work, not only to ensure their accountability to the hundreds of thousands of individual donors who had sent money for the post-Mitch activities, but also to help the NGOs improve their practices. However, the involvement of the main funding agency in the evaluation had a number of side-effects that had to be dealt with during the mission.

The Work of the Task Force

The Task Force was a key asset as well as a constraint in the whole operation. It brought together representatives of about 30 NGOs, five or six administrative areas (collectivities) in France, government officers from the Ministry of Defence, Ministry of Finance and Ministry of Foreign Affairs (MAE) and a representative of the Inter-American Bank. The Task Force was co-chaired by the chairman of Groupe URD and the head of MAE's Mission for Liaison with the NGOs (MILONG).

In the initial proposal, and in order to ensure independence of Groupe URD, a transparent but discreet, or low-key, approach was sought. Then, when the process switched from the initial design to preparing for the fieldwork, our strategy had to change. Both the transparency of the approach and the ownership of the process by the major stakeholders, i.e. the headquarters of the concerned NGOs, their field offices and the main donor agencies, became major concerns. As a result, networking in France and Central America became an overarching operational priority for the preparation of the field mission. We recruited a desk person with good field experience for that purpose and she was based at Groupe URD headquarters. The evaluation proposal we prepared was widely circulated. Regular Task Force meetings took place in Paris.

This transformation from a low-key, inter-NGO approach and framework to a broader forum had several positive and negative repercussions. On the one hand, it enlarged the range of people and institutions involved from purely NGOs to include central government and territorial collectivities, which increased both the scope of the debates and the chance for coordination. On the other hand, there was a risk of political manipulation that increased the need for vigilance by the civil society representatives, i.e. the NGOs.

A number of events delayed the start of the fieldwork for the evaluation but also enriched our overall preparation. A key one was the meeting in April 1999 in Stockholm of the main bilateral and multilateral donors involved in Central America. This was to design a blueprint for reconstruction in Central America and to act as a pledging meeting for donors. At the parallel forum of the NGOs, those agencies involved in the URD-led evaluation presented a rather elaborate position paper that was proposed to the Task Force in order to have a common position. The French government also joined in the debate, with an influential speech being delivered by the French minister for international cooperation. This debate led to an agreement for collaborative NGO/government involvement in the process, with the French Embassies in the region instructed to facilitate the work of the evaluation team. URD's Team Leader for the evaluation was requested to give a full debriefing to an assembly of all the French ambassadors based in Central America and the ministerial staff involved with the region. This NGO–government collaboration created an interesting precedent in France and gave our evaluation process unexpected weight and authority. However, switching from an inter-NGO evaluation marked by notable discretion to a more system-wide mechanism was a real challenge, and changed the rules of the game. Both Groupe URD and those of us on the evaluation team had to adjust without 'losing our souls'.

The Period Prior to the Mission

Once the NGOs and the Task Force had agreed that Groupe URD should be responsible for the evaluation, URD had to draft its own Terms of Reference (TOR). These comprised three cross-cutting (transversal) points, three sectoral ones and a methodology to be followed for organized feedback to the agencies.

The cross-cutting points were:

• analysis of the linking of relief to rehabilitation and development, including the validity of the pace for switching from one to the other;
• analysis of the sustainability of the programmes implemented and the issue of the transition from free distributions to more sustainable mechanisms, including cost recovery in health and credit for agriculture;
• analysis of the management of the land tenure issue by the NGOs in the process of reconstruction and rehabilitation; and
• analysis of the various forms of partnerships that were established, or avoided, between the international NGOs and other actors, including the relations of the French NGOs with other international and national NGOs, and with local authorities and civil society organizations, and the relations of French and local national agencies with the civil society in the disaster area.

Sectoral points to be considered in the evaluation were:

- habitat, shelter and human settlements;
- food aid, agriculture rehabilitation and food security; and
- health and social vulnerability.

The methodological approach to feedback and follow-up was to include:

- regular meetings with all relevant staff in the headquarters of the NGOs prior to departure;
- a 'sandwich' approach to the field mission with a meeting with all actors upon arrival in one of the visited countries, and a feedback meeting to conclude the visits;
- provision of in-depth information at the feedback meeting, including translation into Spanish of the relevant texts;
- opportunities for intense exchanges early on in the visits with local NGOs and national coordination bodies in both Nicaragua and Honduras in order to ensure their support; and
- a series of steps for feedback, learning and capitalizing on the knowledge to be followed up on return, including a series of numbered drafts to be circulated in order to stimulate responses and reactions.

The TOR were discussed by team members, but did not engender major debate between Groupe URD and the NGOs concerned or the government bodies involved in the Task Force and the FDF. However, a certain *flou artistique*, or potential for interpretation, remained between what was the main goal of the mission as elaborated by URD, and the perception of the funding agency (FDF). While URD was much more interested in transversal issues, such as the quality of problem diagnosis, relevance of the action, partnerships, sustainability, and prevention of future vulnerability, FDF was more interested in information about the way the funds had been spent and the coincidence of the field activities with the project proposals by the NGOs for funding. However, these latter accountability points were not explicitly included in the TOR that the Task Force accepted for the evaluation. As a result, the scope of the work was not fully clarified before the fieldwork began and, as will be seen later on, this had repercussions for our post-mission phase.

The issues to be looked at in the mission covered a wide spectrum of sectors and inter-sectoral areas. These included reconstructing the time-frame of the various operations and the involvement of the many actors (national, international, military and civilian); the design and implementation of building schemes along with the social engineering behind the creation of new human settlements; the recovery of food security using food aid and agricultural rehabilitation as well as urban income-generating activities; diverse aspects of health from emergency treatment to public health, and the establishment of cost recovery schemes; and the coordination between the various actors involved. As a result, from the outset URD wanted to have a strong multi-disciplinary team.

Fortunately, the majority of the necessary human resources were already available within Groupe URD. This was crucial, as it ensured a very good cohesion within the evaluation team itself. In the end, our team consisted of an agriculture/food security/resettlement specialist, who was also Team Leader, a medical doctor and public health specialist, a lawyer specializing in land rights issues (so important in Central America) and two emergency specialists, one looking more into the relation between civil and military actors, as well as the 'disaster management cycle' perspective, and the other, who was the manager of the Mitch Task Force, focusing on the inter-actor coordination issue. A key consideration from the outset in selecting the team was the need for a gender balance. The previous experience of some of the URD staff in Central America made them familiar with the 'macho' culture of the 'Latinos'. That influenced the search for a largely female team, with finally only one-third of the members being male.

In addition, after the main team had been selected, it was decided that it would be helpful to add a photographer to the team to ensure more creative post-mission feedback. This was decided after having witnessed an emotional presentation of an evaluation mission based on a slide show. A photographer well known for his work in Rwanda and Albania, Philippe Merchez, expressed an interest in the challenge and joined the team for the whole mission.

We had six team meetings through the eight-month preparation period, either in Paris or in the URD headquarters and training centre in the south of France, although only three of these focused on the actual mission alone. This was probably not enough: more interaction would have improved further our cohesiveness as a team. The distance between Paris, where most of the activities of the Task Force took place, and the location of the URD headquarters was both an intellectual challenge and a logistical nightmare. Yet it was helpful in some ways as URD could keep a distant overview of the Task Force work and avoid being involved in the inter-agency conflicts and day-to-day operations.

Networking with the European and Central American NGOs, donors and coordinating agencies was indispensable. This ensured that the evaluation by URD could be coordinated with other similar initiatives and enriched by the findings of those carried out earlier. Contact with Voluntary Organizations in Cooperation in Emergencies (VOICE), the co-ordination body of European emergency NGOs, UN agencies involved in the field – the World Food Programme (WFP), the Food and Agriculture Organization

---

Box 9.1 Roles and actors prior to the mission

Initiative Groupe URD launched the process and framed the Terms of Reference around sectoral and transversal issues.

External support The Task Force provided a place for peer review and discussion on any issue relevant to the evaluation.

Financial support and guidance on specific issues The Fondation de France played a key role in stimulating thinking.

Assuming responsibility Groupe URD was fully responsible for its methodological choice.

(FAO), etc. – were established, as well as with civil society organizations based in Latin America.

Massive quantities of information were collected at this stage that were crucial for the preparation of our mission and its itinerary. The establishment of relations with the Central American network was the corner-stone of the whole *démarche*. Not only was this consistent with the methodology of Groupe URD, which focuses on partnerships and the development of local capacities, but it also turned out to be another essential ingredient for the success of the whole operation. Networking proved essential for establishing relationships with the national actors from the NGO sector. In turn this affected the quality of the fieldwork.

The review of documentation was an important part of this pre-mission phase. Although we had most of the existing information on Mitch and its aftermath, including all the project documents of concern for the mission, we could analyse only a part of it in the time available. Through the activities of the Mitch Task Force, URD's involvement in European and international networks, including the Active Learning Network for Accountability and Performance in Humanitarian Action (ALNAP), and a regular review of the resources available through the Internet, we had access to more information than we could really digest. Choices had to be made. Nevertheless, this information provided a valuable 'capital' base for the mission. A database of this has been set up, and can be accessed from the URD web site <www.urd.org>.

The Mission

When we finally reached Managua in August 1999, Hurricane Mitch was no longer in the limelight. Disbursement and implementation for most of the projects financed by the Fondation de France was coming to an end. Nevertheless, this seemed an ideal timing for the evaluation since most of the international actors were still there. With the Albania/Kosovo crisis growing, however, some key staff had already been relocated to that area. The short duration of contract for other emergency workers meant that some had already moved on to the next job. This is a known difficulty for all evaluators of emergency assistance programmes, although today to some extent the Internet permits the tracking down of a missing head of project or medical personnel around the world weeks after they have left the crisis being evaluated.

The Task Force and URD has agreed that the mission should visit only Nicaragua and Honduras, although it was recognized that Costa Rica and El Salvador would have been worth visiting (Map 9.1). While this affected the methodology and our work plan, later triangulation reinforced the fact that this was an appropriate choice in terms of both time and resource management and lesson-learning.

It should first be remembered that this mission was much more of a 'learning evaluation' than an 'accountability evaluation'. This perspective was indeed crucial in the methodological choice made early in the process. The fieldwork was organized in two phases. During the first two-week tour of the both countries, all of us on the team functioned as a unit, zoning and classifying the field situation and actors. This involved agro-ecological zoning, zoning on the basis of the degree of impact of the disaster and zoning on the basis of political parameters. It also involved creating typologies of projects, actors, and the realities of their work.

The above provided the basis for our first level of analysis and helped determine issues and problems to be further analysed. Our second tour, again of both countries, thus could be much more focused, addressing certain issues or programmes that were seen as having a capacity to illustrate important issues. The key point of this two-phase approach was that, at the end of the first phase, even though we had been split into sub-teams for short periods, we all had a global and shared view of the area and of the problems, with the key themes clearly identified and prioritized.

During the first phase, the methodology was based on specific approaches to the various stakeholders:

- 'beneficiaries';
- local actors (local NGOs, local and national authorities); and
- international actors (NGOs, international organizations and donors).

During the second phase, as the focus had been narrowed to specific issues, areas or actors, the methodology relied much more on individual interviews.

In order to cope with the very diverse situations, we had to develop specific methods. Two main methods of recording the views of the beneficiaries were utilized: focus group meetings tackling issues such as timeliness of the actions, and semi-structured interviews with individuals. These individuals or sampled families were chosen because they were representing not 'the average case' but one segment of the existing diversity: for instance, large families and small families, complete families or single-parent families. We felt that what was important was whether or not assistance was able to meet highly diversified needs in a heterogeneous environment.

Networking was another key method of maintaining the involvement of the many local actors and ensuring that their views were included. We met with national authorities, local authorities, local trade unions, farmers' associations, women's associations, national NGOs and their federations time and again. We also interviewed UN agencies, embassies, representatives of the European Union, and international NGOs (not only the French ones funded by the FDF, but also other nationalities) and recorded their views. This information from interviews, focus groups and networking was included as raw material for discussion in our 'evaluative brainstorming'. This informal, but regular, team exercise was based on two questions: 'Where are we?' and 'Where do we go from here?'

The design of the itinerary and approach of the mission itself was also a joint team exercise. We had established beforehand a methodology and prepared a draft schedule based on our evaluation strategy. This resulted in a 'position paper' that we shared with the NGOs upon arrival. From this discussion, a tentative programme was then drafted, and logistical aspects of the mission prepared accordingly. The result was a rather inclusive approach, which was very different from the normal top-down exclusive strategies of most evaluation teams previously seen in the region. This ensured prompt and sustained support from all stakeholders and greatly facilitated smooth and cost-effective logistics for the mission.

We undertook regular feedback to specific stakeholders to ensure their ownership of the whole exercise. This was especially important as there was a fear within the evaluation team that the wrong message could have been sent by the donor. In particular it was feared that a defensive rather than open dialogue could result due to fears that a classical accountability-type evaluation was planned, rather than one emphasizing the cross-cutting issue approach. In order to diffuse any such misunderstandings, we had to put a strategy in place. This involved organizing introductory and feedback meetings whenever we entered or left a country. This was found to be quite efficient for achieving the minimum level of confidence among the 'evaluees' and bringing them into the evaluation process. We made a special effort to bring in the national NGO coordinating body. For instance in

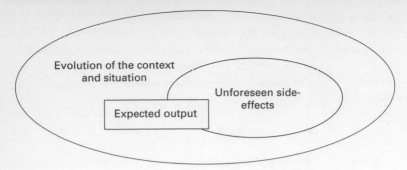

FIGURE 9.1 What did we observe in the field?

Nicaragua, we co-organized with the Coordinadora Civile a series of three mini-workshops – on reconstruction, health and food security. The purpose of these was to provide feedback to the local constituency. These meetings or workshops provided excellent opportunities at which we could get the views of the local actors on our findings.

Meetings also took place with government officials both in Nicaragua and Honduras to understand the situation from their perspective and to bring them into the discussion of learning lessons for better practice in the future. In Nicaragua, the state position was developing a discourse so politicized and against the civil society that little progress could be made in the discussion. In Honduras, the situation was far better and interesting points could be exchanged on public health and disaster prevention.

In such a wide-ranging evaluation, it was essential to maintain a high level of teamwork while preserving individual sector responsibilities. This was achieved by a dual approach that, on the one hand, gave a clear area of responsibility to each of the team members in their area of expertise so that they felt empowered, and, on the other hand, established a mechanism for sharing views, elucidating disagreements and coming to a common approach in order to keep coherence and complementarity in the research, as well as cohesiveness in the team. Keeping a team spirit was fundamental, especially when the quantity of work we faced was huge, the living conditions and transportation sometimes precarious and the climatic conditions hazardous. This was not always easy. Increased efforts in this respect were needed at times.

Reaching conclusions involved a retrospective reflection by the team of why we had launched this evaluation and what had been our TOR. From there we progressively reformulated the findings from our field observations, interviews and discussions with various actors. We framed our analysis of the 'impact' of the activities in terms of:

- the expected outputs;
- the unexpected side-effects; and
- the evolution of the context and situation (see Figure 9.1).

In the rapidly changing circumstances, it was crucial for us to separate these various layers of the situation after intervention, so that the real effects of the programme would not be confused with other influences. This led to another interesting stage of debate with FDF which, as a donor, was stuck in the classical debate between 'learning and account-ability'.

After the Mission

As the main and central theme of the mission was to stimulate lesson-learning, we decided on our return that our work would have the greatest impact if we did not identify specific agencies but focused on stimulating collective thinking and reflection. This was central to all the subsequent stages and the way we handled them. We were helped in this endeavour by the way the TOR were initially drafted: they looked more into the cross-cutting aspects and the overall process rather than the tasks of specific agencies. This was reflected in our conclusions and recommendations (Box 9.2)

Box 9.2 Summary of the conclusions and recommendations

Nature of the actors   The French actors in the post-Mitch operation, excluding the military, belonged to two categories:

- those with already lengthy involvement in Central America, including mainly development and so-called 'solidarity organizations' with good knowledge of the region and good integration within the civil society; and
- those who arrived after Mitch, often called the emergency specialists, who are masters of technical fields but have no or little idea of the local contexts, their historical social tensions and their lines of power.

This division is not anodyne and affected the way the crisis was dealt with.

Quality of the diagnosis   In most instances, the diagnosis of needs and situations was weak. It was driven more by the NGO knowledge or was donor-driven, rather than being based on a sound analysis of local

---

needs, capacities and constraints. Actors have frequently designed their interventions more on the basis of preconceived needs and standards than on the reality of the situation. This point was first identified during the desk phase, when project documents were reviewed.

Coordination In terms of operational coordination, it appeared that the French 'emergency NGOs' had by and large been absent from the main coordination mechanisms, either for the other international NGOs or for the local NGOs. This was bitterly felt by the latter. Yet the French 'development NGOs', who were already in the existing coordination networks, felt equally left out by the emergency operators. This is observed in many theatres of operations, and raises serious questions.

Health This region has been pioneering in the field of public health, especially in Nicaragua. Hence it is not surprising that most of the required measures had been taken by the states to prevent the often feared, but rarely seen, 'post-catastrophe' epidemics. Certain NGOs developed programmes to support this epidemiological monitoring. More difficult was the rehabilitation of the curative health system. While reconstructing health posts and hospitals was easy, the transition from free access to medicine to cost-recovery mechanisms, which is crucial in countries where the state has only a limited resource base and weak tax-collection mechanisms, was much more problematic. Here again, the well-known negative secondary impact of free assistance could be observed fully, although it was aggravated by governmental policies (in Nicaragua, medical aid is still supposed to be free in the state-run institutions).

Habitat and shelter Diagnosis capacity in this sector was dramatically weak. The know-how and creativeness of the NGOs in the design of the shelter programmes had been up to the required level. Technical standards were often of a high quality. But the NGOs poorly managed the whole issue. New villages were created in areas where there were no jobs. Land-titling mechanisms were approached with little or no knowledge of the land problem and led to a dramatic price increase that affected the population. Many costly new villages had already been deserted, the beneficiaries preferring to occupy their agricultural plot rather than a ghetto where overcrowding would result in social and health problems. NGOs were confused about the need for either a village or refugee camp. This poorly conceived approach was already leading to a number of negative impacts in places where the beneficiaries had stayed, with increased urban and inter-gender violence, water and human waste management issues and problems with social cohesion.

Food aid, agricultural rehabilitation and food security The Central American population was for once lucky. WFP food supplies which had arrived belatedly in response to El Niño problems in 1997–98 were immediately available for the first weeks or months of the post-Mitch food aid programmes. The alternative would have been considerable migration to Costa Rica. Indeed, there was a tendency by many farmers to try to find incomes in neighbouring countries. This process was seen by many as being detrimental to local reconstruction. Thus food-for-work programmes for local road construction or reclamation of fields were important in keeping people close to their home areas. Fortunately, the main actors in the food aid business switched relatively quickly from free distribution to more food-for-work mechanisms. In certain areas, this was critical for ensuring a food allocation to people who had to reconstruct everything. More important were the various programmes focusing on agricultural rehabilitation, especially the limited number that established partnerships with local universities and farmers' associations.

Politicization of aid Aid that arrives in large and sudden quantities in an area where resources are scarce often becomes a resource to control. Governments and local officials tried to manipulate it in an almost caricature fashion. The Nicaraguan government, by delaying the declaration of the State of Emergency, by attempting to limit the flow of aid through the civil society and by directing aid to its favourite electoral zones illustrated all the risks. NGOs did not necessarily react in a concerted manner.

Missed opportunities Much of the literature on Mitch concludes that this hurricane underlined existing social and ecological vulnerability. While this is true, the agencies that prepared these documents did not draw conclusion about the real solutions. The real response needed is agrarian reform involving land reallocation to the poor farmers, complemented by a comprehensive credit programme. The French President Jacques Chirac, visiting the area just after Hurricane Mitch, cancelled the public debt of the affected countries to France.

While courageous and generous in appearance, this cancellation without conditions resulted in a missed opportunity to push the local governments towards better governance and, more specifically, to address the land issue properly. The money saved by the countries could have then be reinvested in rural credit schemes. This missed opportunity was bitterly received by the local NGOs and peasants' movements, which were trying to pressure their own authorities to take action. As a result, NGOs and private foundations had to buy land from rich landlords for settling internally displaced people. The opportunity was also missed to lobby for a reduction in the military budget and for control of the illegal trade of light weapons.

Recommendations There were numerous recommendations at the end of the mission. Among the most important were:

- The need to evaluate/coordinate/learn during emergency relief operations, and to delineate between each of these is critical. A mechanism such as the learning office, as proposed by ALNAP, seems to address these needs.
- There is a need to reinforce the diagnosis capacity and related programme design. The current tendency to have programmes shaped more by existing and sometimes externally imposed standards reduces the diagnosis input and hence the quality of the work.
- The will and capacity of international NGOs to enter into partnership with local actors must be enhanced. This is regularly forgotten by the emergency NGO and, in the case of post-Mitch operations, had a dramatically negative impact.
- The capacities of all actors in the field of urban and peri-urban human settlements need to be developed. This sector is more and more a new area in relation to complex emergencies and natural disasters, but NGOs mainly have experience in the rural sector.
- Databases should be established on locations and technologies, as well as on crisis management in specific areas or domains. Lessons could have been learned for the post-Mitch situation from other similar crises in the region or elsewhere as well as from access to existing knowledge on land tenure and local construction techniques.
- A second visit to the areas was recommended in order to confirm or refute conclusions by the evaluation team and to deepen the analysis of the effect of the aid not only over an eight-month timeframe but also over a twenty-month period.

Feedback to the Task Force, which included the NGO stakeholders and French government bodies, took place on three occasions in order to ensure the appropriate timeframe for assimilation and a multi-layer feedback process specializing in different aspects each time.

The first occasion for feedback was just after the return of the mission. It was organized by the French Ministry of Foreign Affairs for its ambassadors and top-level management from the Central America desk. This resulted in a keen interest being expressed by the officials in an interagency evaluation process involving the state and civil society actors on an equal footing.

The second feedback was organized a few weeks after the return of the mission, when our initial ideas were on paper and ready for circulation. The drafting of this summary draft report was a relatively easy process, because many of us were involved with URD and so stayed in contact despite the formal disbanding of the team. First reactions to this summary report were in some cases quite strong, but in two different directions. Comments such as 'Let's do it again' showed the interest of certain actors in this kind of process. Other responses, such as 'Are you sure you really visited our project?' showed a concern for the critical points. Our response to both was: 'Wait for the draft report, where you will see what we have just said but in a more substantiated manner.'

The road from the initial summary draft report to the final product was a lengthy, and sometimes frustrating, process. While waiting for feedback on the first draft, we each went on to other work. As a result it was left to the TL to incorporate the views expressed either during the later technical workshop or sent by email. The new technology, and the Internet in particular, made life much easier. Members were able to complete their part of the report roughly on time for the dissemination of the full draft only one week after the scheduled date for this.

The third feedback event we organized was some time later. The idea was that this meeting would be useful only after people had read the second draft of the mission report that incorporated the comments on the full draft. This last phase of the feedback process took the form of a day long workshop bringing together more than forty people representing thirty NGOs and two universities. Minutes were prepared and circulated a few days after the exercise. This was a more technical workshop that discussed in detail the results of the mission. Unfortunately the first venue and date had to be cancelled for unforeseen reasons, and reconvening the meeting proved difficult. In fact most people had switched in their mind to East Timor, Kosovo or Venezuela by the time it was reconvened. However, as a discrete event, involving a small and very technical discussion, this last workshop provided a useful opportunity to discuss the mission findings, its recommendations, and, even more importantly, the answer to the question 'Where do we go from here?'

This comprehensive multi-phase feedback process proved to be a powerful learning tool and an important catalyst for the overall ownership of the results of the evaluation by both the NGO community and the relevant state actors. As a result, a group called a 'Quality Platform' was established along with an 18-month process for developing methodologies for *ex-ante* assessments (diagnosis, situation analysis, need assessment) and *ex-post* evaluation (impact assessment, end-of-project evaluation).

The typical 'Loch Ness Monster' of any evaluation reappeared during the feedback process: the unclear, non-clarified and hidden agenda behind the evaluation. The funding body, FDF, was not totally satisfied with the report. The classical accountability approach it expected from the evaluation was missing. It was not that the issues of coherence, effectiveness and efficiency were not treated, but that they were given much less importance than the questions of relevance, sustainability, coordination, vulnerability reduction, partnership, and the like. In addition, instead of the results of the evaluation being analysed and presented NGO by NGO and project by project, they were presented in a manner that focused on cross-cutting issues and sectors. The work of individual NGOs was used more to illustrate the main discussions, rather than as a basis for judgement of a particular NGO or project.

The photo-display process was a success. The photographer managed to re-create the atmosphere of the visited area extremely well and to illustrate the challenges faced by the region eight months after Hurricane Mitch. It powerfully illustrated the results of the evaluation mission and received a lot of praise.

Conclusions

We learned many lessons from the mission. The following seem most important in the context of this book.

Evaluation, of the broad and inclusive type described here, is a powerful tool for progress and improving humanitarian assistance. A large number of areas were identified for improvement in the technical and management aspects of humanitarian aid programmes during emergency and post-emergency activities. Numerous implications for the future are already foreseen, including the creation of a 'Quality Project' and improved training of field actors.

The lesson-learning approach can have two strategies, one short-term and the other long-term. The short-term one involves exchanges and debate with the aid actors, both in the field and upon return. This can involve various feedback meetings and technical seminars. This is where the actual formal direct learning takes place. This can impact directly on NGOs, who redesign their programmes. In this case it also resulted in a proposal for a similar exercise to be undertaken in the context of one of the next large-scale crises, with an initial mission much earlier in the course of events. Longer-term learning involves recognizing that many of the errors made are due to a lack of certain skills among the aid actors. Incorporating the lesson learned into existing and future training sessions with aid volunteers and aid managers is seen as one of the most efficient mechanisms for improving the quality of the programmes.

Creating empathy between the evaluees and the evaluation team is a *sine qua non* for a successful evaluation. It is critical to understand the field situations through the eyes of the actors, to gain their trust and support and to share information with them in a transparent manner. This will facilitate the mission and help ensure that critical remarks and recommendations will be well received and seen from the beginning as constructive. The way the evaluation team created a climate conducive to building confidence to facilitate the exchange of views and transparency in the sharing of information was based on a three-pronged strategy:

1. initial information collection and involvement of the NGOs through the work of the Task Force;
2. a website specially set up to keep everybody informed on the whereabouts of the mission; and
3. the 'sandwich strategy' in the field, with briefings at the start and finish of a visit to each country.

Achieving this empathy required considerable effort from the team as a large part of the work of the Paris-based Task Force was not transmitted by the NGO headquarters to their field offices. This resulted in the need for us to undertake lengthy explanations in the field.

The creation of empathy is equally important within the evaluation team itself. Working under pressure, possibly with jet lag or other physical ailments, always affects the relations between a group of people. An experienced person to support the TL in the creation of this internal empathy proved highly useful during this evaluation. A crucial issue is developing a method to ensure that the whole team progresses simultaneously and in a coherent manner. Regular team meetings and collective analysis of the status of the information gathered and of the state of progress are essential.

Clear and accepted TOR are essential for the smooth running of an evaluation mission. There needs to be a shared understanding of the TOR by all stakeholders (donors, field agencies and the evaluation team), not least to avoid the need to explain and re-explain the mission's focus after the work is completed and the reports are being read.

Maintaining multiple accountabilities to both a donor and a network of field actors is essential but not without difficulties. Our experience suggests that transparency and clarification are crucial. In this case, each time there was either a perception of a hidden agenda or a lack of clarity, it required a strong effort to clarify the situation.

A thorough evaluation process requires that adequate time and means are available. The costs involved for the whole of this evaluation process (Task Force management, mission preparation, fieldwork and feedback) were not very high. Over a twelve-month period this amounted to roughly US$100,000. It should be said that a lot of voluntary work was also provided, which means that such a low-cost operation is not necessarily replicable. To undertake thorough evaluation should be seen as an opportunity not to be missed and using the equivalent of 1 per cent or 2 per cent of the humanitarian assistance costs should be quite acceptable.

Note

1. Groupe URD, based in the south of France, is an inter-agency structure composed of one-third 'emergency NGOs', one-third 'developmental NGOs' and one-third academics. Its activities can be conceptualized as a series of concentric circles, with research and evaluation being the inner circle, debate and publication the second one and training and teaching the third and outer circle. Its philosophy is that to improve humanitarian practices the three following steps are necessary: (a) 'generation of knowledge' (research and evaluate); (b) 'capitalization' (accumulate and build on knowledge); and (c) 'valorization' (promote knowledge through dissemination, e.g. books, publications and training sessions).

10

UNICEF–DFID Joint Evaluation of UNICEF's Kosovo Emergency Preparedness and Response

John Telford

The joint evaluation by the UK Department for International Development (DFID) and the United Nations Children's Fund (UNICEF) of the emergency preparedness and response by UNICEF during the 1999 Kosovo crisis aimed to assess whether the relevant programme objectives had been achieved, and to identify the strengths and weaknesses of UNICEF's performance (see Box 10.1). DFID had contributed £5.25 million towards the UNICEF activities in the Kosovo region during the crisis (Map 10.1). DFID also, and completely separately, had been funding a sizeable project to strengthen UNICEF's global emergency preparedness and response capacities. The Kosovo funding was not earmarked. For ease of budgeting and reporting UNICEF allocated the amount to chosen protection and assistance sectors. It was agreed that as well as looking at these, the evaluation would attempt to get a holistic view of operations, and thus would study UNICEF's preparedness and response to the crisis in general. The evaluation covered more than just programme issues. Aspects of the wider institutional role of UNICEF in emergencies were also examined.

For practical reasons it was decided that the evaluation would focus on the funded activities in Albania, Kosovo and the former Yugoslav Republic of Macedonia (fYROM). DFID funding to UNICEF during the crisis was also utilized in both Montenegro and Bosnia Herzegovina. The total duration of the evaluation was approximately one month, spread over the three final months of 1999, and involved a multi-disciplinary team of four persons.

UNICEF has often been seen more as a 'development' than as an 'emergency' agency. Its mandate is based on the Convention on the Rights of the Child. The agency promotes the development of a healthy and wholesome environment for children and women. However, it does this in all conditions and has responded to emergencies for decades, including the chronic southern Sudan crisis through Operation Lifeline Sudan. The

MAP 10.1 Kosovo

DFID-funded capacity-building programme in UNICEF was a related stimulus to our evaluation. This programme, funded by DFID to the tune of several million US dollars, aims to improve UNICEF's emergency preparedness and response. An important additional question for the evaluation was just what is and should be UNICEF's role in emergencies? Did its more developmental background give it specific strengths and weaknesses in this crisis? As it turned out, this was an interesting, challenging and refreshing question.

Box 10.1 Summary of the Terms of Reference for the DFID–UNICEF joint evaluation of UNICEF's Kosovo emergency preparedness and response

The overarching purposes of this evaluation were:

- to assess the extent to which UNICEF's programmes met their objectives and to draw lessons from this assessment for future improvements; and
- to assess the extent to which UNICEF's programme objectives fed into DFID's overall strategy for the region.

The secondary purpose was:

- to identify areas of UNICEF management and delivery capacity requiring strengthening, thereby helping UNICEF further define its work plan for the recent funding DFID is providing to strengthen the capacity of the organization to respond to crises globally. Also, to provide a benchmark of performance upon which any future improvements can be measured.

The study was to pay particular attention to:

- the appropriateness of programme appraisal, design and implementation and whether this matched UNICEF's perceived comparative advantage in the region;
- the effectiveness, efficiency, impact and sustainability of interventions;
- local management and delivery capacity;
- the cost-effectiveness of the contribution and whether the programme approach provided the most effective means of achieving the programme purpose;
- how UNICEF adapted to the changing refugee caseload, including the return process;
- UNICEF's level of coordination with other agencies, government, NGOs and external links with other stakeholders;
- quality of internal reporting to HQ and reporting to DFID/other donors;
- any particularly significant social, economic and political impacts of the programmes that were not explicit in the programme objectives, considering in particular the programme's impact on a) inter-ethnic relationships; b) relations between host and refugee populations; and c) on poverty and vulnerability in the area;
- DFID's relationship with UNICEF – what DFID could have done better.

The 1999 Kosovo Crisis and UNICEF Strategy

Since the outbreak of open conflict between the Kosovo Liberation Army and Yugoslav military and special police forces in early 1998, Kosovo had been the scene of massive forced population movements. In February 1999 the talks between Yugoslav and Kosovar Albanian representatives at Rambouillet broke down. The countries of the North Atlantic Treaty Organization (NATO) launched an air attack on 24 March. Between April and May over one million people fled from Kosovo. Of these some 800,000 ethnic Albanians took refuge in neighbouring countries, including Albania, the fYROM, Bosnia and Herzegovina, Croatia and the Federal Yugoslav Republic of Montenegro. Within Kosovo, the conflict forced people into isolated mountainous areas without shelter, food and basic survival supplies.

International agencies, governments and Albania Force (AFOR–NATO force to support humanitarian operations) constructed dozens of camps for refugees in anticipation that the refugees would be spending many months in exile. An estimated 444,600 refugees fled to Albania, 244,500 to the fYROM and 69,900 to Montenegro. As many as two-thirds or more of the refugees in Albania and fYROM were hosted not in camps but within the local community, either as guests or paying for their own accommodation.

On 3 June Yugoslavia accepted a peace plan requiring the withdrawal of all forces from Kosovo and the entry of NATO peacekeepers under a United Nations (UN) mandate. Russian and NATO forces entered Kosovo on 13 June. The next day the first humanitarian convoy followed. By 14 June refugees had begun to flood back to Kosovo – within the first three weeks over 600,000 refugees returned mostly to badly damaged homes. As the Albanian Kosovars streamed home, however, it is estimated that over 200,000 Serbs and Roma were displaced, seeking refuge in Serbia and Montenegro or in enclaves within Kosovo.

UNICEF was well placed to support the humanitarian efforts. Offices had already been established in Kosovo before the exodus. Country programme offices existed in Albania, the fYROM, Montenegro, Bosnia and Herzegovina and Serbia.

Prior to the massive spontaneous return in June 1999, UNICEF's strategy was to focus on refugee and internally displaced children and women in camps, collective centres and with host families, while simultaneously strengthening social sector infrastructure and services in areas receiving refugees. Post-return, the UNICEF strategy in Kosovo has been to support the establishment of new civil structures in the education, health and social welfare sectors. UNICEF also provided essential and lifesaving relief assistance to children and women.

Setting up the Evaluation and Recruiting the Team

The DFID desk officer who managed relations with UNICEF, and the UNICEF donor relations staff, took the lead in setting up this evaluation, as opposed to their respective evaluation units. (Those units were consulted on the Terms of Reference – TOR – and the evaluation in general.) DFID made a lot of the early running, so to speak, drawing up draft TOR for circulation, contracting a Team Leader, consulting on and proposing time-frames. As preparations progressed, what was initially seen as a quite modest exercise gradually became more extensive and demanding. While it had originally been a DFID initiative, the evaluation soon became a joint effort. However, joint evaluations are especially susceptible to multiple expectations, and to being 'all things to all people'.

In this case, the exact nature of such a 'joint' endeavour was never completely clear and the precise roles and participation of the respective organizations were never spelt out to all parties. While not sufficient to derail the evaluation, this degree of vagueness caused problems with some UNICEF staff and managers when it came to presenting the conclusions. Some UNICEF staff hinted that they saw the evaluation as a donor-motivated, if not imposed, initiative. They wondered whether it was a response to any specific DFID concern regarding UNICEF's emergency performance in the 1999 Kosovo crisis in particular, and in emergencies in general. The significant and ongoing DFID funding of UNICEF capacity-building in emergency preparedness and response, definitely tilted the 'power' relationship during the evaluation in DFID's direction and raised the question of whether it was a DFID 'inspection' of UNICEF's emergency capacity. Despite these realities, the evaluation was 'joint' in many concrete ways, not least in terms of the team membership.

Our four-person team consisted of two DFID-funded consultants, a DFID staff member who was based in Pristina and a UNICEF emergency officer. UNICEF also provided the important logistical support. The team members were:

- a British female consultant specializing in psycho-social issues, education, mines awareness and 'child-friendly spaces';
- a Finnish female UNICEF emergency officer with responsibility for operational support and institutional issues;
- a British male doctor employed by DFID and based in Pristina as a health adviser with responsibility for health, nutrition, water and sanitation; and
- myself, an Irish male economist/social scientist consultant who was Team Leader. I addressed operational support and institutional issues.

All of us knew the region quite well and had experience with a variety of UN, non-governmental organization (NGO) and donor humanitarian and human rights agencies worldwide. We were supported throughout by the DFID focal point and desk officer.

Both the DFID and UNICEF team members were assigned under a degree of duress. Both had pressing commitments, one professional in Pristina (to complete a DFID report) and the other family matters. In fact, were it not for the professionalism of both, serious team problems might have developed in that neither was joining under ideal conditions.

Starting Work: Reviewing the TOR and Planning

The evaluation began with a meeting in London at DFID's headquarters two days prior to departure to the region. The other DFID consultant and I were the only team members present. A UNICEF manager from the region also attended, given that the UNICEF team member could join the evaluation only in the field: her 'home leave' was being cut short so that she could join the mission, an unexpected requirement for her and her family! The DFID staff member based in Pristina was also unable to come to the meeting. At that one-day meeting we reviewed our draft terms of reference, and made practical arrangements. We were also briefed by DFID's London staff.

The original TOR amounted to analysing whether the programme objectives had been achieved, and identifying any relevant strengths and weaknesses along the way. They also included the usual wide range of questions on appropriateness, effectiveness, impact, efficiency and even sustainability. As a result of our discussions we agreed a revised set of TOR, which included evaluation of the role of the donor (DFID) in the field performance. The revised TOR were circulated with a short report of the meeting to the other team members and to DFID and UNICEF. This helped allay, but not entirely, some of the fears among UNICEF staff regarding the seemingly ambitious breadth of the TOR to be covered in such a short time.

During the meeting we also clarified key points and objectives, including prioritizing questions. This was a recognition that not all the criteria and questions could be covered in equal depth. Methods were also considered and the participatory nature of the evaluation was agreed – that UNICEF staff and partners would be involved as much as possible through consultations, meetings and email contacts.

While the meeting was invaluable, it was insufficient. Significant issues and concerns remained inadequately addressed. The planning of the drafting, editing and review process, in particular, remained vague. In addition, the meeting failed in its planning to recognize the time required for getting information and input to and from UNICEF staff in a multitude of field, regional and central locations. This became a serious problem during the fieldwork. Hard data on programme achievements might have been prepared prior to the arrival of the team. Some were available upon arrival, but the data were incomplete, especially in certain offices. This lack of data weakened the evaluation, especially when it came to the presentation of criticisms in the draft report. It left room for attempts to dismiss the findings as weak, and insufficiently substantiated.

The lack of time for planning, and especially for collecting information with which to plan, raises questions about whether there was a reasonable alternative. More meticulous and involved preparations were definitely needed. Yet, at that stage at least, they would have delayed the evaluation to the point that it might not have taken place. The evaluation had to be carried out rapidly so as to have access to the already reduced presence of key UNICEF sources in the region and at central locations (Geneva and New York). Staff were moving on, files (especially invaluable records of email traffic) were being lost, deleted or thrown out and, in general, memories fading. It might not have happened at all, if greater time for preparations had delayed the field mission until after the Christmas holiday season.

Field Methods and Organization

The other consultant and I, having more flexibility, arrived in Tirana two days ahead of the other team members. This gave us time for reading and preparations, which, though never enough, did help immensely. Lack of reading among the team was compensated for by the knowledge of the region, the people and the issues that we had each acquired during our previous work. This knowledge also compensated to some extent for the shortage of detailed quantitative information and the rotation of UNICEF staff out of the region.

The methodology we applied was standard for such evaluations, reflecting both UNICEF's evaluation guidelines (UNICEF 1991) and internal DFID humanitarian guidelines for organizational appraisal. The then recently published Organization for Economic Cooperation and Development (OECD)/Development Assistance Committee (DAC) guidelines for the evaluation of humanitarian programmes were also helpful (OECD–DAC 1999).

The methods we used included the following:

• preparatory generic literature and documentation search and review;

- interviewing, for opinions and triangulation, mainly semi-structured, of programme beneficiaries, agency staff and partners;
- email and telephonic consultations with key people not available for interviewing (including a 'strengths, weaknesses and recommendations' questionnaire);
- short participatory workshops and group consultations with UNICEF partners and staff;
- attendance at programme coordination meetings; and
- field visits, including Serb enclaves in Kosovo.

We also established a set of ground rules for team reporting and meetings. A standard one-page reporting form was designed for summarizing interviews. This included space for a bulleted summary of main conclusions and details of interviewees. This form was helpful, but not as useful as I had imagined. Practical difficulties, mainly time pressures for completing and actually absorbing its contents, reduced its potential utility as a tool. There were also problems with the form itself. It demanded too much detail and allowed for repetition, e.g. details of interviews and conclusions emanating therefrom. As a result, it was overly time-consuming. A daily record of interviews and visits – who, where, when and main conclusions – might have been better. A shorter, simpler format is recommended.

We also formalized clear divisions of responsibilities once we had assembled in Pristina. These were based on technical, sectoral and cross-cutting issues criteria. These worked quite well, as they were largely mutually exclusive. Differences of approach or methodology did arise within the team and this generated a degree of stress. The differences stemmed from the fact that the objectives and expectations were not entirely identical for the two organizations and their members of the team: a hard-hitting, 'accountability'-focused evaluation was expected by some staff of the donor agency, while a less contentious 'lessons-learned' exercise was sought by the implementing agency. As a result, 'hard' quantitative data were sought initially by the technical expert in particular, who represented the donor agency, as a means of verifying achievements and effectiveness.

Three things facilitated the resolution of what was a potentially significant difference in approach. First, the hard data were hard come by – they either did not exist, or were impossible to get in such a short time. Second, as concrete strengths and weaknesses emerged despite the relative absence of such 'evidence', the need for quantitative data diminished. Sufficient evidence to support firm conclusions began to emerge, both from direct observation and from interviewing and reading of more narrative documentation. Third, continual, close team discussions reduced the possibility of seriously diverging positions on issues and approaches. Through daily debate and mutual consultation, emerging conclusions seemed gradually to converge rather than diverge. The issue of approach became secondary and a more qualitative approach was eventually accepted by us all.

Fieldwork

The fieldwork was frenetic. We spent five days in Albania, three days in fYROM and seven days in Kosovo. The TL and the UNICEF team member also continued discussions and interviews in New York (two days) and Geneva (five days).

A specific attempt was made to undertake beneficiary interviews. These did not involve a systematic sampling system as the information was not available but did involve a planned attempt to cover rural and urban dwellers, male and female respondents, and a variety of locations. Some interview opportunities occurred by chance. Some included people who, although they had been refugees, had not necessarily been beneficiaries of UNICEF programmes.

These interviews provided insights on issues and questions that had been emerging in the evaluation and corroborated or contradicted views and conclusions of other interlocutors. They also highlighted the glaring fact that the massive relief operation 'missed' as much as 60 per cent of the refugee population who were in private accommodation, many of whom did not receive aid. Had we remained in the international environment for interviews and research, the temptation to focus just on camps and collective centres would have been great and much would have been missed.

In these interviews one beneficiary spoke of how disturbing it had been to cross the border and find international staff at the reception centres working in a jovial, almost playful mood. This one statement illustrated the trauma on the one hand, and the unthinking remoteness of some aid 'professionals' on the other. It was a reminder that it is not just the aid that is important, but also how it is provided. The need for old-fashioned solidarity and empathy may equal the need for physical aid and protection. It is often just a matter of listening.

Along the way in our fieldwork we faced the usual range of problems. The perspectives of those evaluated were, naturally, diverse. This group included primarily UNICEF staff, but also DFID staff. They were interviewed in some depth, office by office. As ever, different opinions and even recounting of the same facts emerged. Triangulation (comparing interviews) was required, but frequently the time constraints did not allow for sufficient follow-up, and value judgements had to be made in the absence of absolutely conclusive evidence.

The move from Albania to Macedonia brought its demands. The day-long trip was pleasant, along the stunningly beautiful Ochrid lake. But as one of the team began to fall sick, timetables and transport arrangements had to be altered. The team had to split up to allow him to go on to Skopje to recuperate. UNICEF was exceptionally flexible and supportive. Nevertheless, logistics and team coordination became more complicated.

The Macedonia leg of the mission lasted less than three days. One full day was all that was available, plus the three-quarters of a day upon arrival, and the half-day upon departure, but we used that for an intensive debriefing. This was too short, but it was better than originally foreseen, as Macedonia had been excluded altogether from initial plans. It was added to the schedule following our protestations that it would be too important to miss. And this position was vindicated: the specificity of the Macedonia programme provided a rich source of complementary and contrasting information, issues and opinions, without which the evaluation would have been the poorer.

The logistics of entering Kosovo (and subsequently exiting) were complicated and time-consuming. While Albania and Macedonia had no visa restrictions for our all-EU team, the infamous congestion at the Macedonia/Kosovo border required deft work from the UNICEF drivers from both sides to negotiate their way through throngs of people and queues of trucks extending to tens of kilometres. This was a clear lesson that logistics should not be underestimated in the planning for evaluations.

The gradually accelerating pressure of time complicated team coordination. We held evening meetings when one or more team members had still not arrived back from the field. The rigorous reporting procedures, both verbal and written on the one-page standard sheet we had custom-designed for the task, were not always held to, as we came straight from the field without the necessary time to collect our thoughts.

Illness struck for the first of what was to be a succession of bouts of flu and gastro-intestinal upsets. The only answer was straight to bed, followed by a reduced workload until the patient recovered. Luckily, it was one of us at a time. However, the relatively short distances from one country to another allowed for only intermittent rest and recuperation.

In the rush of the final week in Pristina, the report sheets were harder to collect, as we went straight into overall conclusions in the evening meetings, rather than beginning with the findings of the day. And illness struck again. While field conditions were nothing compared to the testing conditions of some African, Latin American and Asian locations, the late nights, early mornings, pressured days all pointed to the need for exceptional psychological and physical stamina. While the team was not 'elderly', and age had probably nothing whatsoever to do with the illnesses, all team members were at an age (thirties and forties) when such stamina is no longer what it might have been a decade earlier. A classical trade-off is evident – experienced evaluators will, almost by definition, not be of an age when unrelenting, high-pressure field missions can be conducted without taking a heavy toll.

Team Dynamics

As a team, we had the great good luck to get on excellently throughout, despite not having worked together before. Our common experience in the region and with international humanitarian organizations helped with this, and the development of a team spirit which was a major asset in the very short and hectic field visits. The team 'gelled' and a growing, if initially hesitant, friendship developed among all four of us. When it came to teasing out conclusions, naturally, this team spirit presented its own dilemmas. On the one hand it facilitated clear and frank discussion. On the other, it heightened the feeling of playing a 'double-hatted' role for the representatives of the two agencies concerned.

In essence the team came to include the DFID desk officer focal point, who was most unobtrusively supportive. His short visit to the field for a few days with the mission was very positive. He helped to refocus the team on key questions, and also to reassure them about the overall progress of the evaluation. This helped in the coordination and planning of the remaining period of the evaluation. It also contributed to closer understandings of issues, incipient conclusions and overall directions.

We were helped in our work by the fact that the UNICEF team member was also the designated UNICEF focal point for the evaluation, thus again facilitating coordination and general understandings. In particular, she could flag possible issues that needed to be approached with particular sensitivity. She also provided invaluable historical knowledge as to how and why certain things within her agency had evolved in the way they had. However, she had to cope with the position of being 'judge and judged', as a staffer of the implementing agency being evaluated. Fortunately she was exceptional in her professionalism and honesty in facing this ambiguity. She managed it superbly through being both meticulous to detail and fair in judgement. Nevertheless, to attempt to bridge this gap was a difficult task indeed when facing colleagues with whom she would continue to work.

All in all, therefore, while in this case team dynamics were not an impediment, but rather a strength, it must be recognized that they do require as much preparation and attention as TOR, logistics, administration and methodologies for the mission.

Coming to a Team Position

The final week in Pristina was welcome for many reasons, not the least of which was the full day set aside (a Sunday) for us to prepare our conclusions. While essential, it was not, however, sufficient. Differences of opinion did emerge, in particular on the overall strengths and weaknesses of UNICEF in emergencies and the relative weight to be given to them in the overall conclusions. To resolve these differences, a system of scoring the overall response out of an ideal 'five' was conducted, team member by team member. As regards strengths, all four 'marks' came in quite close. This helped to narrow the discussion. The main differences came down to how harshly 'weaknesses' would be judged.

Different perceptions of criteria and the relative importance of aspects of the UNICEF performance lay at the heart of these differences. One school of thought saw the more classical emergency preparedness and response activities as fundamental and therefore determinant in arriving at the overall conclusions. Another school saw the developmental nature of the agency and its focus on children and mothers as a real or potential strength, a counterbalance to the more narrowly focused and more classical emergency agencies. These less visible 'relief to development' and 'people-focused' aspects of UNICEF preparedness and response, it was argued, should have a significance equal to, or even greater than, more traditional emergency functions such as supplies and logistics.

Following relatively short but quite intense discussion, an overall assessment and quantitative result was arrived at. This overall 'mark' was included in the first draft of the report, which proved to be a serious error of judgement on my part, as it was neither methodologically sound nor agreed. It unnecessarily weakened the presentation of the evaluation in that it attempted to produce a quantitative result that the methodology could not sustain.

The process of going from conclusions to recommendations was not unduly difficult. In most cases, they flowed automatically. The more difficult part was reaching a conclusion on strengths and weaknesses. Once that was achieved, the recommendations came quite logically.

The authority and perhaps responsibility that any Team Leader can and should have in formulating overall conclusions is an issue. S/he will generally coordinate the final overall report and often write much, if not all, of this. As such, s/he has both power to influence, and also an unenviable responsibility to reconcile and balance, the findings. Although in this evaluation there were no significant disagreements, other than those noted above, these could quite easily arise.

Writing Up: *Modus Operandi*

It had been agreed from the beginning of the mission that each team member would write up the sectors and issues allotted to him or her. Common conclusions crystallized throughout – at team meetings, and through discussions during travel and meals. However, the relatively consistent concurrence of broad opinions was one thing; concurrence on detail was another. Finer points of interpretation and emphasis emerged only in the first drafts, which were produced at the start of the last week the team was together. Herein lies yet another dilemma. Such early drafting was perhaps too early in that it did not allow sufficient time for considered analysis and teasing out of more finely developed conclusions. Yet it was already late, as was proved, when it came to amalgamating texts and editing them into an initial report for circulation. In short, however premature and tedious it might seem, the earlier the drafting begins while the team is still together, the better.

While UNICEF had suggested to us that a sectoral format was 'not the most appropriate given the child rights framework which guides UNICEF activities', our report nevertheless followed a sectoral approach. This was for two reasons. First, UNICEF itself organizes its programmes and reports according to such sectoral categories. Second, a sectoral approach was a practical way of organizing the report drafting given that it mirrored the division of responsibilities within the evaluation team. The conclusions, related recommendations and lessons learned were authored by the respective team member(s) covering each specific sector.

Most of the overall editing of this material, obviously, had to be done by myself as Team Leader, in this case ably supported by the DFID desk officer. Editing was a challenge. The report is often the only remaining physical embodiment of the evaluation output. The final product should be of a high quality – clear, accurate, incisive and informative. But that is not enough. It should also be engaging, so as to increase the chance that it will be read and used as a tool. The devil is in the detail. This is never as evident as when one must edit materials drafted by others. What is evident to the author (or appears to be evident) is not so necessarily for the reader. The author of a draft can take liberties with a text, knowing that it is not final, that a finalizing editor may not. Gaps in fact and logic become glaringly obvious as text is 'cut and pasted'.

The 'sub-reports' were submitted by each team member. The main challenge was to minimize gaps and potential misunderstandings in the consolidated text, despite not having access to either the base material (notes and documentation collected by each individual author) or the logic of each of the authors (except for one's own text). This required a frenzied process of emails, cross-checking, reformatting (very time-consuming), and complicated 'wordsmithing' in order to come up with formulae that could overcome the inevitable level of ambiguity. Finally, the inherent tensions of being 'all things to all people' (multiple expectations on the evaluation by the various potential readers) suddenly became glaringly obvious. Panic nearly set in. Greater clarity on the drafting process throughout the evaluation would have reduced these difficulties, perhaps, and more time should have been allocated to the writing process.

Feedback makes matters worse. Contradictory comments on the drafts from the team initially, and then from DFID and UNICEF, must be reconciled, new drafts received, new circulations coordinated, and so on, with what can easily become an endless round of consultations and revisions. There has to be an easier way. If one is not careful, at a certain point one can lose track and even perspective of the document.

In short, more time for sharing drafts back and forward within the team, and at least one other day-long meeting (or professionally facilitated workshop), would have helped. So too would a clear plan of when drafts would be submitted, by whom, circulated for comments to whom, and within what realistic timeframe. (Field offices should be given at least a week to review documents.) This would have helped us avoid some of the difficulties we encountered with the review of what was an unduly premature initial draft.

Debriefing and Finalization

UNICEF was invited to reply formally to the initial draft. The agency took the whole evaluation process, but especially this stage, very seriously. Senior staff were called to Geneva for the review. Despite deadlines that were too short for a large bureaucracy (they had to be extended), UNICEF replied in detail orally (in meetings and interviews in New York and Geneva) and in writing. While its responses were measured, courteous and diplomatic, underlying tensions were evident, and questions of fact (or error, rather) emerged, albeit limited. The main complaints, made repeatedly, were to do with emphasis and general balance. Some UNICEF staff seemed to see the evaluation as overly critical, and at times unjustifiably so. Considerable rewriting was proposed. UNICEF recommended that the first draft be renamed a 'zero draft'.

DFID's feedback reflected its interest in an evaluation that would include an 'accountability' focus. The feedback asked for specific answers to questions such as whether objectives had been met and how well. DFID officials wanted a more explicitly worded, rather than nuanced, text.

The issue of criteria arose – do you evaluate against ideal standards, including those of the agency itself, and to what extent do you make allowances for constraints, including the inadequacies of other actors, in what is an increasingly interdependent web of operations and activities and programmes? Do you compare performance against that of peers, and take a 'least worst performance' approach, as opposed to a more critical evaluation of accountability against set objectives and standards?

Follow-up consultations were necessary by email, phone and additional interviews to clarify comments and questions raised in the responses to the draft report. These fed into the subsequent drafts. While many differences of perspective, some substantive, were addressed by UNICEF staff, DFID and the evaluators, interestingly enough, most of the overall conclusions and recommendations were gradually both implicitly and explicitly agreed. In fact, final comments emphasized that the problems highlighted were the same old weaknesses that had not been rectified. 'Old hands' in UNICEF expressed resignation or surprise or a degree of cynicism that here were the same hoary old chestnuts being rolled out again.

The linkage, albeit indirect and secondary, between the evaluation and the ongoing DFID-funded UNICEF capacity-building project was important. Without the latter, the evaluation might not have taken place at all. Also, it prompted discussions and focus. That being said, clearly UNICEF was correctly concerned that the Kosovo case should not be generalized unduly. As stated above, a high degree of consensus was arrived at that many of the strengths and weaknesses identified had in fact been encountered previously. This was heartening, in that the capacity-building project could continue to address these issues, but it was disheartening that it should still have to!

Reflections on Method and Process

All in all, this was a 'quick-and-dirty' evaluation. The total time working as a team was less than one month from start to finish. Could it have been otherwise? Should it have been otherwise? Would a longer and more expensive process, such as the United Nations High Commissioner for Refugees (UNHCR) independent evaluation of its operations in the Kosovo crisis (Suhrke et al. 2000) have led to more sound and worthwhile findings and results?

The role and involvement of evaluation units in evaluations that emanate from other departments (e.g. operational or geographic units) is relevant to this case. While they did comment on the TOR, should they have been involved earlier and in a more substantive manner? Should the evaluation have been set up in a different way? This question of centralized

responsibility for evaluations versus Country Desk initiative and responsibility is not unique to this case.

The experience and knowledge of the team went a long way towards
making up for the short time available. The quality of any team is more
important than quantity; coordination of a large team is complex and

---

Box 10.2 Main conclusions and recommendations

UNICEF – general

1. Based on its strengths, UNICEF has had, and should continue to
   have, an important role in emergencies. Greater clarity is required
   on the desired scale and specific expertise of that emergency capacity
   in UNICEF.
2. UNICEF's strengths in emergencies need to be exploited and developed more systematically. Every country office should be capable
   of and required to engage in comprehensive preparedness measures,
   as an integral part of its country programme. Similarly, the quality
   of UNICEF's guidance on core UNICEF emergency issues and the
   depth and systematic professionalism of its preparedness activities
   need to be improved.

Despite UNICEF's declared objective to 'mainstream' emergency
preparedness and response in its institutional capacities and general
programming, this is far from having been achieved. A comprehensive
review of all the major components of emergency preparedness and
response is required. This should lead to an action plan for improving
significant weaknesses that exist at the institutional level.

DFID – lessons on evaluation in emergencies Evaluation of humanitarian aid is increasingly frequent, not to say fashionable. There are a
number of lessons to be learned from this particular evaluation.

1. Though rarely conducted, joint donor/partner agency evaluations
   are feasible. The shared analysis can be enriching. A multi-disciplinary team including both 'insiders and outsiders' of both donor
   and partner agencies can produce a healthy mixture of perspective,
   knowledge and experience.
2. International relief coordination and management are increasingly
   complex, involving a multitude of increasingly interdependent actors.
   The effectiveness and results of any one actor depend on those of
   others. Additionally, overall impact can often be measured meaning-
   fully only at the level of a particular situation.

time-consuming – the rule of diminishing returns kicks in rapidly. This team had many strengths, including flexibility and the capacity to empathize, while retaining a professional stance. Many evaluators do not, however. Training and broader development of a cadre of evaluators would be logical and desirable, as it is for virtually any profession. From our

3. *Ex-post* evaluations in emergencies are limited by the rapid loss of institutional memory. Rapid staff rotation compounds the problem. It is recommended that pilot 'real-time' evaluations be conducted. This would require the deployment of a small evaluation team in support of agencies during emergencies as a capacity for participatory analysis and strategy development with staff at all levels, especially the 'deep field'.

4. Just as coordination among agencies in actual operations is important, so too is coordination of evaluations among donors. The Kosovo crisis has so far led to almost thirty formal evaluations. Joint efforts are potentially more efficient and less taxing on agency staff in that the effort is concentrated into a shorter time period.

DFID – general Catastrophe was avoided for the Kosovars in Albania and fYROM. Apart from the immense contribution of the refugees and those who welcomed them, the level of funding made available to a wide range of agencies during this emergency contributed to containing the crisis. It allowed for an unusual and welcome range of services to refugees (such as mobile phone calls for tracing relatives). UNICEF has played its part, including in Central Serbia, in favour of victims and refugees, in line with international humanitarian, refugee and human rights law, especially the Convention on the Rights of the Child (CRC).

1. It is expected by beneficiaries and practitioners alike that new ground has at last been broken in raising the standards of relief in emergencies and catastrophes worldwide. The very core of humanitarianism is that protection and relief benefit all victims irrespective of colour, creed, ethnicity and geographic (or strategic) considerations. Were this not to be the case, the laments emanating from the plethora of currently underfunded emergencies (in western Africa, India and the Caucasus, for instance) might lead to cynicism. Humanitarian values and basic human rights belong to all humanity, to be applied universally and transparently. The focus on Kosovars should not be to the detriment of other victims worldwide.

experience, it would seem to be essential for evaluators of humanitarian programmes to have seven skills. They should be:

- analytical;
- knowledgeable about the people, and relevant languages, topic and geographical area;
- patient;
- skilled and experienced in evaluation methods and techniques, both qualitative and quantitative;
- good listeners;
- good communicators, including being good report writers; and
- have emphathy and concern for others.

A detailed plan of the evaluation would have been an asset. In joint evaluations, where there are varying expectations and perspectives, this is particularly recommended. The plan would go beyond the TOR, and could become an annex to it. It would set out possible roles, approaches, schedules, practical matters and report-writing arrangements. It would also outline the process of arriving at conclusions and finalizing the report. However, unduly detailed planning at the start of an evaluation is neither feasible nor desirable, especially when the team is still building up confidence in itself. A balance has to be struck, but one that ensures that adequate thought is given by all in the team to these issues.

Evaluations are generally front-loaded. Most time and effort seem to go into preparations, design, agreement on the TOR, and initial reading and interviewing. The designers of TOR are often overly optimistic about what can be covered. The fundamentally important final phase – getting to detailed conclusions, drafting, review and revision of drafts – is, as a rule, underestimated. Time simply runs out and ambitious methodologies and coverage smash into the concrete wall of reality – a report must be written, and finalized fast. Although the evaluation process is central, the report is the remaining tangible product!

The usual inadequacy of files and reports in emergencies, especially at the beginning, needs to be anticipated and allowed for in the objectives, methodologies, and the TOR and plan in general. Adequate time for reading also needs to be allocated.

'Listen to the beneficiaries as soon as possible' is the single most important message. It is feasible and usually less difficult than one imagines. By planning it and giving it priority, contact can be made. The experience is invariably rewarding. It sets a realistic framework for impressions and conclusions and in our case did orient conclusions, especially the fact that the international actors addressed only a relatively small portion of overall needs. Skills, practices, methods and general guidance on this need to be developed, as a priority within the overall efforts to develop and improve evaluation expertise and capacities.

The report format was based on the sections to be drafted by each team member. This practicality obliged the structure to follow a sectoral approach, although comments were made that a more 'holistic' structure should be followed (integrating the sectors around cross-cutting themes). Innovative ways, as well as formats, for 'findings, conclusions and recommendations' might be explored to make reports more accessible (enjoyable and engaging!) to audiences.

The process of commenting on drafts and addressing those comments would need to be included in the proposed 'plan' of the evaluation. The 'authority' of comments needs to be clearly understood, especially when conflicting ones are received. The degree of independence of an evaluation team, if not spelt out prior to an evaluation, can get confusing, even complicated.

What follow-up on conclusions and recommendations there will be is rarely spelled out, much less planned for. The objectives of evaluations need to be linked to follow-up. Who are the potential users and for what will it be used? The more focused an evaluation, debatably the easier it is to conduct and the easier it is to follow up.

Donor inputs, performance and agendas need to be explicitly addressed in evaluations. In particular, political and geo-strategic 'agendas' should be evaluated against humanitarian principles, just as much as operational performance. Special expertise and access to specific, sometimes restricted, information is needed to address such issues. Transparency and accountability require this. The TOR and 'plan' should explicitly include such questions.

Humanitarian evaluation is a learning process in terms of methods and practice, as well as in terms of the findings of the case in point. Although this evaluation went relatively smoothly, there is much to be learned from it and much to put into practice in the next evaluations we each take part in.

11

Conclusions

Adrian Wood, Raymond Apthorpe and John Borton

The range of experience from doing humanitarian evaluations is immense. Each year hundreds of people are involved in undertaking these studies, while many more are commissioning and managing them. Thousands of people are interviewed. Many others are the recipients of the reports and have to make decisions based on the findings they produce. This book touches just the tip of the iceberg of this experience, focusing upon the perspectives of those involved in the teams who do these evaluations.

To reflect on this experience, contributors were asked to consider the various aspects of the evaluation process. They were asked to identify what made the process successful or problematic, what struck them as influential on the way they did their evaluations and what influenced the results they obtained. These and other issues have been discussed in the different case studies. Experiences have been identified from which others might learn.

In concluding we will reflect on these different experiences and try to draw some overall conclusions that will clarify this experiential learning process. However, it should be made clear that we are not trying to produce a guide or handbook for humanitarian evaluation. That would require a different frame and discourse and a much more wide-ranging review. Rather, we are trying to explore some of the experience of the doing of humanitarian evaluations as seen by individuals, and to use this to sensitize evaluation practitioners, managers and students. Our goal is to stimulate thought and awareness that can be applied at all times and in all places, not to set up a model of steps that are applicable only under specific circumstances.

The Diversity of the Studies

The experiences reported in this book are diverse. In Chapter 1 we identified a number of variables, such as type of evaluation, agencies involved and field conditions, which at the outset appeared important influences on the quality of humanitarian evaluations. It was on this basis that we chose the case studies to be included in this volume. The actual experience reported in these cases has shown the ways in which these and other variables can influence the outputs from the evaluations. Before reviewing these variables and their impact in the doing and managing of humanitarian evaluations, it is useful to review the case studies and to identify the most striking features of each.

Somalia This involved the use of five different consultancy companies in an evaluation process that was coordinated by the Policy and Operations Evaluation Department of the Netherlands Ministry of Foreign Affairs (IOB). Each company was responsible for studying specific programmes or projects funded by the Netherlands government and run by UN agencies or non-governmental organizations (NGOs). One company, ETC-UK, was given the responsibility to look at a wider range of activities. It was involved in a considerable amount of fieldwork, unlike two of the other four individual studies for this evaluation, which were office-based. IOB tried to coordinate this fragmented approach to the work. However, it failed to organize a joint briefing at the start or a common debriefing at the conclusions. IOB staff undertook fieldwork themselves in the context of aid delivery as it affected the Somalia operation and spent several weeks in Somalia and Nairobi to do this, as well as completing a desk study in The Hague. Conditions for the fieldwork were quite difficult due to security, the limited data and their lack of representativeness. In some of the field analysis it was found that to try to focus on the perceptions of the different groups involved offered a useful way of understanding the situation.

The five consultancy studies formed the first part of a two-stage study. The second part involved ETC-UK working jointly with IOB to reach general conclusions. The whole evaluation process was subject to an external peer review process to ensure that the reasoning was robust. The report and the policy reaction by the minister for development cooperation were presented to Parliament and discussed by the Standing Committee on Foreign Affairs. The report was published and a video using a series of slides taken in Somalia during the evaluation was also produced that broadly outlined the evaluation's findings.

Horn of Africa This evaluation was contracted out by the Swedish International Development Agency (Sida) to the Institute of Social Sciences Advisory Service (ISSAS), a consultancy/research company based in the Institute of Social Studies, which is a higher education institution located in The Hague and specializing in teaching and research on the developing world. ISSAS recruited a team of four independent consultants, three of whom were university-based and had considerable research experience in the region. Only one of the team was a full-time consultant. The four consultants worked as a loose net, not a team, each based in different countries in the region. The Team Leader coordinated their activities at a distance and undertook his own fieldwork primarily with the UN agencies and on the coordination of the assistance provided by Sida and its partners.

This evaluation benefited from an initial, four-week, desk study that used recently organized data in Sida's headquarters. This gave some order to the complex situation, with more than 500 projects and over 60 field partners, thereby allowing the team to select a sample of the projects of the various partner agencies. But the diversity of the projects and the passage of time since their implementation meant that it was difficult to contact many beneficiaries and undertake the accountability study Sida had originally envisaged. As a result the Terms of Reference (TOR) evolved, with Sida's approval, to become more of a programme and policy review – rather than a project or even partner review.

This more generalized approach helped Sida headquarters staff answer the question: 'How should we think about humanitarian programmes?' However, the team was not allowed to follow up the issues relating to this policy and programme approach in Sida's headquarters. Draft and final reports were each submitted in two volumes, with accountability issues covered in Volume Two, based on the team members' field studies. Sida was more interested in Volume One, a synthesis of the higher-level findings, which was written primarily by the Team Leader, with two other team members involved to varying degrees. At the end a core team of two remained, using their own time to produce the final report. Volume One was selected by Sida for publication in its evaluation series. Beyond this there was a further publication of the findings in a training and information booklet while a workshop was run in the region in following year, based on that booklet.

Cambodia This study was undertaken by a team commissioned directly by Sida and managed by Sida's evaluation unit. The study evaluated six years of activities by both NGOs and UN agencies in Cambodia, which had been supported by Sida's funds. Most of the team had experience in the country. This was both advantageous and problematic, the latter because of the vested interests some team members had in the findings of the study. The study involved little preparation and the rush to start fieldwork, along with the sector division of responsibility, left it up to the team members to make their own choice about methodologies. This led to conflicts when the team tried to draw together its conclusions and create a synthesis of their findings. As a result, in the report to Sida an annex was included with minority-view conclusions.

Rwanda As an evaluation of emergency humanitarian assistance, this was almost certainly the largest ever in terms of the number of agencies, the size of the teams and the scale of the funding considered. Study 3 was managed by ODA within a Management Group composed of five bilateral donor organizations, which in turn reported to and were guided by the Joint Evaluation of Emergency Assistance to Rwanda (JEEAR) Steering Committee. The study covered all the organizations – NGOs, bilateral donors and the UN – that had been involved in the relief operations following the Rwandan conflict and genocide, and so could be called a system-wide study. The Study 3 team, with 20 members, was probably the biggest evaluation team to study humanitarian assistance. It never operated as a single unit. Seven was the largest number of people who were in the field together at any one time. The study involved several months of preparation that involved careful team member selection by the Team Leader and development of an analytical framework and methodology for the fieldwork that had to be cleared with the Overseas Development Administration (ODA). Two field visits were undertaken, the first by a core team for reconnaissance purposes and the second for the main data collection, during which many team members operated independently.

This disparate team was managed tightly by the Team Leader, who took responsibility for almost all of the writing up of the final report using the reports submitted by each team member. The Management Group acted as a buffer between the team and those agencies whose performance was being evaluated – many of whom were represented on the Steering Committee. This helped protect the team from undue pressure from the more defensive organizations. However, in the case of the major disagreement that occurred with the United Nations High Commissioner for Refugees (UNHCR), the Management Group's buffer role did not function properly and the team were drawn into direct negotiations over the text of the final report.

The Study 3 report was published together with the reports of the other teams and the synthesis report that constituted JEEAR's output. Over five thousand copies were disseminated throughout the humanitarian system. A one-year follow-up process – JEFF – was established by the Steering Committee to monitor the extent to which the recommendations of the evaluation were followed up by the agencies.

Liberia This was set up as an 'independent' evaluation by the World Food Programme (WFP) to assess the work of its own field offices and their field partners. The team, recruited by WFP, was mixed, including both WFP staff and a representative of one other UN agency, while the majority of team members, including the Team Leader, were independent, university-based consultants. The study focused on policy issues despite its original TOR, which required an emphasis upon the individual project activities. This adjustment of the TOR evolved in the field without direct reference to the WFP headquarters. This change caused some tension in the team, especially on the part of the UN staffers, who considered themselves to be not emergency specialists but 'development people'.

The study addressed a six-year period during which multiple forms of assistance had been provided. This timeframe, combined with insecurity in the field, made it difficult for the team to focus on the project activities. The team was able to draw key lessons about the conceptualization of the field situation by the WFP field and headquarters staff that radically altered the framework for thinking about and planning food aid. The team's work was well received at its debriefing in Rome, although it was subject to attack, for which no defence was allowed, at a later meeting of the WFP Board. The report, which was an internal document, has never been published despite commitments to do so.

Papua New Guinea   This study, commissioned by the Australian Agency for International Development (AusAID), was undertaken by a team of consultants recruited by a university-based consultancy company (ANU–TECH). This was the most 'timely' study in this volume, as it was meant to look at ongoing relief activities and the team did reach the field just after the last distributions had been completed. It included some Papua New Guinea (PNG) specialists, especially the Team Leader, but only one emergency specialist who, however, played a key role and was very in-fluential with the Team Leader in the design of the fieldwork.

These two worked closely together, especially in the report-writing stage, and became the core team. The team developed a clear field method that focused on the end of the supply chain and a survey of sampled bene-ficiaries in some of the more remote locations, an approach that AusAID approved before the fieldwork started. The team did not really function as such, with individuals or sub-teams doing their work separately for the most part. However, all the teams and sub-teams reported regularly and in detail to the Team Leader, who in turn kept all members informed by email about all developments, especially during the difficult drafting stages.

There was a major conflict with the commissioning agency when the draft report was first submitted. This battle involved eight drafts of the report, before it was accepted. While the consultancy company supported the team in this fray, it proved difficult to overcome a lack of communication between the evaluation team and the commissioning agency and some misunderstandings over the TOR. A summary report was published by AusAID. This was prepared by an ex-AusAID staffer in her new role as a journalist and with an introduction by the chief technical adviser.

Tajikistan This study was commissioned by the International Federation of Red Cross and Red Crescent Societies (IFRC) Secretariat to assess its work in relation to the Tajikistan Red Crescent Society (TRCS), a member national society, in preparation for a newly funded programme. The study was funded by two Western Red Cross Societies, which supplied the core members of the evaluation team. The team was put together by IFRC. It also included representatives from the Tajikistan Red Crescent Society, the head of the Federation's local office, an expert from the IFRC Secretariat and an independent Team Leader. The team did not work entirely together. One member travelled independently, and the representative of the Tajikistan RCS was not with the team during the briefings and debriefing in Geneva. A further problem was that three members of the team had their own agendas during the mission.

The fieldwork primarily involved meeting IFRC and TRCS field staff and managers rather than the beneficiaries of any aid programmes. Although not in the TOR, the team was able to look at management issues that affected the programme, including the relationships between the various IFRC offices. The Team Leader wrote most of final report with contributions from team members. It was an internal document for the IFRC and has not been published.

Hurricane Mitch This evaluation originated in a different way from the others. It was developed in response to requests from the French NGOs for a study to learn lessons from their field experience after Hurricane Mitch. They approached an organization, the Groupe Urgence-Rehabilitation-Développement (Groupe URD), with whom they were associated and which they trusted. URD then set about mobilizing funds for the study and assembled a team composed primarily of its own staff. The study was funded by the Fondation de France (FDF), which had provided a significant part of the funding used by the NGOs in their operations. There were some conflicts between the accountability approach that FDF sought in the study and the lesson-learning approach that the NGOs wanted and the URD followed. URD used a networking approach, liaising with the headquarters of the NGOs before going to the field and holding introductory and debriefing workshops as they arrived and left each country.

As a result this is the most inclusive evaluation reported in this volume. A major desk study preceded the fieldwork and a particular approach or methodology for learning lessons and addressing cross-cutting issues was developed. Groupe URD decided that the team should be made up predominantly of women given the field situation. This is the only case in this volume where gender considerations are reported to have explicitly affected the selection of its members. Fieldwork involved two stages, with an initial team tour to get a common view of the situation and then a second one with individuals doing work on their specific areas of expertise. A major feedback process occurred back in France, including three different stages to try to meet the needs of different stakeholders.

Kosovo This was a joint UK Department for International Development (DFID) and United Nations Children's Fund (UNICEF) study, although it was initiated by DFID as an evaluation of UNICEF's use of DFID's funding in Kosovo. The joint team consisted of DFID- and UNICEF-appointed staff with an independent Team Leader recruited by DFID. Despite their different organizational backgrounds the team worked well together and managed to reach agreed conclusions through joint fieldwork and discussions in the field. More problematic were the difficulties that some UNICEF staff had in seeing this as a joint evaluation rather than an accountability check by DFID. This led to some tensions at the debriefing and reporting stages. This report had still not been placed in the public domain when this volume went to press.

The diverse characteristics from these case studies are collated and structured in Box 11.1. It shows how a great number of factors influence the different stages in an evaluation. These influences are often not simple and unidirectional. There is frequently feedback, especially when the behaviours of the various actors are involved. Indeed, the interaction between actors and between the team and field conditions can create such potential for variability that it is hard to imagine a 'normal' humanitarian evaluation ever being described or defined.

Lessons for the Practicalities of 'Doing' Humanitarian Evaluations

The experiences reported in this book suggest that humanitarian evaluations can be improved through many different actions and changes in the way they are undertaken. However, these case studies are a very small sample and it would be dangerous to make recommendations about precisely what to do on the basis of this material alone. Rather, what we will do is to draw attention to six broad areas of concern and within each to discuss a number of issues about which evaluators of emergency humanitarian assistance, and the commissioners of evaluation studies, need to be aware. In some cases suggestions for improvement can be made, but in many cases it is simply a question of raising awareness.

Team selection: getting the right team and making it work Recruiting an evaluation team is a major task. It can take months and it involves exploring networks of contacts to find people who are trusted and able to do the work to an appropriate standard. The question of trust and standards is important at the present time, when guidance about how to do humanitarian evaluations is limited and the final quality and fine-tuning of the work depend very heavily upon the characteristics and attributes of the Team Leader. It is thus very important that specialists with appropriate networks and knowledge about the performance of individuals, and especially those being considered as Team Leaders, are consulted. But above this, the selection process must be given adequate time so that availability does not become the sole criterion by which people are chosen, as is often the case at present. Hence the need for evaluation should be considered from the outset of a humanitarian programme and a much earlier start made in setting up an evaluation process.

A second question concerns the balance of specialists and evaluation generalists. Clearly there is a need for subject specialists to address particular issues, such as logistics or nutrition, while area specialists can provide in-depth understanding of the reality in the field and unravel the complexity of these situations. However, the general feeling of many of the authors is that expertise in evaluation is the core skill that team members must have. Having too many specialists can make it difficult to come to an agreed view and write a balanced report. Quality evaluation contributions by team members, rather than excessive specialist analysis, are what a Team Leader needs.

The origins of team members are also a debatable matter. In some cases a mixed team of insiders (from the commissioning agency) and outsiders is effective in addressing a situation, perhaps especially for ensuring that lessons are followed up. In other cases an external team is needed. In all cases the vested interests of the evaluators need consideration, along with their ability to place these on one side in order to achieve an independent evaluation. It is important that team members do not have personal or professional interests in the findings that the study reaches. Consultants trying to set up the next job and university-based researchers trying to explore an old field area should be avoided.

Remarkably, the issue of gender within the team seems not to have become well established in humanitarian evaluation practice as yet. Several teams within the sample in this book were all male and only one contribution makes any explicit reference to the need for a gender consideration in the team design, an issue that is clearly too important to leave to chance.

Evaluation teams are often not really teams, with high levels of cohesion and solidarity. In most cases they seem to operate as a loose network of

Box 11.1 Characteristics of humanitarian evaluations

Characteristics of the study

Nature of the study

Type: lesson-learning, account-ability; internal, external, mixed

Level: project, programme, policy analysis

Focus of the work

Emergency humanitarian assistance alone, wider emergency context

Own performance or field partners' performance

Type of agency commissioning the evaluation

Single agency: UN agency, bilateral donor, IFRCS

Joint agencies: DFID and UNICEF

Multiple agency: JEEAR

Terms of Reference

Range: broad, focused

Relative to resources: manageable, overwhelming guidance over method

Timing of evaluation

Relative to assistance: during ongoing relief, after relief activities

Constraints to timing of evaluation: political, security, weather

Degree of autonomy for the evaluation team in the field

Field travel: managed, free, controlled by circumstances

Subject coverage: able to address areas team feels are relevant

Scale of study

Field area: extent of study area

Time period: period of assistance being studied

Agencies: number and diversity

Evaluation team

Team membership

Origins: internal to commis-sioning agency, external to commissioning agency or mixed team

Background: university-based researchers, freelance consultants, balance of these

Expertise: evaluation specialist, development or emergency

Team operation

Team interaction in general: tight team, loose net, series of in-dependent consultants

During preparation, fieldwork and writing up: level and nature of interaction

Structure: core team, groups, viewpoints

specialist, sector specialist, balance of these

Size of team: small, medium, large, varying

Team management

Team employed: directly by commissioning agency, through consultancy company

Consultancy company: buffer role (active or passive) between team and commissioning agency

Team Leader: role in team management and interactions

Operation of evaluation

Preparation

Time: amount of preparation and desk study time

Support: assistance in data preparation

Records/documentation: availability and their use

Briefing of team members before fieldwork: amount, origin and content

Methodological approach

Methodology: active consideration, implicit, coordinated among team, individual

Use of specific techniques: timelines, checklist, conceptual model, analytical framework

Approach: research orientation, consultancy orientation

Length of assignment

Time in field
Time writing up
Balance of field and write-up

Fieldwork

Time: length, share of total evaluation time

Timeliness: relative to emergency assistance, relative to other variables affecting effectiveness

Field contacts: beneficiaries; field actors, donors' representatives, agency headquarters

Structure of fieldwork: single-stage, multi-stage

Division of responsibilities: sectoral, country/area

Limits: access, security, beneficiary recall, attrition of staff, availability of records

---

Reporting and dissemination

Writing up

Division of responsibility: among team and load on Team Leader

Timing of write-up: in field, post field, time pressure

Reporting

Debriefing: process and people involved

Reaction to report: accepted, rejected

Selling of report: activities by team to ensure report accepted

Follow-up

Dissemination means: published report, published summary, booklet or other dissemination means, or withheld

Follow-up: board or parliamentary discussion and decisions, workshop or training activities, monitoring and review of use of findings

---

individuals doing their specialist work and coming together only at the start and the conclusion. This can be advantageous by offering flexibility, but it can cause problems in achieving coherence and reaching final agreement on the conclusions. In a few cases team members do travel together for all or part of the mission, but this is often not the whole team. In many cases there are core-team and outer-team members, with the core of two or three driving the whole evaluation and doing most of the integrative analysis and final report-writing. The evidence here suggests that teams of strangers when thrown together can work, and do work, in most cases. Prior knowledge of each other and cohesion through previous work can be helpful, but are not essential.

While the ability to work together appears to be in part because the team members are professionals, it is also in considerable part due to the attitude and behaviour of the Team Leader and team members. They must be willing to understand each other and contribute to the process of building up trust and mutual understanding. Team Leaders must be open and inclusive in discussions and willing to strike a balance between allowing team members independence but also encouraging responsibility. A willingness to discuss without imposing preconceived views is also essential in order to bring the best out of a team. Good results can be obtained from a poorly selected and inexperienced team provided they have a good Team Leader. Problems seem to occur when there are major methodological debates or personality problems. Sometimes these can be avoided, but it must be recognized that we all carry some 'baggage' with us and that has to be coped with.

Terms of Reference Addressing the Terms of Reference (TOR) is obviously critical for an evaluation study. The need to return to them throughout, so that the study keeps on track, makes it very important that they have been designed with care. However, it is clear from many of the case studies reported here that humanitarian evaluation teams are often given excessive and unrealistic TOR. This overload is partly the result of applying 'normal' evaluation questions in particularly new and difficult post-emergency or ongoing complex emergency field conditions, where much of the information needed is not available.

The problem of excessive TOR is especially found in joint or multi-agency evaluations. In these cases, all the agencies involved will have had their chance to contribute to the TOR and will have added their own special focus to the work. This situation also happens in single agency studies when the TOR are circulated to different sections within the commissioning organization for comment and addition. The result is often a long, and difficult to manage, list of tasks.

This untidy incremental process may also result in confusion in the TOR, with different types of evaluations sought in one mission. Typically lesson-learning and accountability are sought together, without the recognition that they need different types of fieldwork that can be conflicting. Project-level and policy-level questions may be asked together, as well as programming or planning issues. While these different questions are related, it is best if an evaluation has one major objective that is the focus of the work, rather than a confusing set of somewhat conflicting questions (Patton 1997).

Where TOR overload occurs, there is a very real risk that evaluation teams will either end up ignoring parts of the TOR or will try to cover everything by spreading their efforts more thinly and drawing conclusions on the basis of limited data, thereby suggesting false accuracy. Excessive TOR often reflect a lack of focus and methodological clarity within the commissioning organization and represent the transference of what is, in effect, an internal shortcoming onto the evaluation teams with the consequent likelihood of conflicts within teams and with their commissioning agencies.

As the TOR are usually prepared before recruitment is begun, the team members have little ownership of them. This is very much a consultancy–client relationship where the team comes in to do the job that is already defined and is not meant to ask any questions about it. Such 'mechanistic' and conventional commissioning approaches, coming out of development evaluation, are not usually sufficiently adapted to the much more complex humanitarian evaluation process. We believe that a more negotiated process should characterize such evaluations (as is also desirable in development evaluations). In this, one of the first critical acts for an evaluation team should be to review carefully their TOR and where necessary seek clarification and focus. One of the studies implies that the team needs to undertake an initial reconnaissance mission before the main TOR are finalized. In this way the discussion over the TOR can be informed by field reality and the teams' perspective on the principal issues likely to emerge during the study. If necessary more realistic TOR should be developed with the commissioning agency. Certainly it is important for an evaluation team and its commissioning agency to have a shared understanding of their TOR and for the evaluation team to have some ownership of the process. It is also vital for the team itself to have an agreed understanding of what is required, the focus in their work and what, often in trying and difficult circumstances, can be done credibly.

Preparations: briefings, start-up meetings and documentation Generally the amount of time given to the preparations for humanitarian programme evaluations is inadequate. Often, commissioning organizations seem to spend a lot of time drawing up the TOR but very little in briefing the team and ensuring that they are aware of all the relevant documentation. Time and again evaluators call for more time to collate the various documents from different sources, to read them and prepare for the fieldwork. Obviously there are many pressures to get to the field before everyone who needs to be interviewed leaves. But the answer to this problem is not to skip the preparations, but to start the whole process earlier. Starting earlier is the responsibility of the commissioning agency, as it must involve not just planning the evaluation from the start of the relief work but also keeping appropriate records for the briefing (as well as for the fieldwork).

Briefings with the commissioning agency are essential, but not enough. Establishing a dialogue and a route for communication throughout the study are essential as there will be questions during the study that need reference back to those who commissioned it. Such a dialogue, or rapport, is vital at the outset when the TOR need discussing. It is also vital when it comes to reporting and discussing the findings. Certainly teams should not neglect establishing such a relationship at the outset of the mission. To do this later in the evaluation process is very difficult. Indeed, we believe that a far more inclusive evaluation process is needed, with much more interaction between the commissioning agency and the team throughout the mission in order to obtain the best from the work. One example is the way IOB in the Netherlands, which operates as an independent evaluation department, undertakes some of the evaluation work itself and works jointly with the consultants it commissions.

In terms of briefings, it often proves difficult to get the team together for these, or else the commissioning agency sees it as the responsibility of only the Team Leader to attend such meetings. These are both unfortunate occurrences as the briefings can be critical in developing a sense of team responsibility towards the TOR and the commissioning agency, as well as achieving a common understanding of the situation being addressed and starting the development of a team spirit.

Time spent on preparation should also result in better studies. A number of cases reported in this volume do record several weeks or even months of preparation. This may involve collation and analysis of the data that are available and the development of specific conceptual and analytical frameworks for the study, as well as methodologies. In one case, preparation also involved establishing dialogues with the headquarters of all the NGOs whose field operations were to be studied so that they could be part of the preparation process and have some ownership of the evaluation. Through this, it was hoped, their internal lesson-learning processes after the evaluation would be facilitated.

Methods and methodology for the field Giving sufficient attention to methods and methodology is critical for achieving quality evaluations and for ensuring confidence in the findings on the part of the donors and field agencies. Lack of methodological rigour results in impressionistic findings that are hard to defend and undermine the reputations of humanitarian evaluations.

Methodology is often a matter about which evaluators are sensitive. The 'M-word' is sometimes a neglected issue, on the assumption that everyone understands and agrees, but about which, in reality, everyone has uncertainties. In some cases an evaluation team or team member may in retrospect go so far even to say that the evaluation 'had no methodology'. Peer reviewers have been asked by teams 'to think about methodology for us'. In extreme cases, the failure to agree a methodology can make it impossible for the team to come to a common view and agree upon a single set of conclusions for the study.

It is important for the teams and their commissioning organizations to recognize the multiple layers of methods and methodology. We suggest that four layers exist. The 'methodology' that most evaluation reports do tell us about – let us call this layer M-1 – is the timetable: who was where, when and why during the mission, the basis for the division of labour in the team and the time allocation in the field and other locations. This is method in only the broadest sense on which teams need to agree in order to complete their task on schedule. Less frequently explained are the methods by which problems as they arose in the field were addressed and solved – let us call this layer M-2. This may include whether the TOR, set for and accepted by the mission, were successfully modified, what team management issues arose, what networks were established, and how difficult relations in the field with representatives of governmental and other agencies, as well as those of the client organization, were smoothed.

The layer about which there is usually even less reporting, M-3, includes the conceptual and analytical or methodological frameworks for the study, as well as the precise field methods for data collection. These should include reference to the criteria by which field information was assessed and judgements reached in order to produce the findings from the evaluation. This is probably the most difficult part of an evaluation, especially if there are no clear standards or criteria. It needs particular attention because in small teams the personalities of team members, as optimists or pessimists, can be very influential. Whether it is found to be good for a programme to achieve so much or poor not to achieve everything should not be a totally subjective assessment.

What is normally entirely unstated is the final layer, M-4, the methodology of how exactly a mission proceeded from whatever findings it could establish with confidence, to drawing conclusions about them, and finally making recommendations 'accordingly'.

Developing appropriate field methodologies in advance is certainly not an easy task, especially given the types of field conditions that can be encountered. However, it is no excuse for leaving methodology to evolve in response to circumstances. Indeed, the problems likely to be faced – complex field situations, a multitude of actors, lack of data, variable translation of field interviews, limited access to the field and beneficiaries and difficulties with attribution – make it all the more important that methods to cope with these situations are thought about in advance and appropriate methodologies developed. Similar problems can occur in the analysis stage, especially where quantitative methods are applied to field data that are not robust and accurate enough to support this. Again, prior consideration of methods is essential. One suggestion about how to deal with this, which comes from two of the case studies in this volume, is to undertake two-stage fieldwork, with an initial field visit or tour of the study area in order to prepare the team for thinking about the methods they will use.

Sampling requires preparation rather than being left to the bias of chance in the field. However, this is dependent upon information being available about the whole of the operations so that choices can be made using some criteria, such as agency, activity and field situation. This requires considerable data-processing before the fieldwork starts. In many cases this is not possible and so judgements about representative field situations have to be made based on experience.

Many humanitarian evaluations are weak on institutional and management analysis. While this is possibly a failure of the TOR, which tend to direct evaluators to field situations, this may also be the result of a failure by the evaluation team to undertake initial analysis of the situation with sufficient rigour to identify the need for information in these areas.

The problem of methodology is not uniform and in some of the case studies included in this volume considerable thought was given by the evaluation teams to the methods they used. Focusing in the field upon extreme situations rather than average field conditions, or the end of the supply line, and developing checklists to ensure comparability show some concern with M-3 type methodological issues.

While attention to field methods in advance is necessary, it is also vital that teams can adjust and respond to both issues and ideas that come up in the fieldwork. It is also vital to be able to cope with any resistance to evaluation that is met in the field.

Coming to a team position and writing the report The means by which teams come to agreement about their findings and then take them forward to conclusions and recommendations (M-4) are critical. However, it appears to be a hazy and poorly documented process, lacking in transparency. Even when asked to explain it in their chapters for this volume the authors found it difficult to do. Clearly much more attention has to be given to this part of the evaluation process, as there is by no means a simple, single, or linear process for getting from findings to recommendations.

Team agreement is greatly facilitated if the team holds a common conceptualization of the situation being studied and agrees the methodology and criteria to reach findings, conclusions and recommendations. This should be the result of team discussions at the outset of the evaluation, as well as discussions with the commissioning agency. These conceptualizations and methodological views will also evolve during the mission, but a common understanding is required at the outset and should be sought throughout.

The process of getting to findings and recommendations may be partly formalized through regular review meeting to assess 'Where are we?' and 'How does this relate to the TOR?' These are reported in this volume to take part during the fieldwork, but are less common after this part of the mission is completed. There are also informal processes of sharing information and views that occur during the fieldwork as team members travel around together and discuss the work. These may be supplemented through the exchange of field notes.

Getting to the recommendations may also require more time. Far too often the recommendations, which are the aspects of the report given greatest attention by the commissioning agency, are written by the Team Leader (TL) when he or she is most exhausted and under the greatest pressure. Starting to think about them earlier, without prejudging the findings, and giving more time to the final stages of writing up, with the team, or at least with a core team, together could help to ensure that these vital parts of the evaluation report receive due attention.

The actual reporting process is also subject to many tensions. There is often a major tension between commissioning agencies, which want reports soon after the team returns from the field, and the team wanting time to reflect on what they have seen before drawing a balanced conclusion. Requiring reports within three days of return seems quite unhelpful to the process of achieving a balanced evaluation. On the other hand there are benefits from writing up while the team is together, and that is often possible only in the field.

Typically report writing involves the individual team members writing sections for their specific responsibilities and then leaving it to the TL to combine these into the final report and resolve any conflicts and the usual differences in style. There seems to be a common problem with excessively long specialist inputs that require considerable efforts from the TL to synthesize and integrate into the main report. It is generally agreed that the responsibility for reaching final conclusions rests with the TL. He or she has to have particular skills in synthesizing the vast range of material and also 'changing gear' from the specific case material to the more general conclusions and recommendations. At that stage, a higher level of analysis is usually required, as issues of policy and organizational learning often need to be addressed. In addition, there can be the problem of coping with dissenting conclusions and deciding whether a consensus can be achieved, whether a dissenting annex should be included, or whether one view alone should dominate.

Writing up almost always takes more time than is planned or paid for and many TLs seem to subsidize evaluations at this stage with unpaid days. There is little evidence of a process of agreeing the final report through a meeting of the team members at some finalization stage, despite the fact that in some cases there were major criticisms and feedback from the commissioning agency. This seems to be a burden that the Team Leader or the core team is obliged, inappropriately, to shoulder alone.

However, it is not always a tense situation involving conflict. With a good rapport between the core team and the commissioning agency it can lead to a very healthy mutual learning process.

A final point about writing is the need to communicate, both to one another in the team and to the commissioning agency. While this is partly a question of style, it is also a question of jargon. In one case it is reported that an independent editor was useful for 'untangling' some of the difficult texts. In other cases, the editing was done by the TL or another member of the team.

Selling the report and follow-up   Another aspect of humanitarian evaluations that tends to be given insufficient attention is that of getting the report and its findings accepted and used. To some extent there is a skill in 'pitching' a report to ensure that it is accepted and that some action does occur. If there is too much criticism it will tend to close ears and the commissioning agency will want the report filed and closed as soon as possible. If there is too much praise it encourages organizations to feel there is no need to respond, and little learning will occur. In addition, critical points can be raised in a constructive and forward-looking manner so that they stimulate action rather than encourage people to focus on escaping blame. Overall there are benefits from giving attention to the presentation of findings in a 'saleable' manner.

A key aspect that can help ensure acceptance of an evaluation report and active follow-up is the maintenance of a rapport between the evaluation team and the commissioning agency. This dialogue should help ensure a clear focus in the report as commissioning agencies are often, and understandably, unhappy where accountability and lesson-learning outputs from an evaluation are mixed and the TOR are not strictly addressed. Hence the rapport should help ensure that the report meets agreed TOR and the interests of the commissioning agency, with the work as fine-tuned as is possible to what is wanted.

However, within commissioning agencies, evaluation reports tend to be forgotten quite quickly, especially once the report is no longer new and the pressures that led to the evaluation have subsided. Getting the report published may help ensure some follow-up as it puts the findings into the public domain. Several of the case studies in this volume had their reports published, but the impact of this is difficult to judge. It seems that some form of active follow-up is necessary to ensure that the best use is made of evaluation reports. This was the case in the Rwanda study's follow-up monitoring for a year or to a lesser degree the Horn of Africa workshop and booklet to publicize and make more accessible the findings of that evaluation.

Improving the Approach to Humanitarian Evaluations

The case studies in this volume show that the evaluation of emergency humanitarian assistance is important. It can be done, and done successfully, despite the various problems that are faced. Accountability can be improved and lessons can be drawn from experience so that, if they are acted upon by agencies, performance in the provision of humanitarian assistance can be improved next time an emergency is faced. This actual and potential contribution of evaluations needs to be more fully recognized so that their benefits can be optimized in the donor agencies and the field organizations.

In order to achieve this constructive attitude towards humanitarian evaluations, there is a need for us to develop our approach to these evaluations, as well as changing the 'practicalities of doing' discussed above. Eight key aspects for an improved approach can now be presented to conclude this volume.

To begin with, there must be a greater understanding of the reality faced when applying evaluation methods, designed primarily for economic development projects, into situations of humanitarian assistance. Humanitarian situations are extremely complex and difficult for evaluation procedures. They involve a large number of independent actors with the consequent difficulties of attribution. They lack baseline data that would facilitate assessing impact and performance. They are often highly charged politically, which makes investigation and drawing conclusions sensitive matters. Because of the 'steep learning curve', caused by post-Cold War intervention in ongoing conflicts, evaluations frequently face a heavy burden of assessment at the policy level, as well as at the project and programme levels. Hence the uncritical application in humanitarian evaluations of methods developed for assessing the impact, efficiency, effectiveness and relevance of development assistance often overloads these evaluations with assessments that are very difficult to make. In particular, trying to address accountability-type questions, as well as learning lessons, in such difficult situations can lead to conflicting priorities and has added to confusion on the part of those undertaking and commissioning humanitarian evaluations. One set of goals can get in the way of achieving others, and the resulting tension can undermine the effectiveness of the evaluation.

In response to this situation, our second point is the need for greater clarity of thinking about the focus of evaluations that are needed, and the prioritization of their objectives. The relative importance to the commissioning agency of accountability-type goals, compared to lesson-learning and knowledge-generation goals, needs to be made clear here as in other types of evaluations (Patton 1997). This will require evaluation managers, who are the 'gatekeepers' in this process, to be prepared to change the ground-rules and to allow a more open discussion of the TOR between the commissioning agency and the evaluators. Ensuring that the evaluation team knows what is wanted and for what purpose, and forcing the commissioning agency, and not just its evaluation unit, to think about this and clarify the usually excessive and sometimes even incoherent TOR is a critical step to achieving more effective and useable evaluations.

This need for discussion between evaluation teams and commissioning agencies makes it necessary for the relationship between these two to change. The third recommendation is for a change from the strait-jacket of imposed TOR that are not discussed and a management consultancy-style mission appointment and direction. Instead of the team being briefed through a single meeting with a one-way flow of information and no communication with the commissioning agency until the team submits its report, a continuing dialogue is vital. This would recognize the fact that humanitarian evaluation is an evolving process where adjustments need to be made as the work progresses. The dialogue should also recognize that there is a mutual learning process going on throughout the evaluation and that both the commissioning agency and team should be involved. In other words, a more inclusive and open way of managing the evaluation process is needed. This dialogue could include specific learning mechanisms, such as a workshop for the commissioning agency and team at the end of the fieldwork, before writing up starts, and also once the report is submitted.

An early part of this dialogue should be about what needs to be studied, how this can be done and with what resources. This type of understanding evolves as knowledge of the evaluation situation develops and especially once the field is visited. Hence our fourth proposal is for a two-stage evaluation process that allows a renegotiation of the TOR and the contract once an initial assessment of the field situation has been made. This is mentioned in the Organization for Economic Cooperation and Development (OECD)–Development Assistance Committee (DAC) guidance but is rarely implemented as far as we are aware (OECD DAC 1999).

Fifth, if evaluations are to be undertaken better, they need adequate resources. At present the resources expended on evaluations are minuscule relative to the funds disbursed for humanitarian assistance. The need for greater clarity of purpose has been noted and this should lead to clarification of the resources necessary to achieve the tasks set out for an evaluation. The request we are making here is not for more resources *per se*, but rather for adequate resources to match the task. This may mean smaller and more focused evaluations within the resources available, or greater resources in order to undertake thorough work to match the requirements of agreed TOR.

Another important step in improving the approach to humanitarian evaluations is to change the attitudes towards evaluations in donors and humanitarian organizations. Instead of evaluations being feared and seen as sticks to be used to beat an unsatisfactory organization or as hurdles to be jumped, evaluations must be looked upon in a positive light, as opportunities for learning. Gaining from evaluations rather than losing from them should be the aim. Evaluation departments should be seen as critical in determining the future, and the future success, of the organizations undertaking humanitarian assistance. As units generating the ideas and approaches for the future of these organizations, we would suggest that evaluation activities be relocated and integrated more closely into the learning and operations structure of an organization, rather than being out on an 'accountability limb' as so many of them appear to be.

Our seventh point is that if humanitarian evaluation is to be thorough, it must not work with its hands tied. To date there has been a tendency by commissioning organizations to require evaluations to 'look out' to the field as the place where most lessons can be learned. However, lessons are not learned only in the field, as some of the case studies have suggested, and 'looking up' within the commissioning agencies and within their headquarters is also necessary. Open and thorough evaluations must be undertaken addressing all dimensions of the humanitarian process, including the commissioning agencies with their policies, organizational frameworks and procedures, if we are to improve the effectiveness not only of evaluations but also of the overall performance of the humanitarian system.

Finally, serious efforts are also needed to ensure that humanitarian evaluations are better used. Too many studies are not utilized effectively, and some are barely read beyond the draft stage. Follow-up tends to be patchy and informal, and there is often a lack of clarity about the role of the evaluation team and the evaluation department in ensuring action on the findings of such studies. While accountability and lesson-learning outputs from an evaluation will need different forms of follow-up, in both cases this should not be left to chance. Key lessons need to be identified and methods for ensuring their adoption established through training courses, staff development manuals and monitoring procedures along with agreed action routes. As some of the case studies show, the follow-up itself can be a major process, with accessible booklets or films produced to supplement workshops and training programmes. These efforts can help ensure that lessons are learned not just within the commissioning organization, but also by field partners and other interested parties. Such follow-up actions are essential if we are to complete the full learning process from humanitarian evaluations.

Overall we would argue that a win–win scenario can be established where lessons about evaluation are learned so that better-designed and conceptualized humanitarian evaluations, with adequate resources and sound methodologies, can be undertaken in situations where learning is sought and the structures to facilitate this are in place. However, this must be a continual process as the range of humanitarian evaluation work is rapidly expanding and the gap between practice and guidance is growing. Doing humanitarian evaluations better through an ongoing process of reflection and learning is the most cost-effective way for ensuring that humanitarian programmes improve.

References

Allen, B. J. and R. M. Bourke (1997a) 'Report of an assessment of the impacts of frost and drought in Papua New Guinea', unpublished report, Port Moresby, PNG: Ministry of Provincial and Local Government Affairs, National Drought Committee and NDES.

Allen, B. J. and R. M. Bourke with others (1997b) 'Report of an assessment of the impacts of frost and drought in Papua New Guinea – Phase 2', unpublished report, Canberra; AusAID.

Allen, B., H. C. Brookfield and Y. Byron (1989) 'Frost and drought through time and space, part II: the written, oral and proxy records and their meaning', *Mountain Research and Development*, Vol. 9, No. 3: 252–78.

Anderson, M. (1999) *Do No Harm: How Aid Can Support Peace – or War*, Boulder, CO: Lynne Rienner.

Apthorpe, R. (1997) 'Some relief from development: humanitarian emergency aid in the Horn of Africa (including Sudan), Rwanda and Liberia', *European Journal of Development Research*, Vol. 9, No. 2: 83–106.

— (1998) 'Confessions of a consultant: some personal experience of the art', reproduced in R. Apthorpe (ed.), *Towards Emergency Humanitarian Aid Evaluation, Development Issues*, No. 12: 67–84, Canberra: Australian National University, Asia Pacific Press.

— (ed.) (1998) *Towards Emergency Humanitarian Evaluation, Development Issues, No. 12*, Canberra: National Centre for Development Studies, Australian National University, Asia Pacific Press.

— (1999) 'Introduction' in D. A. M. Lea, B. Broughton, B. Murtagh, M. Levett, C. McMurray and J. Amoako, ed. A. McLaughlin, *Review: Australian Assistance to the 1997–98 PNG Drought*, internal discussion document, Canberra: AusAID.

— (2000) 'Kosovo humanitarian programme evaluations: towards synthesis, meta-analysis and sixteen propositions for discussion', background paper for the ALNAP Symposium 'Learning-from-Evaluation: Humanitarian Assistance and Protection in Kosovo', Geneva, 17–18 October 2000, London: ALNAP.

Apthorpe, R., H. Ketel, M. Salih and A. Wood (1995) *What Relief for the Horn: Sida-supported Emergency Operations in Ethiopia, Eritrea, Southern Sudan, Somalia and Djibouti*, Sida Evaluation Report 1995/3, Stockholm: Sida.

Apthorpe, R., H. Ketel and A. P. Wood (1996) *Beyond Relief? Towards Best Practice for Disaster Prevention, Preparedness and Relief in the Horn of Africa*, Stockholm: Sida.

Apthorpe, R., P. Atkinson, A. Waeshle and F. Watson (1996) *Protracted Emergency Humanitarian Relief Food Aid: Towards 'Productive Relief'; Programme Policy Evaluation of the 1990–1955 WFP-assisted Refugee and Displaced Persons Operations in Liberia, Sierra Leone, Guinea and Côte d'Ivoire*, Rome: World Food Programme.

Bernander, B., J. Charny, M. Eastmond, C. Lindahl and J. Ojendal (1995) *Facing a Complex Emergency: An Evaluation of Swedish Support to Emergency Aid to Cambodia*, SIDA Evaluation Report 1995/4, Stockholm: Sida.

Borton, J. (1993) 'Recent Trends in the International Relief System', *Disasters*, Vol. 17, No. 3: 187–201.

— (1996) 'The Rwandan refugee influx into Goma in mid-July 1994: an assessment of the performance of contingency planning and early warning arrangements within the international humanitarian aid system', mimeo, London: Overseas Development Institute.

Borton, J., R. Stephenson and C. Morris (1988) *Evaluation of ODA's Provision of Emergency Aid to Africa 1983–86*, Evaluation Report EV 425, London: Overseas Development Administration.

Borton, J., E. Brusset, A. Hallam, S. Collins, J. Pottier, D. de Lame, A. Chalinder, J. Shoham, L. Lee, R. Connaughton, T. Ishøyet, J. Telford, F. Goetz, G. Shepherd, L. Hilsum, B. Jones, D. Turton, L. Jackson, N. Shellard and A. Welsh (1995) 'Masking a policy vacuum: humanitarian aid and the 1994 crisis in Rwanda', Draft Report of the Study III Team, London: Overseas Development Institute.

— (1996) *Humanitarian Aid and Effects*, Study III of *The International Response to Conflict and Genocide: Lessons from the Rwanda Experience*, Copenhagen: Steering Committee of the Joint Evaluation of Emergency Assistance to Rwanda.

Broughton, B. and J. Hampshire (1997) *Bridging the Gap: A Guide to Monitoring and Evaluating Development Projects*, Canberra: Australian Council for Overseas Aid.

Broughton, B. and D. A. M. Lea (1999) 'Monitoring of emergency relief: the PNG experience, 1997–1998', unpublished AusAID seminar paper, 2 March.

Chambers, R., P. Cutler, S. Morris-Peel, C. Petrie, N. Russell and S. York (1986) *An Independent Review and Evaluation of Africa Drought Relief Operations, 1984–86 of the League of Red Cross and Red Crescent Societies*, Report 1, Sussex: Institute for Development Studies.

Cracknell, B. (2000) *Evaluating Development Aid: Issues, Problems and Solutions*, New Dehli: Sage.

Dabelstein, N. (1996) 'Evaluating the international humanitarian system: rationale, process and management of the joint evaluation of the international response to the Rwanda genocide', *Disasters*, Vol. 20, No. 4: 286–94.

Danish Red Cross (ed.) (1995) *Record from the Copenhagen Workshop on Programming Relief for Development*, Copenhagen: Danish Red Cross.

de Waal, A. (1997) *Famine Crimes: Politics and the Disaster Relief Industry in Africa*, Oxford: James Currey.

ECHO (European Commission Humanitarian Office) (1999) *Manual for the Evaluation of Humanitarian Aid*, Brussels: ECHO.

Frerks, G. E., T. J. Kliest, S. J. Kirkby, N. D. Emmel, P. O'Keefe and I. Convery (1995) 'A disaster continuum', *Disasters*, Vol. 19, No. 4: 362–67.

Glantz, M. (ed.) (1976) *The Politics of Natural Disaster: The Case of the Sahel Drought*, New York: Praeger.

Glasgow Media Group (1995) 'British television news and the Rwanda crisis, July 15th 21st 1994', unpublished report, Glasgow: Glasgow Media Group.

Goie, A. (1986) 'Natural disasters surveys and studies: frost', *Department of Enga Province Technical Bulletin*, No. 1, Wabag, PNG: Division of Primary Industry (Subsistence Unit), Department of Enga Province.

Greene, M., R. Stevens, K. Madi and J. Telford (2000) *UNICEF Preparedness and Response in the 1999 Kosovo Refugee Emergency: A Joint UNICEF/DFID Evaluation*, London: DFID.

Groupe URD (2000) *8 Mois après Mitch. Bilan des Actions et Premières Leçons. Capitaliser sur la Réponse aux Grandes Catastrophes Naturelles*, Plaisians, France: Groupe URD.

Guba, E. and Y. Lincoln (1989) *Fourth Generation Evaluation*, Newbury Park, CA: Sage.

Hallam, A. (1998) 'Evaluating humanitarian assistance programmes in complex emergencies', *Relief and Rehabilitation Network (RRN) Good Practice Review No. 7*, London: Overseas Development Institute.

IASC (Inter-Agency Standing Committee) (2000) *Global Humanitarian Assistance 2000*, Geneva: Office for the Coordination of Humanitarian Assistance.

Jawad, N. and S. Tadjbakhsh (1995) *Tajikestan: A Forgotten Civil War*, London: Minority Rights Group.

JEEAR (Joint Evaluation of Emergency Assistance to Rwanda) (1995) 'Terms of reference for evaluation of emergency assistance to Rwanda', mimeo, Copenhagen: Danida.

— (1996) *The International Response to Conflict and Genocide: Lessons from the Rwanda Experience*, 5 vols, Copenhagen: Steering Committee of the Joint Evaluation of Emergency Assistance to Rwanda.

JEFF (Joint Evaluation Follow-up, Monitoring and Facilitation Network) (1997) 'The joint evaluation of emergency assistance to Rwanda: a review of follow-up and impact fifteen months after publication: report by JEFF in conformity with a decision by the Joint Evaluation Steering Committee at its final meeting on 14 February 1997 in Copenhagen', London: Overseas Development Institute.

Kent, R. (1987) *Anatomy of Disaster Relief*, London: Pinter.

Kirkby, J., T. Kliest, G. Frerks, W. Flikkema and P. O'Keefe (1997) 'UNHCR's cross border operation in Somalia: the value of quick impact projects for refugee resettlement', *Journal of Refugee Studies*, Vol. 10, No. 2: 181–98.

Kjekshus, H. (1991) 'Evaluation policy and performance: the state of the art' in Olav Stokke (ed.), *Evaluating Development Assistance: Policies and Performance*, 12, London: Frank Cass, pp. 60–70.

Lea, D. A. M., B. Broughton, B. Murtagh, M. Levett, C. McMurray and J. Amoako (1998a) *Draft Review of Australian Assistance to the PNG Drought* (third draft), submitted to AusAID by ANUTECH Pty Ltd, May.

— (1998b) *Review of Australian Assistance to the PNG Drought (Revised Draft)* (seventh draft), Canberra: Office of Program Review and Evaluation, AusAID, October.

Lea, D. A. M., B. Broughton, B. Murtagh, M. Levett, C. McMurray and J. Amoako, ed. Andrea McLaughlin (1999) *Review: Australian Assistance to the 1997–98 PNG Drought*, internal discussion document, Canberra: AusAID.

Minear, L. (1994) 'The international relief system: a critical review', paper presented to the Parallel National Intelligence Estimate on Global Humanitarian Emergencies, Meridian International Center, Washington, DC, September.

Netherlands Ministry of Foreign Affairs (1993a) *A World in Dispute*, The Hague: Ministry of Foreign Affairs.

— (1993b) *Humanitarian Aid between Conflict and Development*, The Hague: Ministry of Foreign Affairs.

OECD–DAC (1986) *Methods and Procedures in Aid Evaluation. A Compendium of Donor Practices*, Paris: OECD–DAC.

— (1988) *Evaluation in Developing Countries. A Step in a Dialogue*, Paris: OECD–DAC.

— (1992) *DAC Principles for Effective Aid*, Paris: OECD–DAC.

— (1999) *Guidance for Evaluating Humanitarian Assistance in Complex Emergencies*, DAC Working Party on Aid Evaluation, Paris: OECD.

Operations Review Unit (1994) *Humanitarian Aid to Somalia*, The Hague: Ministry of Foreign Affairs.

Paquet, C. (1995) 'The 1994 epidemic of dysentery in the displaced populations of Central Africa', paper prepared for Study 3 of JEEAR, Paris: Epicentre.

Parsons, A. (1995) *From Cold War to Hot Peace: UN Interventions 1947–1995*, London: Penguin.

Patton, M. (1997) *Utilisation-Focused Evaluation: The New Century Text*, 3rd edn, Thousand Oaks, CA: Sage.

Pottier, J. (1996a) 'Relief and repatriation: views by Rwandan refugees; lessons for humanitarian aid workers', *African Affairs*, Vol. 95, No. 380: 403 29.

— (1996b) 'Why aid agencies need better understanding of the communities they assist: the experience of food aid in Rwandan refugee camps', *Disasters*, Vol. 20, No. 4: 323–36.

— (1999) 'In retrospect: beneficiary surveys in Rwandan refugee camps, 1995: reflections 1999', in G. Frerks and T. Hilhorst (eds), *Evaluating Humanitarian Aid: Politics, Perspectives and Practice*, Wageningen: Disasters Studies Unit, University of Wageningen, pp. 115–26.

Roberts, A. (1996) *Humanitarian Action in War: Aid, Protection and Impartiality in a Policy Vacuum*, Adelphi Paper No. 305, London: International Institute of Strategic Studies, and Oxford: Oxford University Press.

Scriven, M. (1991) *Evaluation Thesaurus – Fourth Edition*, Newbury Park, CA: Sage.

Sen, A. (1981) *Poverty and Famines: An Essay on Entitlement and Deprivation*, Oxford: Oxford University Press.

Shawcross, W. (1984) *The Quality of Mercy: Cambodia, Holocaust and Modern Conscience*, London: André Deutsch.

Sheets, H. and R. Morris (1974) *Disaster in the Desert: Failures of International Relief in the West African Drought*, Washington, DC: Carnegie Endowment for International Peace.

Suhrke, A., M. Barutciski, P. Sandison and R. Garlock (2000) *The Kosovo Refugee Crisis: An Independent Evaluation of UNHCR's Emergency Preparedness and Response*, Geneva: UNHCR.

Trigger, D. S., M. Robinson and L. Gladstone (1998) 'Anthropologists and consultancy contracts in the 1990s: who owns your brain?', *Australian Anthropological Society Newsletter*, No. 74: 5 10.

UNICEF (1991) *Making a Difference?* New York: Evaluation Office, UNICEF.

USAID (1977) *United States Response to the Sahel Drought: 3rd Special Report to Congress*, Washington, DC: US Agency for International Development.

— (1986) *The US Response to the African Famine, 1984–86: An Evaluation of the Emergency Food Assistance Program* (Dennis Wood, Albert Brown and Vincent Brown), Washington, DC: US Agency for International Development.

Watts, M. J. and H. G. B. Bohle (1993) 'The space of vulnerability', *Progress in Human Geography*, Vol. 17, No. 1: 43–67.

Wayi, B. M. (1998) 'Interim report on the impact of frost and drought in Papua New Guinea – Phase III', Konedobu, PNG: Papua New Guinea Department of Agriculture and Livestock.

Weiss, T. (1999) *Military–Civilian Interactions: Intervening in Humanitarian Crises*, Lanham, MA: Rowman and Littlefield.

Wiles, P., R. Brennan, D. Horobin and R. Rogers (1996) *International Federation of Red Cross and Red Crescent Societies: Review of the Tajikestan Programme*, Geneva: International Federation of Red Cross and Red Crescent Societies.

Wiles, P., M. Buchanan-Smith, B. Bradbury, S. D. Collins, J. Cosgrave, A. Hallam, M. Mece, N. Norman, A. Podanociv, J. Shakman and F. Watson (2000) *Independent Evaluation of Expenditure of DEC Kosovo Appeal Funds, Phases 1 and 11, April 1999–January 2000*, London: Overseas Development Institute.

Wohlt, P. B., B. J. Allen, A. Goie and P. W. Harvey (1982) 'An Investigation of Food Shortages in Papua New Guinea, 24 March to 3 April, 1981', *IASER Special Publication No. 6*, Port Moresby: IASER.

Wood, A. (1996) *From Ideas to Practice: Learning Lessons from the 1994 Evaluation of the SIDA-funded Relief Activities in the Horn of Africa*, workshop guide, Stockholm: Sida, Department for Cooperation with NGOs and Humanitarian Assistance.

— (1999a) 'The 1995 Addis Ababa post-evaluation workshop on SIDA projects in the Horn of Africa', in R. Apthorpe (ed.), Canberra: National Centre for Development Studies, Australian National University, Development Issues no. 12, pp. 85–95.

— (1999b) 'Making it count! Using the findings of the evaluation of Sida-supported emergency operations in the Horn of Africa, 1990–1994', in G. Frerks and T. Hilhorst (eds), *Evaluating Humanitarian Aid: Politics, Perspectives and Practice*, Wageningen: Disasters Studies Unit, Wageningen University, pp. 193–206.

Wood, A. P., R. Apthorpe and H. Ketel (1996) *Beyond Relief? Towards Best Practice for Disaster Prevention, Preparedness and Relief in the Horn of Africa*, Stockholm: Sida.

Index

ALNAP Annual Review 2001
Humanitarian Action: Learning from Evaluation
Publication date 1 May 2001

The number of evaluations of international humanitarian action has increased significantly in recent years and represents an important investment in learning and performance improvement efforts by humanitarian agencies. However, the reports produced by such evaluations are rarely shared across the community and the potential for shared learning is often lost. This first *ALNAP Annual Review*, of approximately fifty evaluations of humanitarian action completed and placed in the public domain in 1999–2000, aims to redress this deficit by providing a synthesis of their principle findings and recommendations. The analysis reveals cross-cutting issues and trends and in turn the learning and accountability implications facing those within the humanitarian sector, whether practitioner, policy-maker or evaluator.

A centrepiece of this first *Annual Review* is an in-depth and critical consideration of 16 evaluations and one synthesis evaluation undertaken of the response to humanitarian crisis produced by the 1999 Kosovo conflict, together with 45 other 'evaluative' documents on the same subject. Through synthesis and meta-analysis this section draws together common and recurrent strands and challenges for the sector, as well as providing a critique of the evaluation process itself.

Evaluation provides an exceptional learning and accountability mechanism for all within the sector, yet it is currently undermined by the highly variable quality of both process and product. Drawing on current guidance and a growing body of what is increasingly acknowledged as good practice in evaluation, the *Annual Review* introduces a 'pro forma' tool against which the quality of individual evaluations can be assessed. Its application to the 1999–2000 *ALNAP Annual Review* selection reveals the strengths and weaknesses of current practice from conception and design, through the process of doing the evaluation, to the dissemination of evaluation findings and recommendations.

The *ALNAP Annual Review* can be obtained from the ALNAP Secretariat, c/o ODI, 111 Westminster Bridge Road, London SE1 7JD.

Retail price £15.

Order form available on ALNAP Website <www.alnap.org>